D1310300

CREATING Keepsakes
SCRAPBOOK MAGAZINE

scrapbooking FRIENDS & FAMILY

Presenting over 825 of the best scrapbooking ideas from *Creating Keepsakes* publications, with layouts, tips, and techniques for heartwarming memory pages starring your loved ones.

take time to

LAUGH

– it is the music of the soul

PRODUCED EXCLUSIVELY FOR LEISURE ARTS

CREATING Keepsakes

Founding Editor	Lisa Bearnson
Co-founder	Don Lambson
Editor-in-Chief	Tracy White
Special Projects Editor	Leslie Miller
Copy Editor	Kim Sandoval
Editorial Assistants	Joannie McBride, Fred Brewer
Administrative Assistant	Michelle Bradshaw
Art Director	Brian Tippetts
Designer	Joleen Hughes
Production Designers	Just Scan Me!, Exposure Graphics
Publisher	Mark Seastrand
Media Relations	Alicia Bremer, 801/364-2030
Director of Sales and Marketing	Tara Green
Web Site Manager	Emily Johnson
Assistant Web Site Editor	Sarah Thatcher
Production Manager	Gary Whitehead
Business Sales Assistants	Jacque Jensen, Melanie Cain
Advertising Sales Manager	Becky Lowder
Advertising Sales, West Coast	Debbie Hanni, 801/583-1043
Advertising Sales, West Central	Barbara Tanner, 801/942-6080
Advertising Sales, East Central	Jenny Grothe, 801/377-1428
Advertising Sales, East Coast	RaNay Winter, 801/796-7037
Wholesale Accounts	800/815-3538
	Donna Hair, stores A–G, and outside of U.S., ext. 235
	Victoria James, stores H–R, ext. 226
	Kristin Schaefer, stores S–Z (except "Scr"), ext. 250
	Sherrie Burt, stores starting with "Scr," ext. 244
	Kim Robison, distributor accounts, ext. 251

PRIMEDIA
Consumer Magazine & Internet Group

Vice President, Group Publisher	David O'Neil
Circulation Marketing Directors	Dena Spar, Janice Martin
Promotions Manager	Dana Smith

PRIMEDIA, Inc.

Chairman	Dean Nelson
President & CEO	Kelly Conlin
Vice-Chairman	Beverly C. Chell

PRIMEDIA Consumer Media and Magazine Group

Chief Operating Officer	Daniel E. Aks
EVP, Consumer Marketing/Circulation	Steve Aster
SVP, Chief Financial Officer	David P. Kirchhoff
SVP, Mfg., Production & Distribution	Kevin Mullan
SVP, Finance	Kevin Neary
SVP, Chief Information Officer	Debra C. Robinson
SVP, Consumer Marketing	Bobbi Gutman
VP, Manufacturing	Gregory Catsaros
VP, Business Development	Jasja de Smedt
VP, Direct Response & Classified Advertising	Carolyn N. Everson
VP, Single Copy Sales	Thomas L. Fogarty
VP, Manufacturing Budgets & Operations	Lilia Golia
VP, Database / e-Commerce	Suti Prakash

PRIMEDIA Outdoor Recreation and Enthusiast Group

SVP, Group Publishing Director	Brent Diamond
VP, Comptroller	Stephen H. Bender
VP, Marketing and Internet Operations	Dave Evans
VP, Human Resources	Kathleen P. Malinowski

SUBSCRIPTIONS

To subscribe to *Creating Keepsakes* magazine or to change the address of your current subscription, call or write:

Phone: 888/247-5282
International: 760/745-2809
Fax: 760/745-7200

Subscriber Services
Creating Keepsakes
P.O. Box 469007
Escondido, CA 92046-9007

Some back issues of *Creating Keepsakes* magazine are available for $5 each, payable in advance.

NOTICE OF LIABILITY

The information in this book is distributed on an "as is" basis, without warranty. While every precaution has been taken in the preparation of this book, neither the author nor PRIMEDIA Inc. nor LEISURE ARTS, Inc. shall have any liability to any person or entity with respect to any liability, loss or damage caused or alleged to be caused directly or indirectly by the instructions contained in this book.

TRADEMARKS

Trademarked names are used throughout this book. Rather than put a trademark symbol in every occurrence of a trademarked name, we state we are using the names only in an editorial fashion and to the benefit of the trademark owner with no intention of infringement of the trademark.

CORPORATE OFFICES

Creating Keepsakes is located at 14901 Heritagecrest Way, Bluffdale, UT 84065. Phone: 801/984-2070. Fax: 801/984-2080. Home page: *www.creatingkeepsakes.com*.

Scrapbooking Friends & Family
Hardcover ISBN# 1-57486-408-4
Softcover ISBN# 1-57486-424-6
Library of Congress Control Number 2004102013

Published by Leisure Arts, Inc., 5701 Ranch Drive, Little Rock, Arkansas 72223, 501-868-8800. *www.leisurearts.com.* Printed in the United States of America.
Vice President and Editor-in-Chief: Sandra Graham Case
Executive Director of Publications: Cheryl Nodine Gunnells
Senior Publications Director: Susan White Sullivan
Director of Designer Relations: Debra Nettles
Licensed Product Coordinator: Lisa Truxton Curton
Special Projects Director: Susan Frantz Wiles
Special Projects Designer: Lisa Laney-Hodges
Associate Editors: Steven M. Cooper, Susan McManus Johnson, and Kimberly L. Ross
Senior Art Operations Director: Jeff Curtis
Art Imaging Director: Mark Hawkins
Imaging Technicians: Stephanie Johnson and Mark Potter
Publishing Systems Administrator: Becky Riddle
Publishing Systems Assistants: Clint Hanson, John Rose, and Chris Wertenberger
Senior Director of Public Relations and Retail Marketing: Stephen Wilson

Publisher: Rick Barton
Vice President, Finance: Tom Siebenmorgen
Director of Corporate Planning and Development: Laticia Mull Dittrich
Vice President, Retail Marketing: Bob Humphrey
Vice President, Sales: Ray Shelgosh
Vice President, National Accounts: Pam Stebbins
Director of Sales and Services: Margaret Reinold
Vice President, Operations: Jim Dittrich
Comptroller, Operations: Rob Thieme
Retail Customer Service Manager: Stan Raynor
Print Production Manager: Fred F. Pruss

a common bond

Friends and Family

As I TRAVEL the country talking with scrapbookers, I find there's one thing we all have in common: each of us has family and friends who are important to us. After all, it's the memories we create with our loved ones that motivate us to continue scrapbooking.

Creating Keepsakes is dedicated to providing you the inspiration you need to create scrapbook pages that will be cherished for years to come. In this volume, we've collected some of our favorite ideas and techniques you can use to make your scrapbook pages a reflection of you and your loved ones. You'll find limitless ideas for every month of the year and every stage of life.

So sit back and get ready to be inspired. With the ideas in this book and your own life stories, you'll be well on your way to creating memorable scrapbook pages that will last a lifetime and beyond. ❤

Tracy

JACKIE BONETTE

86

JENNI BOWLIN

249

CREATING Keepsakes

contents

SCRAPBOOKING FRIENDS & FAMILY

31

144

Through the Months

Through the Years

212

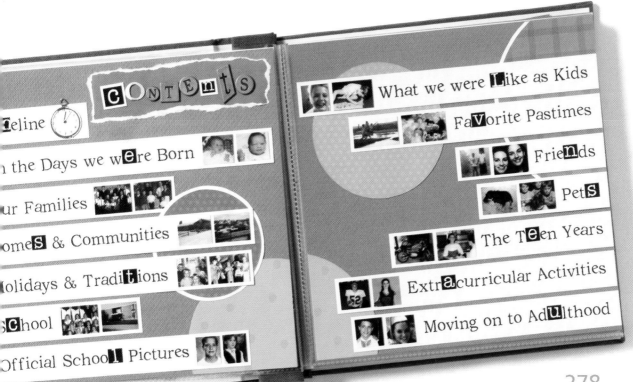

278

Be such a man, and
live such a life,
that if every man
were such as you,
and every life
a life like yours,
this earth would be
God's paradise.

OLD NAVY

2002

...and justice for all. ...and justice for

JULY 2002

Joshua and Chandler

great

Perfect

Savoring a sweet
Moment in Time
Grandpa Dennis & Brina
SLC. October 2002

january

SHANNON WATT

new beginnings

From New Year's resolutions to fresh-fallen snow, January is all about new beginnings. Capture the inspiration and hope of the month, as well as the warm, cozy moments you share with others, in photographs you'll treasure. Here are 15 ideas to get you started:

- Icicles sparkling as they hang from rooftops
- Clear, blue skies reflecting light on the clean snow
- Firewood piled high, ready to provide warmth and light
- The snowman alone in the backyard when everyone's come in for the night
- Tightly packed snowballs ready to be launched from little hands

- Driveways and sidewalks being shoveled before the sun comes up
- Brightly colored oranges at the peak of their sweetness
- Ice-skating outdoors for as long as you can bear the cold
- Beds covered in puffy quilts and comforters
- Rubber snow boots in a row by the back door

- Feet snuggled in warm, woolly slippers
- Bundled-up kids sledding down hills
- Knit mittens, scarves and hats that match
- Fresh footprints (and paw prints) in the snow
- Smoke drifting from every chimney on the block

ARTICLE BY CATHERINE SCOTT

new year's eve and kids

Spice your scrapbooks with holiday cheer

Dearest Keaton;

As your parents, we want so many things for you. Nothing but the best seems good enough and we find such joy in giving you all that we can. Of all the things we will give you in your life, we hope that the most cherished gift we will pass on to you is the ability to live a full and very happy life. Gifts are wonderful and fun to get, but the things that really matter in life are often free. We want you to appreciate every day and never take life for granted. We want to instill in you the value and importance of being a positive and kind person. Treat others as you'd like to be treated and remember that you can positively make this world a better place just by being you and being respectful, joyful, thoughtful, helpful, and true. Keep true to yourself .... know that we love you as you are .... and always will.

Love Mom & Dad

Be such a man, and live such a life, that if every man were such as you, and every life a life like yours, this earth would be God's paradise.

Supplies *Patterned paper:* Doodlebug Design; *Computer font:* Batik Typewriter Regular, downloaded from the Internet; *Fibers:* Fabulous Fibers; *Adhesive:* Hermafix tabs; *Other:* Beads and hand-cut stars. *Ideas to note:* For the peel-back frame, Leslie cut a cardstock "photo mat" on three sides, then tore the fourth side and rolled the edge for artistic effect. She hung the stars by wrapping fiber around the bottom of the frame cutout.

"Be Such a Man"
by Leslie Lightfoot
Stirling, ON, Canada

Photo by Peg McCarthy

It's not every day that a baby turns one, and Keaton's parents wanted to "capture some good photos while he was still so little." They took him to a professional photographer, who shot roll after roll of film.

This is just one of the many layouts Leslie has scrapbooked for her son's "One Year Photo Shoot" album. The letter is from the many discussions Leslie and her husband have had since their child's birth. Notes Leslie, "We want Keaton to know he is loved and that he can impact the world by just being positive and true to himself."

ARTICLE BY LANNA WILSON

Supplies *Vellum:* Paper Adventures; *Lettering template:* Block, ABC Tracers, Pebbles for EK Success; *Computer font:* CK Journaling, "The Best of Creative Lettering" CD Combo, *Creating Keepsakes; Beads:* Darice (royal blue), Mill Hill (red), Halcraft USA (purple), Westrim Crafts (orange, yellow, pink and teal) and Wangs (green); *Craft wire:* Artistic Wire Ltd.; *Pen:* Zig Writer, EK Success; *Chalk:* Craf-T Products; *Sequins:* Crafts Etc.! *Idea to note:* Alisa sewed beads and sequins onto felt letter cutouts for her title.

"The Magic of Midnight"
by Alisa Bangerter
Centerville, UT

Alisa's children were thrilled to visit their grandparents and cousins one New Year's Eve. As the midnight hour drew near, everyone waited anxiously, armed with confetti, streamers, party hats and horns.

Recalls Alisa, "The clock struck midnight and the celebration began—amid a yawn or two!" When she scrapbooked the event, Alisa chose black for her page background to create a sense of midnight. She speckled her titles and accents with beads, sequins, wire and bright paper for a festive look.

"Winter"
by Susan Cliett
Belvedere, SC

Snow is a rare treat in South Carolina, and Susan shot four rolls of film of her kids playing in the powdery delight. "The idea for this page came to me one night after I went to bed," she recalls.

Susan layered vellum over the denim cardstock for a softer look, then tore openings for the vellum "frames" after printing the journaling. "I love how the results frame my kids' faces and match the rough lines of the snowballs," says Susan.

Supplies *Specialty paper:* Denim and Natural Rain, Patchwork Memories; Marco Paper (silver); *Computer font:* CK Script, "The Best of Creative Lettering" CD Combo, *Creating Keepsakes; Vellum:* Hot Off The Press (printed) and Marco Paper (overlay); *Snowflake punch:* Marvy Uchida; *Eyelets:* Doodlebug Design; *Other:* Sheer ribbon. *Idea to note:* Susan threaded the ribbon through eyelets she punched through the vellum and cardstock.

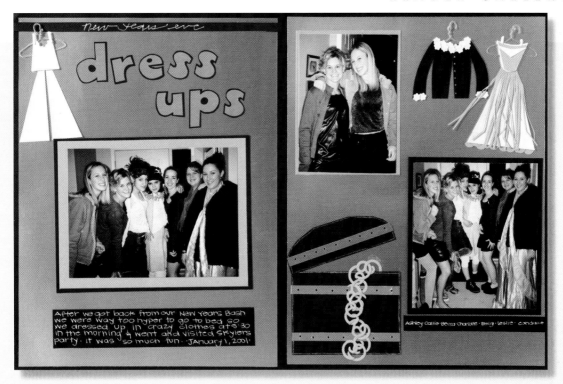

"New Year's Eve Dress-Ups"

by Ashley Schow
Cardston, AB, Canada

Supplies *Specialty cardstock:* Making Memories (silver and pink foil) and Paper Adventures (sparkly); *Punches:* Darice (mini flower and big flower), Family Treasures (medium swirl), and Marvy Uchida (dot); *Tape:* Hermafix, Tape Runner; *Stickers:* me & my BIG ideas; *Glue:* Zig 2-way Glue Marker, EK Success; *White pen:* Milky Gel Roller, Pentel; *Craft wire:* Artistic Wire Ltd.; *Hangers, clothing and trunk:* Ashley's own designs

New Year's Eve warrants an all-night party, and Ashley and her friends weren't ready to call it quits. They found a trunk filled with old clothes, dressed up and headed out. "I wanted this layout to communicate my excitement," says Ashley, "so I chose hot pink! The clothes are my designs. I just looked at the pictures and got ideas from our outfits."

"The Joys of Having Boys"

by Susan Kresge
Temple Terrace, FL

Underwear on her boys' heads? "This was just a typical day in our family," says Susan. "The boys are always coming up with something silly."

While Susan likes to take photos on special days and holidays, she admits that pictures of everyday activities are her favorites. For this layout, she used patterned paper that matches her bathroom wallpaper.

Supplies *Patterned paper:* Frances Meyer; *Lettering template:* Wacky, ABC Tracers, Pebbles for EK Success; *Computer fonts:* Kabel (title), Microsoft Works; CK Journaling (journaling), "The Best of Creative Lettering" CD Combo, *Creating Keepsakes*; *Embroidery floss:* DMC; *Tags:* Susan's own designs

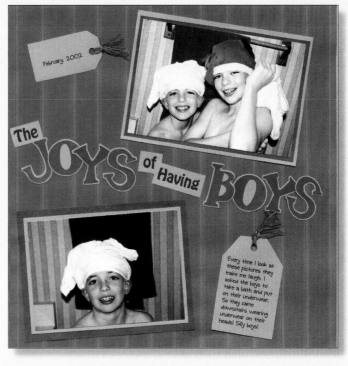

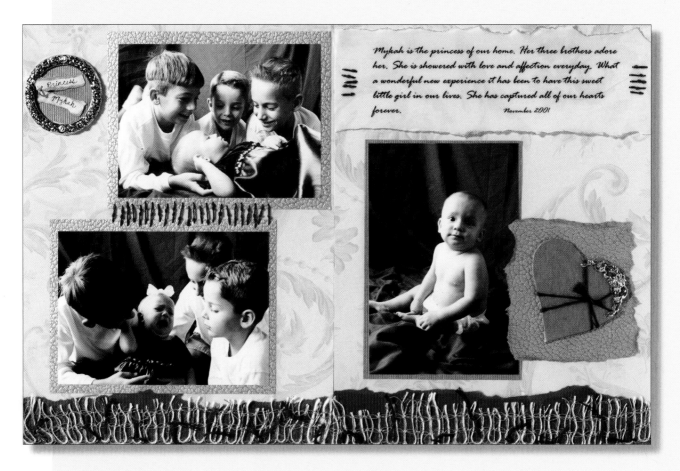

Mykah is the princess of our home. Her three brothers adore her. She is showered with love and affection everyday. What a wonderful new experience it has been to have this sweet little girl in our lives. She has captured all of our hearts forever.

November 2001

"Princess Mykah"

by Shannon Jones
Mesa, AZ

When Shannon's friend Sarah asked her to take photos of her children, Shannon readily agreed. "I was so impressed by the way the boys treated their new sister," Shannon recalls. "They doted on her and indulged her every whim. She is obviously the princess in their house."

While scrapbooking the pictures, Shannon used different gold textures and deep-purple accents to create a royalty motif. "The outcome," she says, "is pages fit for a princess—Princess Mykah, to be exact."

Supplies *Patterned paper:* Anna Griffin; *Gold and purple specialty paper:* Memory Lane; *Computer font:* Page Italics, Microsoft Office; *Floss ribbon and frames:* Memory Lane; *Pen:* Zig Millennium, EK Success; *Heart:* Shannon's own design; *Embroidery floss:* DMC. *Idea to note:* Shannon cut the gold floss ribbon in half, then tied it to the page with floss.

Story Time

Record the stories that make your family unique

While driving through Las Vegas on a recent vacation, I stayed with cousins I don't see very often. My favorite cousin, Anthony, and I have a habit of talking into the wee hours of the morning.

On this particular occasion, Anthony pulled out the family Bible and showed me the names, birth, marriage and death dates of family members I've heard of but never known. He showed me where my mother wrote my name, and I added my son's information to this crumbling family annal. We laughed and relived family stories (and legends) until almost 4 a.m.

Listening to these crazy tales helped me appreciate the spice my family adds to my life. Whether you're gathering with family this holiday season or another time of the year, take time to record your family's stories. (See samples that follow.) Future generations will remember and retell the stories for years to come!

by Danna Carter

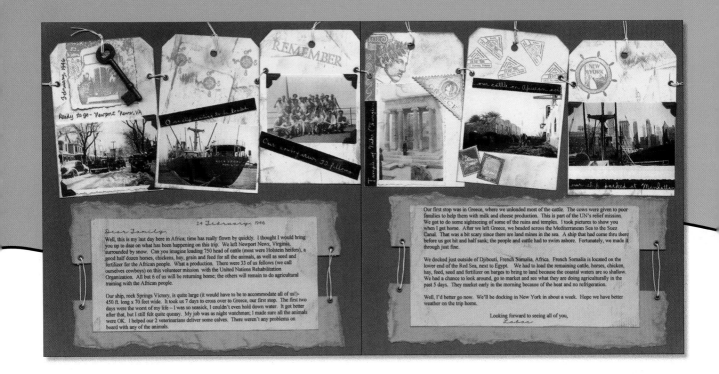

"International Cowboy"

by Carol Wingert • Gilbert, AZ

Supplies *Waxed linen and eyelets:* Memory Lane; *Stamping ink:* Adirondack, Ranger Industries; *Rubber stamps:* Hero Arts (Africa), Inkadinkadoo (compass), Stampa Rosa ("Remember"), Stamp Francisco (New York), Stampington (vintage car) and Toybox (Greece); *Skeleton key:* Stampington; *Computer fonts:* CK Cursive, "The Best of Creative Lettering" CD Combo, *Creating Keepsakes*; Times New Roman, Microsoft Word; *Postage stamps:* PostalZ. *Idea to note:* Carol connected the tags with eyelets to form a pictorial storybook.

Journaling excerpt: "Can you imagine loading 750 head of cattle (most were Holstein heifers), a good half dozen horses, chickens, hay, grain and feed for all the animals, as well as seed and fertilizer for the African people? What a production! There were 33 of us fellows (call ourselves cowboys) on this volunteer mission with the United Nations Rehabilitation Organization. All but six of us will be returning home; the others will remain to do agricultural training with the African people...."

Ideas for Recording Family Stories

The story has been told and retold about how my third great-uncle was born in a leaky tent while his family crossed the plains in 1851. Do you struggle to find the important stories in your family? Consider the following ideas to help you find and record family stories from bygone eras:

* Take a tape recorder to your next family get-together. Prompt someone to talk about old family stories passed down through the generations.

* Don't lose your own stories. Set aside a time each week to write down a memory.

* Scour old letters. You'll be surprised at how much stories evolve over the years.

* Read journals for insightful and meaningful accounts. Use the accounts as the journaling on your pages.

* Peruse old wills. They can be incredibly informative, especially those written in past eras.

* Check the backs of photographs for notes. They can also trigger memories.

* Did a family member do something newsworthy? Check your local newspaper or town history.

* Flip through family baby books for cute anecdotes.

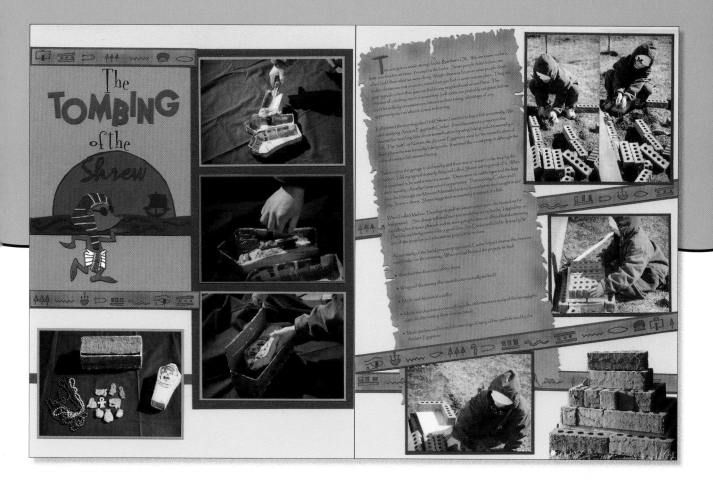

"The Tombing of the Shrew"

by Kendra McCracken • Bolivar, MO

Supplies *Clip art of shrew pharaoh and ship:* PrintMaster; *Computer fonts:* Babe Bamboo (title), Mariah, Papyrus (journaling) and fontdinerdotcom, downloaded from the Internet; *Pens:* Zig Writer, EK Success; Le Plume, Marvy Uchida; *Stamping ink:* Archival Ink. *Ideas to note:* Kendra drew the hieroglyphics on cardstock strips and hand cut the papyrus journaling sheet. She sponged ink onto the sheet for a more realistic look.

Journaling excerpt: "Shawn, Caelan and I were studying Ancient Egypt. I discovered a neat project on the Internet for using baking soda on fish to teach kids about mummification.

"When I went out to the garage to do laundry, I found a mouse in the trap by the washer. The 'mouse' turned out to be a shrew. Shawn suggested we mummify it instead of a fish.

"When I called a friend to tell her about our project, she teased me for being weird. I egged her on by telling her the shrew was a pharaoh and we were going to have an official burial ceremony. We did, and it was one of the most educational home-school projects we've done."

"Catholic Missal"
by Pam Canavan • Clermont, FL

Supplies *Leather paper:* Paper Pizazz; *Stamping ink:* Close To My Heart; *Eyelets:* Dritz; *Computer font:* Lucinda Blackletter, downloaded from the Internet; *Other:* Fibers. *Ideas to note:* Pam dragged her cardstock across a sepia inkpad to give the paper an archaic look. She photographed the missal next to a pen to give viewers a reference on size.

Journaling excerpt: "These are pictures of the Catholic missal that John Canavan brought over when he immigrated to the United States. We are pretty sure the missal is actually his; however, the story that goes along with the missal may be just that, a good story!

". . . John carried his missal with him at all times, including when he went to battle during the Civil War. The 'story' part comes in when supposedly he was hit in the chest by a Confederate bullet and the bullet was 'stopped' by the missal! . . . This may be one case where faith literally saved someone's life!"

"Why Is That Chair There?"
by Gail Newton-Bowman • Orangeburg, SC

Supplies *Computer font:* Garamouche, Impress Rubber Stamps; *Alphabet eyelets and button:* Making Memories; *Ribbon:* C.M. Offray & Son. *Idea to note:* Gail ran her ribbon through a Xyron machine.

Journaling excerpt: "When Henry and I went to Myrtle Beach for our second wedding anniversary, I was looking forward to taking some great beach pictures. When I saw Henry lounging on the balcony, I thought, 'Here is my chance!' In my excitement to get a candid picture, I slammed the balcony door behind me, locking us out of our room.

"When someone came to help us, I realized that not only did I lock us out of the room, but I also locked our help out of the room. I had the security lock on the door!

"After the guard fashioned a tool to release the security lock, we were rescued. Now, whenever I go on a balcony, I make sure I stick a chair in the door—JUST in case!"

Leona and Edmond Kruse were first cousins to my mom. Their mother was the much older sister of my grandmother Anna. While my mother didn't really know her cousins as children, because they were many years older than she was, the story about their donkey, Nellie, was told again and again.

Nellie was purchased from a neighbor when Edmond was just a baby. The Kruses used Nellie to pull carts of small harvests to market. She was also a friend to Edmond and took him for rides whenever she wasn't pulling carts. After Leona was born, she too, would take rides on Nellie for entertainment. They were very good friends with the donkey.

One winter day when Edmond was a bit older, he got in trouble for accidentally letting the chickens out of the hen house. He was so upset, that while his ma and pa were rounding up the chickens, he and Leona took off on Nellie across the fields. It was snowy and very cold. They came across a frozen pond and attempted to cross it.

When they were almost to the other side, the ice broke and Leona fell off into the pond. Nellie got Edmond up to the side and he got off. Then Nellie went back into the pond to rescue Leona. The little girl was able to grab onto Nellie's mane and Nellie pulled her to safety, just as Ma, Pa, and the 2 oldest brothers came looking for Edmond and Leona.

From then on Nellie was considered a part of the family and her main job was entertaining the children with rides.

"Part of the Family"

by Mary Larson • Chandler, AZ

Supplies *Patterned papers:* Bo-Bunny Press (flecked) and K & Company (flowered); *Letter blocks:* My Mind's Eye; *Letter stickers:* Nostalgiques ("Part of the"), Sticko by EK Success; *Chalk:* Craf-T Products; *Ribbon:* C.M. Offray & Son; *Computer font:* Bookman, Microsoft Word; *Other:* Buckle, lace, numbers, buttons and metal ring.

Journaling excerpt: "One winter day, Edmond got in trouble for accidentally letting the chickens out of the hen house. He was so upset that he and Leona took off on Nellie, our donkey. They came across a frozen pond and attempted to cross it.

"When they were almost to the other side, the ice broke and Leona fell into the pond. Nellie got Edmond to the side, then went back to rescue Leona. The little girl was able to grab on to Nellie's mane and the donkey pulled her to safety, just as Ma, Pa and the two oldest brothers came looking for Edmond and Leona.

"From then on Nellie was considered a part of the family. Her main job was entertaining the children with rides."

RENEW????
YOU HAVE TO RENEW YOUR LICENSE?

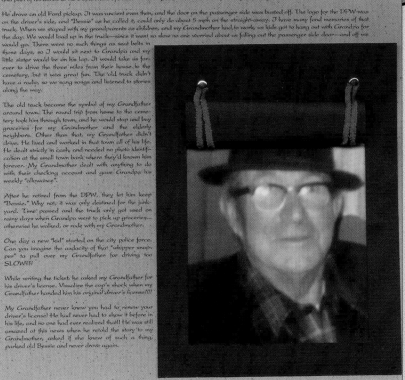

"Renew?"

by Kathie Rinehart • Port Orchard, WA

Supplies *Fibers:* Brown Bag Fibers; *Computer fonts:* Rubber Stamp and President, downloaded from the Internet; *Other:* Brads. *Idea to note:* Kathie's son drew a picture of the car, which he copied from a picture on the Internet.

Journaling excerpt: "One day a new 'kid' started on the city police force. Can you imagine the audacity of that 'whippersnapper' pulling my grandfather over for driving too SLOW?

"While writing the ticket, he asked my grandfather for his driver's license. Visualize the cop's shock when my grandfather handed him his original driver's license!

"My grandfather never knew you had to renew your driver's license! He'd never had to show it before, and no one had ever realized that! He was still amazed at this news when he retold the story to my grandmother. He parked old Bessie, his truck, and never drove again."

12 FRESH LAYOUTS THAT CELEBRATE

My name is Lisa Bearnson, and I'm 38 years old. My life is approximately half over. If I didn't have a tomorrow, do I have a scrapbook that tells about me? Have I created pages that tell about my likes and dislikes or who I am and what I stand for?

While browsing through my children's scrapbooks, I realized that the books—while incredible in what they cover—don't tell much about me. How will my posterity know what was important to me?

I know, you're probably thinking, "Another scrapbook to create? I can't even keep up with the photos I already have!" Or perhaps you're thinking, "Would people think I'm conceited?" or "But my life is too boring."

Let me share my thoughts. First, I've kept this project simple and doable, with easy suggestions for success. All you have to do is create *one layout* a month, and at the end of the year you'll have a beautiful album that highlights *you.*

Please don't feel it's conceited to create a book about yourself. You'll find it revealing, and family and friends will consider your efforts a priceless gift for years to come. And don't worry about having a boring life. As you create these pages, you'll find out that you're a lot more interesting than you thought.

The new year is here. Let's get started on your first page!

BY LISA BEARNSON

A title page sets the tone for your book. Don't be shy about including your photo! *Page by Jocelyne Hayes.*
Supplies *Computer fonts:* Crumbly Gingersnap, Vintage and Broken Flower Pot, all downloaded from *www.twopeasinabucket.com; Cardstock and vellum:* Accent Designs; *Fibers:* On the Surface; *Other:* Brads and specialty paper.

JANUARY

January is a natural time for beginnings, so why not start by creating a title page? You'll find a heartwarming example above by Jocelyne Hayes, plus suggestions and an inspiration starter.

"WHY I'M ME"

To create a title page for your album:

1. Get a photo of you taken. (This is a must!)

2. Write why this album is important for you and your posterity. Include the date.

3. Jot down 15–20 words that describe what will be included in the album.

4. Dedicate the album to a special someone.

INSPIRATION STARTER

Here's what Jocelyne wrote on her page:

"The other day, my mother and I were rummaging through some old photographs of our ancestors. Luckily, on the back of many photos we found a name and a date. However, even with a name, there were many stories left untold and unanswered questions. What were they thinking? What were their dreams, their ambitions, their goals? I will never be able to find these answers, but I can prevent you from having the same questions as you look back through photos of your ancestors.

"Come and take a peek into my life. Enclosed you will find my dreams, my values, my strengths, my memories, and my thoughts. Together these are my own personal legacy, and the purpose is so that those who come after me will know what makes me who I am— what makes me 'me.'

"Take it as advice, both on what to do and what not to do. Enjoy reading about my dreams and goals. Laugh at some of my funny and embarrassing moments. But most importantly, enjoy knowing more about me than a simple name and date! I encourage you, the reader of my album, to create your own legacy. Trust me, your future generations will be so touched that you thought about them, and cared enough to give them a peek into your life."

FEBRUARY

February is full of admiration for those who've touched our lives. Like Kristy Banks, above, scrapbook the most influential people in your life!

"MOST INFLUENTIAL PEOPLE"

To create this layout:

1. Make a list of the people in your life who have influenced you most.

2. Gather a photo of each person. (If you only have one photo or no photos, that's okay, too.)

3. Jot down one word that describes how each person influenced you to be the person you are today.

4. Write in more detail how each person has made an impression on your life.

5. Incorporate all these thoughts on a layout.

INSPIRATION STARTER

Has one of the following influenced your life?

- Parent
- Sibling
- Child
- Friend
- Teacher
- Spiritual leader
- Babysitter
- Stranger
- Doctor
- Co-worker
- Celebrity
- Coach
- Boss

Include the people who have influenced you the most. *Pages by Kristy Banks.* **Supplies** *Sage paper:* Paperfever; *Computer fonts:* CK Typewriter, CK Elusive, CK Gutenburg and CK Inky, "Fresh Fonts" CD, *Creating Keepsakes; Letter stickers:* Flavia, Colorbök; *Vellum:* Paper Adventures; *Eyelets:* Dritz; *Metal charms:* Making Memories; *Flower bradlets:* Provo Craft; *Paper clip:* Doggie Treats, Boxer Scrapbook; *Silver embossing powder:* Timeless Images; *Quotes:* Downloaded from *www.quotegarden.com; Other:* Wishing stone and tiny brads.

> ## ALL I NEED TO KNOW
> *in life*
> ## I LEARNED FROM
>
> **BENJAMIN HUNSAKER**
>
> My next-door neighbor, 24-year-old Ben, has probably taught me more about life than any other person. While most would call his Down Syndrome physical challenge a burden, I call it a strength. Ben has touched so many lives for good and taught lessons unlike any other person. Here's what I've learned from Ben:
>
> ### Love your favorite things with a passion
>
> Ben's favorite person in the whole world is Michael J. Fox. He has every movie Michael's starred in, every magazine that has ever mentioned his name and his latest book that talks about his disability. Ask Ben any trivia question about his "best friend" Michael Fox and he doesn't even skip a beat when he answers it. Ben's also passionate about his huge movie collection and the memorabilia he got when he appeared on Touched by an Angel.
>
> ### The best way to have a friend is to be one
>
> Every time I get a letter from Ben, it makes my day. Even though he only lives next door, he often delivers hand-written notes to let me know he's thinking of me, to thank me for being his friend and to ask me if I've figured out a way from him to meet Michael J. Fox yet.
>
> ### Take the Scenic Route—Explore, Dream, Discover!
>
> I often watch Ben walk to the bus stop. He's never in any hurry to get there—he's always stopping to discover the extraordinary things that to most of us are ordinary. Maybe it's a new flower that's bloomed ... maybe a bug that's crawling across the pavement.
>
> ### Show your real emotions
>
> While Ben is happy most the time, he's also a real person who's not afraid to show when he's mad, sad, angry or glad. He's also quick to forgive when someone's offended him.
>
> ### Enthusiasm is the key to true happiness
>
> Whether Ben is off to a day of school, performing in his dance group, going to the movies with his girlfriend, Amy Witherton, or packing his own lunch, he's always enthusiastic about what he's doing—no matter how mundane. I gave him the double of the photo on this page and you'd have thought he'd won the lottery!
>
> "Life consists not in holding good cards but in playing those you hold well."
> Josh Billings

Highlight the lessons you've learned from the people around you. *Page by Lisa Bearnson.* **Supplies** *Tag, button and ribbon:* Doo-Dads, Colorbök; *Computer fonts:* CK Twilight, CK Chemistry and CK Fresh, "Fresh Fonts" CD, *Creating Keepsakes; Chalk:* Stampin' Up!; *Corners:* FreshCuts, EK Success.

MARCH

March is a time for remembering life's lessons. Scrapbook yours, like I did above with what I've learned from my neighbor Ben.

"LIFE'S LESSONS"

To create this layout:

1. Think of one person in your life who has taught you some important lessons.

2. Write down the lessons he or she has taught you (one sentence per lesson). Share what you've observed with this person.

3. Get a picture of this person, either alone or with you.

4. Combine the photo and lessons on a scrapbook page.

INSPIRATION STARTER

Maybe a lesson you learned came from a stranger who stopped to change your tire on a cold, rainy day. Maybe it came from a physically challenged friend like my neighbor Ben. Maybe it came from your newborn baby who's so dependent on you for everything.

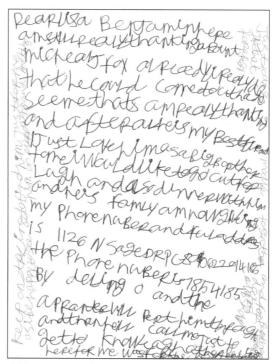

This is an example of the notes I regularly receive from my neighbor Ben.

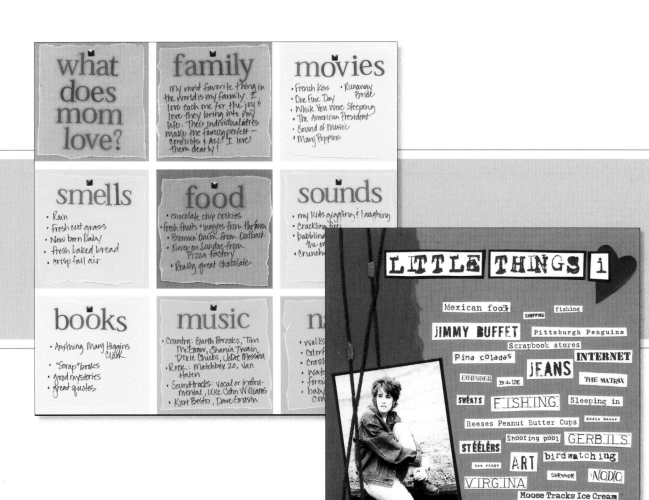

what does mom love?

family
My most favorite thing in the world is my family. I love each one for the joy & love they bring into my life. Their individualities make the family perfect — conflicts & all! I love them dearly!

movies
- French Kiss
- Runaway Bride
- One Fine Day
- While You Were Sleeping
- The American President
- Sound of Music
- Mary Poppins

smells
- Rain
- Fresh cut grass
- New born baby
- fresh baked bread
- crisp fall air

food
- Chocolate chip cookies
- fresh fruits & veggies from the farm
- Bloomin Onion from Outback
- Never on Sunday from Pizza Factory
- Really great Chocolate

sounds
- my kids giggling & laughing
- crackling fire
- babbling the ...
- Crunch...

books
- Anything Mary Higgins Clark
- "Scrap" books
- good mysteries
- great quotes

music
- Country: Garth Brooks, Tim McGraw, Shania Twain, Dixie Chicks, Jo Dee Messina
- Rock: Matchbox 20, Van Halen
- Soundtracks: Vocal or instrumental, like John Williams
- Kurt Bestor, Dave Grusin

n...
- walk...
- color...
- crash...
- wate...
- forei...
- baby...
- cow...

LITTLE THINGS I ♥

Mexican food · SHOPPING · fishing · JIMMY BUFFET · Pittsburgh Penguins · Scrapbook stores · Pina coladas · JEANS · INTERNET · LOBSTER · BLUE · THE MATRIX · SWEATS · FISHING · Sleeping in · Reeses Peanut Butter Cups · Eddie Bauer · Shooting pool · GERBILS · STEELERS · ice rings · ART · birdwatching · VIRGINA · SURVIVOR · AC DC · Moose Tracks Ice Cream · SHRIMP · CAMPING · SPRING · FAMILY · X-ACTO KNIFE

Create a "What I Love" page that's divided into categories. *Page by Kerri Bradford.* **Supplies** *Paper and stickers:* SEI; *Silver square embellishments:* Scrapyard 329.

Take a "random" yet artistic approach when sharing what you love. *Page by Pam Kopka.* **Supplies** *Paper glaze:* Aleen's Paper Glaze; *Fibers:* On the Surface; *Computer fonts:* Mail Bomb, Facelift, Stamping, Ticket Capitals, Metallic Avocado, Hootie, Blue Baby, Mechanical Fun, Trash and Splendid, downloaded from the Internet; *Paper beads:* Pam's own creation.

APRIL

April brings sunshine . . . and showers. Like Kerri Bradford and Pam Kopka, you can capture the things you love on a scrapbook page. But don't stop there—also scrapbook the things that bug you.

"THINGS I LOVE"

1. For the next few days, make a list of all the things you love. (I have a "Things I Love" page that accompanies my "Things That Bug Me" page in my editor's note this issue.)

2. Scrapbook what you love. As shown here, you can divide your page into categories (note Kerri's page and how it incorporates her own handwriting). Or, present the things you love in a random order, as shown by Pam Kopka.

Scrapbook the favorite spot where you feel "at one" with yourself. *Page by Ashley Gull.*
Supplies *Computer font:* Dragonfly, downloaded from *www.twopeasinabucket.com*; *Mesh:* Magic Mesh, Avant Card; *Compass stamp:* All Night Media; *Stamping ink:* VersaMark and InkXpressions; *Colored pencils:* Prismacolor, EK Success; *Mini brads, Vellum:* Paper Adventures. *Idea to note:* Ashley used VersaMark inkpads over the tan paper to make it appear like an old map. She also chalked and inked the torn edges to create a burned look.

MAY

May is a perfect time to scrapbook a favorite spot. Like Ashley Gull, above, share where you go to "get away" from it all.

"A FAVORITE SPOT"

To create this layout:

1. Reflect on a favorite place that makes you feel secure, serene and "at one" with yourself.

2. Write down the sights, sounds and smells associated with this spot. How do you feel when you're there?

3. Have someone take a picture of your favorite spot (with you in it, of course!).

4. Create a page that will remind you and your family that the simplest places in life can be the best of all.

INSPIRATION STARTER

Does your favorite spot include one of the following?
• A grandparent's home
• A lake, stream or waterfall
• A cozy spot by the fireplace
• A front-porch swing
• A sporting event
• A Jacuzzi
• A garden
• A cabin
• A craft room
• A church
• A park bench
• A library
• A shopping mall
• A spa
• Disneyland (just joking!)

ASHLEY'S JOURNALING

"The waves crashing in at our feet while we stare out at the vast ocean before us creates a sense of peace. I feel at one with myself when I stand on a shore. The unknowns before me seem insignificant to that very moment. I realize how precious each breath is as I inhale the salty ocean air. Everyone needs a place they can escape to and feel at peace. This is my place. I am so glad to have been able to share it with you."

Knead

My memories of being four years old are fragmented--blurred really. But every time I smell bread baking I am instantly transported back to that time with Mom.

The kids were at school and Mom was my captive audience. Once a week we'd bake bread, but it was more than just baking bread it was a ritual. In one afternoon we turned our house into a warm, aromatic haven that buffered the kids from the pressures of grammar school.

Once the warm, yeasty dough had risen in its shiny, silver container, Mom placed the big bucket on the floor. I kneeled between her knees, placed my dimpled four-year-old hands on the wooden handle, then felt her strong hands wrap around mine. After she secured my hands, we slowly turned the handle. My little arms stretched out before me then back again as we methodically kneaded the bread. I could have never turned that handle on my own, but her help made it easy.

Rise

Bake

No, I no longer bake bread. But on tough days I know I can rely on Mom. Whether she physically puts her hands on mine, or metaphorically, her love and support can make my life just a little easier.

Random Memories of living in Turlock picking grapes with Mom at the neighborhood vineyard • singing "On Top of the World" above the sunken living room • riding super-fast on my trike, hurrying to pass the "haunted" house on the corner • listening to the 1812 overture over and over with the boy next door • getting my "Cabbie doll" for Christmas • refusing to take a nap at preschool • blushing because I accidentally called the preschool teacher "Grandma" • playing croquet in the backyard • being the baby of the family

JUNE

With its laid-back days, June is just the month to scrapbook a tangible item you treasure. Above, Tracy White chose to highlight a well-worn, well-loved bread maker.

Tell how a favorite tangible treasure invokes memories of intangible treasures. *Pages by Tracy White.* **Supplies** *Computer font:* My Old Remington, downloaded from *www.free-typewriter-fonts.com.*

"A FAVORITE TREASURE"
To create this layout:

1. Identify your favorite tangible treasure.

2. Ask if it invokes a special memory.

3. Take photos of your treasure. (Note how Tracy found different, interesting ways to photograph the same object.) Write down why the object is so meaningful to you.

4. Include the photos and journaling on a scrapbook page.

INSPIRATION STARTER
Tracy's page beautifully captures her childhood memories of baking bread with her mom. The old bread maker (still in Tracy's possession) is her tangible treasure. The intangible treasures? Memories of one-on-one time with mom and developing a strong, lasting relationship with her.

Time-saver: Print your title and journaling directly on your background paper, then adhere your photos without matting them.

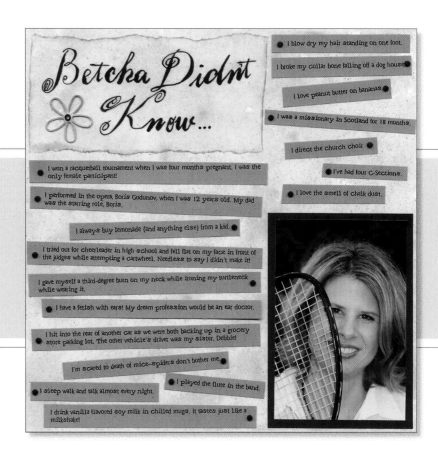

Jot down interesting items most people don't know about you. *Page by Lisa Bearnson.* **Supplies** *Patterned paper:* Provo Craft; *Computer font:* CK Evolution, "Fresh Fonts" CD, *Creating Keepsakes; Letter stickers:* Flavia, Colorbök; *Brads:* Doggie Treats, Boxer Scrapbook; *Chalk:* Stampin' Up!; *Metal charm:* Making Memories.

JULY

July is a time to abandon cares and just play. I had fun creating a layout about things people don't know about me.

"BETCHA DIDN'T KNOW"
To create this layout:

1. Make a list of the things most people don't know about your life. These can include funny experiences, trips, fears, talents and more. Be "real" and include some embarrassing moments, too (like the time I tried out for cheerleader and fell flat on my face in front of the judges).

2. Get a picture taken with an object that's associated with one of your "betcha didn't knows."

For example, note the picture of me with a tennis racket.

3. Create a quick page with your list, photo and "Betcha Didn't Know" title. People will love your page—I guarantee it!

"You are the author of your life's adventure. Weave your tales of wonder, save a place to dream and believe in your brave heart." — BRANCY BRITTON

Highlight your favorite hobby, plus your likes and dislikes about it. *Page by Kristy Banks*. **Supplies** *Patterned paper*: Scrap-Ease; *Letter stickers*: Colorbök; *3-D stickers*: Jolee's Boutique, Stickopotamus.

AUGUST

August is an ideal time to scrapbook your favorite hobby, be it practicing tae kwon do, refinishing furniture, or sewing (see the page above by Kristy Banks).

"YOUR FAVORITE HOBBY"

To create this layout:

1. Identify your favorite hobby. Choose something besides scrapbooking—your posterity will know you loved it just by looking through your books.

2. Record your likes and dislikes. Why are you willing to spend time and money on your hobby? What frustrates you about it?

3. Include your thoughts and feelings—along with any photos of finished projects—on a scrapbook page.

INSPIRATION STARTER

Like Kristy, include twice the journaling and another photo by creating flaps under some of the paper and photo blocks.

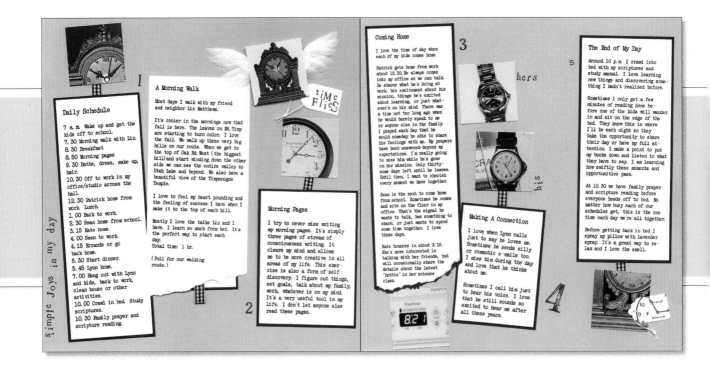

SEPTEMBER

Come September, it's time to get back on schedule. Scrapbook your daily routine, choosing a "Time Flies" theme like Kim McCrary's above.

"YOUR DAILY ROUTINE"
To create this layout:

1. Write down your daily routine. Be specific with times and events.

2. Identify five favorite parts of your daily routine.

3. Take photos of some of the things you do each day. Or, use Kim's clever idea and take pictures of all the different clocks in your home. (Kim included her formal living-room clock, her casual family-room clock, "his" and "her" watches and her stove's digital clock.)

4. Include all these elements on a page layout.

INSPIRATION STARTER
Include a pull-down tag under your journaling block. Like Kim, detail the walking route you take each day. Future generations will love walking the same route as great-grandma!

No matter how mundane, share your daily routine on a page layout. *Pages by Kim McCrary.* **Supplies** *Computer font:* Another Typewriter, downloaded from the Internet; *Feather wings:* Midwest; *Tags:* Accu-Cut Systems; *Letter stamps:* PSX Design; *Square punch:* Marvy Uchida; *Number stamps:* From Kim's collection of print blocks; *Other:* Ribbon.

OCTOBER

October is the month for creepy-crawlies. Counter that with a "Secrets to a Happy Life" layout. It's one of my favorites!

"SECRETS TO A HAPPY LIFE"

1. Take several days to meditate, then jot down your secrets to a happy life. It's fine to inject a little humor.

2. Highlight one word that can easily describe each secret.

3. Gather and use several photos that relate to your "secrets."

4. Search books or the Internet for quotes that describe how you feel about life. I got the inspiration for this layout from an e-mail written by Andy Rooney and forwarded to me by a friend.

5. Have fun creating a layout that shares your secrets.

INSPIRATION STARTER

Gather a variety of photos for this layout. Since most will have been taken at different times, consider using a Kodak PictureMaker machine to change all your photos to black and white or sepia.

Your secrets to a happy life will be invaluable for generations to come. Don't be afraid to use your own handwriting. *Pages by Lisa Bearnson.* **Supplies** *Computer font:* Times Roman, Microsoft Word; *Paper:* SEI; *Chalk:* Stampin' Up!; *Alphabet stickers:* David Walker, Colorbök.

NOVEMBER

November is a time to be thankful . . . for a favorite "girl toy." Whether your toy is a funky cell phone or an SUV, scrapbook it!

"FAVORITE GIRL TOY"

To create this layout:

1. Forget the fallacy that only boys have cool toys. Look at your own life and see what brings you fun and pleasure.

2. Think of how your toy makes you feel and why you love it so.

3. Get pictures of you with your toy.

4. Create a page that shows you having the time of your life!

INSPIRATION STARTER

Is your favorite toy on the following list?

- Inline skates
- Big-screen TV
- Tanning bed
- Cooking set
- Computer
- Cosmetics
- Golf clubs
- Top-of-the-line oven

Cars can be "girl" toys, too. *Pages by Jocelyne Hayes.* **Supplies** *Computer font:* Stained Glass, downloaded from *www.twopeasinabucket.com.*

Reflect about the hardships and struggles concerning family, faith and friends. Remember to be "real" in what you write about. *Page by Julie Scattaregia.* **Supplies** *Pen:* Zig Writer, EK Success; *Chalk:* Craf-T Products and Stampin' Up!; *Computer font:* Lucida, WordPerfect; *Craft wire:* Artistic Wire Ltd.; *Eyelets:* Making Memories and Stamp Studio; *Eyelet charm, eyelet word, vellum square, button, page pebble and flower snap:* Making Memories; *Fibers:* On the Surface and Making Memories; *Tag:* Paper Reflection; *3-D stickers:* Jolee's Boutique, Stickopotamus; *Letter stickers:* David Walker, Colorbök; *Decorative leaf:* Black Ink; *Botanical stickers:* Maurice; *Heart and medium square punches:* EK Success; *Large square punch:* Marvy Uchida; *Stamps:* Stamp Craft (letters), Stampabilities (large key, pocket watch), Hero Arts (Italian poetry background, block letters), Limited Edition (small key) and Dawn Houser (heart locket); *Stamping ink:* Close To My Heart and Tsukineko; *Copper embossing powder:* Ranger Industries; *Cross charm:* Pincharmingo, Inc.; *Other:* Microbeads, brads, charms, key tag ring, Velcro and pop dots.

DECEMBER

December marks the end of the year and is a great time for reflection. Like Julie Scattaregia, above, scrapbook your trials and triumphs.

"REFLECTIONS ON FAITH, FAMILY AND FRIENDS"

To create this layout:

1. Write down your reflections on faith, family and friends. Did you go through a particularly difficult experience that tried your faith? Did you meet new friends? Are you staying in touch with old acquaintances? What does your family mean to you?

2. Gather photos, memorabilia and other items that relate to faith, family and friends. Create a collage for your page.

3. Personalize the layout more by including some of your own handwriting.

INSPIRATION STARTER

Create interactive flaps and tuck your heartfelt journaling behind your collages. Remember, your family will appreciate your honesty in this book about you!

Here's what Julie wrote for her "Family" section:

"What do you get when you combine a self-assured, opinionated, Italian man with a stubborn, self-sufficient graduate student? Cinderella and Prince Charming? Get real! But what a wonderful and wild roller coaster ride it has been for the past 15 years.

"I don't think I'll ever have this marriage thing entirely figured out, but I suppose that's what keeps our relationship so exciting, so frustrating, so alive! I'm happy we're still in love. Hearing the words 'I love my wife' makes me happier today than on the first day we were married. And who would have guessed that this overachieving, corporate career woman would find such unexpected joy as a stay-at-home mom? I want to absorb every minute of it. For now, this is where I want to be. I adore my precious family."

february

matters of the heart

Snow may be covering the ground, but in February our hearts are warmed by the romance in the air. As you celebrate "love, sweet love" this month, don't forget to enjoy—and scrapbook—the following sights, moments and experiences:

- Holding hands with the ones you love
- Sitting down to a candlelit dinner for two
- Spelling out messages with conversation hearts
- Filling the whole house with the scent of cinnamon
- Devouring a box of gourmet chocolates by yourself
- Making plans for your spring garden

- Reading a Jane Austen romance with family or friends
- Spending an afternoon making valentines with children
- Renting an evening's worth of romantic movies to laugh and cry over
- Composing an original love poem for your partner or dream partner
- Surprising someone with a dozen red roses when they least expect it

- Coating sweet sugar cookies with pink frosting and sprinkles
- Decorating someone's door with messages of love and friendship
- Bringing a smile to someone's face with a simple good deed
- Treating yourself to a bottle of fragrant perfume

ARTICLE BY CATHERINE SCOTT

love and chocolate

Sweet layouts for the season

Supplies
Vellum: The Paper Company; *Craft wire:* Artistic Wire Ltd.; *Foil paper:* HyGloss *Metal sheeting:* ArtEmboss; *Pigment ink:* Hampton Art Stamps; *Lettering template:* Pebbles in my Pocket; *Embossing powder:* Embossing Tinsel, Ranger Industries; *Computer font:* AucoinLight, downloaded from the Internet. *Idea to note:* To create the random pattern for the heat-embossed stripes, Shannon wadded plastic wrap, dabbed it in pigment ink, then sponged it onto her cardstock.

"A Moment Here with You"
by Shannon and David Landen
San Antonio, TX

Unexpected moments sometimes afford the most precious memories. "While snapping pictures of my son's soccer game, I turned toward the bleachers and captured this sweet moment between my husband and daughter," Shannon says.

Since this moment belonged to David, Shannon asked him to write the journaling. Notes Shannon, "His letter was so heartfelt that—after I stopped bawling—I told him he could do all the journaling from now on!"

ARTICLE BY LANNA WILSON

"A Letter to My Love"

by Kim Bailey
Twin Falls, ID

Kim is quick to exclaim that her husband Paul is "the hardest person to shop for!" When she couldn't find anything for Paul for Valentine's Day, she decided to make a love letter layout for him. "I started with a simple layout plan but kept coming up with new ideas," she says.

Six hours and a lot of embossing powder later, Kim completed her layout. Did her husband like his gift? "He loved it!" she smiles.

Supplies *Vellum:* Paper Accents and The Robin's Nest Press; *Mulberry paper:* PrintWorks; *Gold paper:* Golden Oak; *Pen:* Gelly Roll, Sakura; *Beads:* Create-a-Craft; *Eyelets:* Stamp Studio; *Brads:* Office Max; *Ribbon:* C.M. Offray & Son; *Embossing powder:* Stamp Craft; *Embossing pen:* Close To My Heart; *Stamping ink:* VersaColor, Tsukineko; *Rubber stamps:* Stampendous! (heart) and Rubber Stampede (love); *Other:* Charms, mesh ribbon and gold thread. *Ideas to note:* To create the heart at lower left, Kim stamped the image, then cut out the center and mounted it to the side. She then embossed the ripped cardstock and vellum for a gilded look. For the heart at top left, she wove strips of gold paper and vellum, then cut out a heart shape and embossed the edges.

"Celebrate Love"

by Lisa Rice
Scott City, MO

Dressing up isn't Lisa's idea of fun. When she and her husband embarked on a dinner cruise, Lisa says "we rented these formal outfits." Pictures were a must! And, Lisa already had the perfect journaling for her layout—song lyrics included in an e-mail from her husband.

"I used woven jewel tones because they reflect the formal feel of the night," Lisa explains. The envelope conceals the journaling on the tag.

Supplies *Vellum:* Paper Adventures; *Rubber stamp:* Stampa Rosa; *Embossing powder:* PSX Design; *Watermark ink:* Tsukineko; *Eyelets:* Stamp Doctor; *Computer fonts:* Mistral AV (title) and Tempus Sans ITC (journaling), Microsoft Word; *Tag and envelope:* Lisa's own designs; *Other:* Beads and copper wire. *Idea to note:* To create the metallic lettering, Lisa heat-embossed her hand-cut title.

Supplies *Vellum:*
Paper Adventures;
Pen: Milky Gel Roller,
Pentel; *Craft wire:*
Darice; *Other:* Eyelets

"Prisms of Love"

by Sharon Whitehead
Vernon, BC, Canada

Sharon's parents waited a long time for their pink bundle of joy. When Sharon was born, her parents were thrilled. "We waited five years for you," said her mother. "You are so loved."

Although the layout looks time-consuming, Sharon says it was "super easy to put together." Since most of the pieces of paper are different shapes and sizes, they didn't require measuring. Sharon simply made them large enough to accommodate the lettering but small enough to maintain the prismatic effect.

Sharon shaped covered craft wire to form her lettering and hearts. She did her journaling with a white gel pen to resemble the wire letters. To create the double-matted photo in the center, Sharon output two copies (one larger) of the same photo on her Epson 870 printer. The smaller white-rimmed photo is adhered in the center of the larger white-rimmed photo.

"Young Love"

by Lisa Pilkington
Waynesville, NC

When Lisa's son took a walk with his girlfriend one afternoon, she couldn't resist—she grabbed her camera and headed out for an impromptu photo shoot.

Lisa enlarged the photo and changed the tones to sepia "to coordinate with my paper." After attaching the photo and ribbon corners to the layout, she mounted strands of metallic embroidery floss threaded with silver beads.

Ribbon: C.M. Offray & Son; *Computer fonts:* Adorable, downloaded from the Internet; CK Cursive, "The Best of Creative Lettering" CD Combo, *Creating Keepsakes; Embroidery floss:* DMC; *Other:* Beads. *Idea to note:* To make ribbon corners, Lisa cut 3" of wired ribbon, then folded the top left corner to the bottom edge to form a triangle. Next, she folded the triangle in half, bringing the bottom left point to the top right point. To finish the triangle, she recommends gluing or stitching it together.

"Chocolate"
by Dawn Stan
Melton, Victoria, Australia

What's more decadent than even the richest chocolate? Dawn smiles as she remembers her husband's birthday celebration at the country club.

"My daughter was enjoying her chocolate mousse so much, I couldn't resist taking pictures," she says.

Dawn wanted a warm and elegant look for her layout. Notes Dawn, "The metallic shimmer cardstock and the Tuscan paper created the perfect combination for my pages."

Supplies *Patterned paper:* Scrap-Ease; *Metallic cardstock:* Regal Paper Mart; *Computer fonts:* Scriptina (large title) and Bradley Hand (journaling), downloaded from the Internet; Little Buddy (small title), downloaded from *www.two-peasinabucket.com*; CK Cursive (date), "The Best of Creative Lettering" CD Combo, *Creating Keepsakes*

"Together"
by Pam Kopka
New Galilee, PA

When Pam met her husband-to-be, Denny, she was 19 and he was 32. She was hesitant to date him, but Denny persisted and won her over. Seventeen years later, Pam and Denny are still going strong!

To create her graphic representation of a couple, Pam drew the line shapes, then cut them out with an X-acto knife. She made a vertical slit in her white cardstock, then mounted adhered black cardstock behind her white cardstock.

For her custom photo borders, Pam cut rectangles in white cardstock, then painted the edges before adhering her photos behind the cut-out sections.

Supplies *Computer font:* Still Time, downloaded from the Internet; *Sketch of couple:* Pam's own creation, inspired by a greeting card; *Paint:* Folk Art. *Idea to note:* The journaling is in Pam's own handwriting. She did the word "together" in all caps and red to draw attention to it.

sophisticated stickers

Create our 14 cool looks with "heart"

Figure 1. Combine different-sized heart stickers for a "homespun" quilt border. *Page by Mary Larson.* **Supplies** *Patterned paper:* Karen Foster Design; *Stickers:* Mrs. Grossman's; *Ink pads:* Stampin' Up!; *Stitches:* Making Memories; *Computer font:* Hypewriter, downloaded from the Internet.

DO YOU SUFFER FROM "STICKER GUILT"? Do you own hundreds of stickers that you haven't used? If you're like me, you enjoy the designs but struggle at times with how best to use them on your pages. Take heart! Here are 14 cool, sophisticated sticker looks that'll set your scrapbook pages apart.

BY MARY LARSON

Antiquing

By combining sanding with stippling, you can make a sticker look more dimensional (Figure 1). Here's how:

❶ While the sticker is still on its paper backing, sand off some of its color.

❷ Dab a dry stipple brush onto a dark-

Figure 1, Step by Step

Step 1. Sand off some of the sticker's color.

Step 2. Dab a dry stipple brush on an ink pad, then pounce the brush up and down on the sticker.

Figure 2. Create dimension with layers of stickers and embossing powder. *Page by Mary Larson.* **Supplies** *Handmade paper:* Ink It; *Stickers:* DMD Industries; *Embossing powder:* StampCraft; *Computer fonts:* Andes ("Eight"), downloaded from the Internet; CAC Leslie ("Contemplate" and journaling), "CreataCard" CD, American Greetings.

brown ink pad.

❸ Pounce the stipple brush straight up and down on the sticker until it's partially covered with little dots of ink.

❹ Repeat with a lighter color of brown ink.

❺ Let dry and place on layout.

Variation: Stipple after the sticker is placed on cardstock.

Embossed Dimension

To create texture and dimension, use leftover sticker-sheet pieces for a layered background. Here's how:

❶ Cut remaining sticker sheets into very small pieces.

❷ Stick the pieces down randomly on cardstock, overlapping them.

❸ Create a top layer by attaching stickers. (I used three heart stickers on top of one another for greater depth.)

❹ After the area is covered, sand off as much color or shine as possible so the ink will adhere to the area.

❺ Use a soft cloth or paintbrush to brush off any dust residue from the sanding.

❻ Turn a wet inkpad upside down, then cover the sticker-remnant area with ink.

❼ Sprinkle on embossing powder, then set it with heat.

Note: If you're using paper-backed stickers, consider inking and embossing a separate sticker in a different color and attaching it as shown (Figure 2).

Mosaic

With just a few snips of your scissors, you can turn a sticker into a mosaic work of art (Figure 3). Here's how:

❶ Using a ruler, draw lines randomly across the back of your sticker sheet. These will be the lines you cut on.

❷ Cut a sticker away from the sheet.

❸ Get your background paper ready, then cut out a piece of sticker, using the lines you've drawn as a guide.

❹ Stick the piece of sticker on your paper, then continue cutting and sticking additional pieces. Don't worry about exact placement; you just want to maintain the general shape of the sticker.

Mix It Up

Cut your stickers into pieces, then put the pieces back together randomly. For Figure 4, I cut four heart stickers into fourths and attached each section to a piece of

Figure 3. Scissor snips give stickers character and interest. *Page by Mary Larson.* **Supplies** *Patterned paper and stickers:* Karen Foster Design; *Computer fonts:* Bric-a-Brac and Broadcast, downloaded from the Internet; *Brads:* Creative Impressions.

Figure 4. Mixing up pieces of stickers is a fun way to accent your page. *Example by Mary Larson.* **Supplies** *Stickers:* Tie Me To The Moon; *Eyelets:* Making Memories; *Fibers:* Rubba Dub Dub, Art Sanctum.

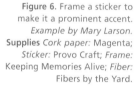

Figure 5. Layer vellum with stickers and tags for a subtle accent. *Example by Mary Larson.* **Supplies** *Patterned paper:* Magenta; *Stickers:* Mrs. Grossman's; *Tags:* Making Memories (vellum square) and Avery; *Brad:* American Tag Company; *Fibers:* Rubba Dub Dub, Art Sanctum; *Other:* Heart eyelet.

Figure 6. Frame a sticker to make it a prominent accent. *Example by Mary Larson.* **Supplies** *Cork paper:* Magenta; *Sticker:* Provo Craft; *Frame:* Keeping Memories Alive; *Fiber:* Fibers by the Yard.

cardstock. I then took one piece from each heart and put them all together by tying them with fiber.

Try These as Well

Don't stop with the ideas above. Consider the following looks as well:

◆ **Tagged.** Stickers are perfect for stylizing tags (Figure 5). Add even more interest with fibers and patterned paper.

◆ **Framed.** Use a small frame around a sticker to give it definition, then add fiber to hang it (Figure 6).

◆ **Reversed.** Place stickers on the back side of vellum and you'll see the shapes in white. Consider this for a small vellum envelope (Figure 7).

◆ **Punched.** Use a punch smaller than the sticker to punch out part

of the middle. Back the resulting hole with patterned paper (Figure 8).

◆ **Clustered.** Place small stickers on several tags, squares, or other shapes and group them together. You can hang the tags for a border or use the shapes as an accent (Figure 9).

◆ **Wrapped.** Wrap fiber or craft wire around the sticker (Figure 10). Secure it on top with brads or on the back with tape.

◆ **Colored.** Use metallic rub-ons, chalks or metallic pens to change the color of stickers (Figure 11).

◆ **Screened.** Tone down bright stickers with wire mesh or screen. After placing the screen over the sticker, anchor the screen with brads (Figure 12).

Techniques Revisited

Many of the techniques presented in previous Supply Savvy columns can be used on stickers. Be sure to try:

◆ Texturizing by crimping or embossing (Figure 13)

◆ Aging with sanding, folding or scratching

◆ Overlaying with beads, glitter, tissue paper or sequins (Figure 14). If the sticker is symmetrical, don't worry about putting adhesive on the front. Just use the back of the sticker where it's already sticky.

So, don't feel guilty about your stash of unused stickers. They've got better days ahead. Just try a few of these ideas, and soon you'll be customizing your stickers in ways you never imagined. ♥

Figure 7. A vellum envelope makes a cute hideaway for extra notes. *Example by Mary Larson.* **Supplies** *Tag:* PrintWorks; *Stickers:* Mrs. Grossman's; *Envelope:* Déjà vu; *Other:* Hemp.

Figure 8. Punch inside a sticker, back it with patterned paper, and you've got a new look. *Example by Mary Larson.* **Supplies** *Patterned paper:* Memory Lane; *Stickers:* K & Company; *Brad:* American Tag Company; *Copper leafing pen:* Krylon; *Other:* Craft wire.

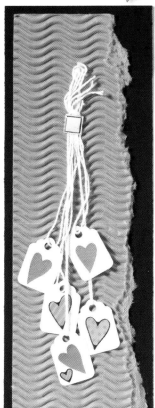

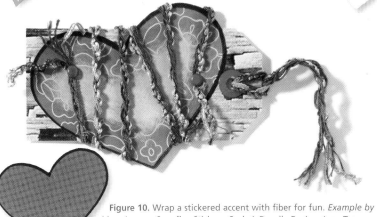

Figure 10. Wrap a stickered accent with fiber for fun. *Example by Mary Larson.* **Supplies** *Stickers:* Cock-A-Doodle Design, Inc.; *Tag:* Shotz Tagz by Danelle Johnson, Creative Imaginations; *Chalk:* Craf-T Products; *Fibers:* Rubba Dub Dub, Art Sanctum; *Eyelet:* Creative Impressions; *Other:* Brads.

Figure 11. Change the look of stickers with simple coloring. *Example by Mary Larson.* **Supplies** *Patterned paper:* Rocky Mountain Paper Company; *Stickers:* K & Company; *Brads:* American Tag Company.

Figure 9. Grab tiny stickers and tags and create a whimsical border. *Example by Mary Larson.* **Supplies** *Crimped cardstock:* Memory Lane; *Stickers:* Whipper Snapper; *Brad:* Creative Impressions; *Tags:* Avery; *Gold leafing pen:* Krylon.

Figure 12. Add interest and texture with copper screening. *Example by Mary Larson.* **Supplies** *Patterned paper:* All About Me, Pebbles in my Pocket; *Stickers:* S.R.M. Press and Tie Me To The Moon; *Screen:* Paragona WireMesh; *Other:* Washer and brads.s

Figure 13. Run your sticker and cardstock through a crimper for quick, cool texture. *Example by Mary Larson.* **Supplies** *Sticker:* DMD Industries; *Tag:* Making Memories; *Crimper:* Li'l Boss, Paper Adventures; *Other:* Fiber.

Figure 14. Take advantage of the adhesive on stickers' backs by over-laying it with fun products. *Example by Mary Larson.* **Supplies** *Patterned paper:* Scrap-Ease; *Sticker:* Mrs. Grossman's; *Computer font:* Chocolate Box Decorated, downloaded from the Internet; *Beads:* Beadz, Art Accents; *Other:* Hemp and silver frame nailheads.

Where to Find Themed Stickers

Whether you want to use stickers as-is or experiment with custom touches, check out the offerings from the companies below:

All My Memories • *www.allmymemories.com*
Bo-Bunny Press • *www.bobunny.com*
Crafty Secrets Publications • *www.craftysecrets.com*
Creative Imaginations • *www.cigift.com*
Destination Stickers & Stamps •
   www.destinationstickersandstamps.com
DMD Industries • *www.dmdind.com*
Doodlebug Design • *See your local scrapbook store.*
EK Success • *www.eksuccess.com*
Frances Meyer • *www.francesmeyer.com*
Hot Off The Press • *www.hotp.com*
Inspire ME • *www.inspiremescrapbooks.com*
K & Company • *www.kandcompany.com*
Kangaroo & Joey • *www.kangarooandjoey.com*
Karen Foster Design • *www.karenfosterdesign.com*
Keeping Memories Alive • *www.keepingmemoriesalive.com*
Magenta • *www.magentarubberstamps.com*
Making Memories • *www.makingmemories.com*
Mary Engelbreit • *www.maryengelbreit.com*
me & my BIG ideas • *www.meandmybigideas.com*
Mrs. Grossman's • *www.mrsgrossmans.com*
NRN Designs • *www.nrndesigns.com*
Okie-Dokie Press • 801/298-1028
Paper House Productions • *www.paperhouseproductions.com*
Paperfever • *www.paperfever.com*
PrintWorks • *www.printworkscollection.com*
Provo Craft • *www.provocraft.com*
PSX Design • *www.psxdesign.com*
Renae Lindgren • *www.renaelindgren.com*
Rocky Mountain Scrapbook Co. • *www.rmscrapbook.com*
Sandylion • *www.sandylion.com*
Scrappin' Dreams • *www.scrappindreams.com*
Scrapbook Times • *www.scrapbooktimes.com*
Scrapbook Wizard • *www.scrapbookwizard.com*
SEI, Inc. • *www.shopsei.com*
S.R.M. Press • *www.srmpress.com*
Stamping Station • *www.stampingstation.com*
Stickopotamus • *www.stickopotamus.com*
Sunbeams etc. • *www.sunbeamsetc.com*
Susan Branch • *www.susanbranch.com*
Suzy's Zoo • *www.suzyszoo.com*
The Gifted Line • *www.giftedline.com*
Tie Me To The Moon • *www.tiemetothemoon.com*
Treehouse Design • e-mail *njatreehouse@aol.com*
Two Busy Moms • *www.twobusymoms.com*
Tumblebeasts • *www.tumblebeasts.com*
Whipper Snapper Designs • *www.whippersnapperdesigns.com*

Show a familiar landscape through the seasons. *Photos by Deb Ringquist.*

Changing Seasons

Everyday, I pass one of the few dirt roads left in our town. The setting is scenic and familiar, and I've always loved watching it change with the seasons. It makes me appreciate all the more the four seasons we enjoy here in Michigan.

I photographed the scene during winter, spring, summer and fall. Looking at the scenes side by side helps me remember all the times I've noticed this spot's beauty.

—*Deb Ringquist, Grand Haven, MI*

march

march moments

The spring thaw is just around the corner, and soon the gentle spring sun will be peeking through the gray winter clouds. Bask in the welcome warmth, then jot down a few moments you don't want to miss capturing on film this month. Here are a few ideas:

- The first trip to the playground after the snow melts
- Bright-yellow daffodil heads peeking through the snow
- Water dripping from the trees and roof as the snow melts
- Children heading outdoors to enjoy the warm afternoons
- Soil loosened for a spring garden

- Searching for the pot of gold at the end of the rainbow
- "Green" everywhere, from new grass to budding leaves and shamrocks
- Enjoying tender baby vegetables with your meals
- Rubber boots and raincoats waiting at the door
- Kites soaring high in open fields

- Handmade pinwheels spinning playfully in the breeze
- Birds returning daily from their winter retreat
- Chasing squirrels through the yard
- Giving the house a good cleaning
- The fresh smell of blossoming trees

ARTICLE BY CATHERINE SCOTT

spring and family ties

Seven layouts and 18 ideas

Supplies
Vellum: The C-Thru Ruler Co.; *Paper yarn:* Emagination Crafts; *Punches:* Family Treasures (square) and The Punch Bunch (leaf); *Eyelets:* The Stamp Doctor; *Letter stamps:* Hero Arts; *Stamping ink:* Impress Rubber Stamps; *Pen:* Pigma Micron, Sakura; *Dragonfly stamp:* Stampin' Up!; *Chalk pencils:* Creatacolor; *Computer font:* Papyrus, Microsoft Word; *Tags:* Amber's own design.

"This is the Day"
by Amber Crosby
Houston, TX

Amber loves this joyful photo of her son and chose a psalm that matched his happy mood.

◆ Create mini pocket tags to hold (and partially conceal) small journaling blocks.

◆ To mimic a banner, thread paper yarn through an eyelet on each end of a title block.

ARTICLE BY LANNA WILSON

"Springtime Buds"

by Jayne Kielman
Waverly, IA

Spring was in the air, Jayne remembers, and she spent the weekend shooting pictures of her kids and their friends.

◆ When outdoor surroundings don't offer a lot of color, opt for black-and-white photos.

◆ Alternatives: Concerned about twigs denting facing pages? Store your pages in raised Protect-A-Page protectors by Dolphin Enterprises. If you prefer not to use real twigs, try foam-tape mounted stickers or paper branches, such as those by Forget Me Not Designs.

Supplies *Patterned paper:* Moody Blues Kit, Club Scrap; *Computer font:* Girls Are Weird, downloaded from the Internet; *Fiber:* Magic Scraps; *Eyelets:* Making Memories; *Other:* Twigs and foam tape.

"Always Together"

by Janice Carson
Hamilton, ON, Canada

Janice is quick to note that Maggie has always had a special bond with her brother Jon. "I wanted to record this closeness between my children," she says.

◆ Change the color of pewter stickers and brads by dipping them in colored ink, then heat-embossing them with clear embossing powder.

◆ Give your sticker color a twist with an antique, variegated look.

◆ Attach medium-width fiber to your layout with mini glue dots.

Supplies *Patterned paper*: Mustard Moon; *Fiber and thread:* Brown Bag Fibers; *Mesh:* Maruyama Paper, Magenta; *Vellum:* R & R Scrapbooking; *Computer fonts:* CK Script ("always"), "The Best of Creative Lettering" CD Combo, *Creating Keepsakes*; Verdanna ("Together") and Mandigo (journaling), downloaded from the Internet; *Brads:* From www.punchcrazy.com; *Stamping ink:* Tsukineko; *Embossing powder:* Stampin' Up!; *Pewter stickers:* Magenta.

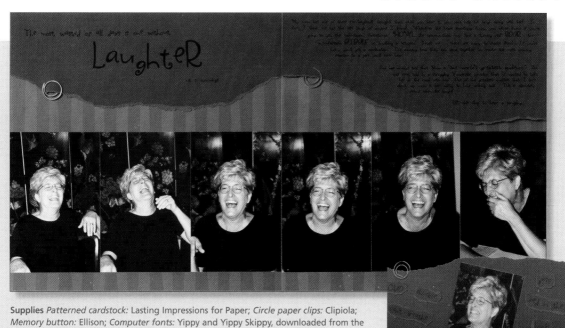

Supplies *Patterned cardstock:* Lasting Impressions for Paper; *Circle paper clips:* Clipiola; *Memory button:* Ellison; *Computer fonts:* Yippy and Yippy Skippy, downloaded from the Internet; *Date stamp:* Stockwell Office Products; *Stamping ink:* Hero Arts; *Other:* Foam core.

"Laughter"

by Kyra Harris
Phoenix, AZ

Kyra caught her mother's laugh on film while experimenting with her new camera. She created this layout because she loves seeing everyday life captured in scrapbook albums.

◆ To create a sense of sequence, line a series of photos across a two-page layout.

◆ Record someone's voice or infectious laugh with a memory button. It can be mounted on foam core and hidden under a flap if desired.

◆ Use muted cardstock to keep the focus on your photos. Select colors that reflect the layout's theme. Kyra chose red because her mother's face "gets so red when she laughs."

"Portland Spirit"

by Cori Dahmen
Portland, OR

When Cori's husband, Brian, won a boat ride for two, they savored their time together away from the kids.

◆ Space your title (and punctuation) across several tags for added attention.

◆ To print a 12" title on a regular printer, select the legal-sized paper option in the page setup box. Choose the landscape feature, which allows you to print the length of the page. As you type and size the text, use the on-screen ruler as a guide. When you're ready to print, cut 12" x 12" paper to 8½" x 12" and feed it through the printer.

Supplies *Vellum:* Close To My Heart; *Tags:* Cori's own design; *Computer fonts:* CK Cursive (Portland) and CK Penman (journaling), "The Best of Creative Lettering" CD Combo, *Creating Keepsakes*; Daddy (March), downloaded from *www.letteringdelights.com*; Angelina ("The"), downloaded from the Internet; *Letter die cuts for "Spirit":* DayCo Ltd.; *Fiber:* Cut-It-Up; *Brads:* Boxer Scrapbook Productions; *Chalk:* Craf-T Products; *Circle punches:* Emagination Crafts.

Supplies
Patterned paper: Mustard Moon; *Vellum:* Paper Adventures; *Embroidery floss:* DMC; *Heart brads:* Magic Scraps; *Square punch:* EK Success; *Computer fonts:* Scrap Rhapsody (script), "Lettering Delights" CD Vol. 2, Inspire Graphics; 2Peas Think Small (sans serif), downloaded from www.twopeasina-bucket.com.

"Dear Jacob"
by Cheryl Overton
Kelowna, BC, Canada

Says Cheryl, "I love how sweet my son and my mom look in this picture. I wanted a special layout to complement it."

◆ Ask your subject to jot down notes to include with the journaling.
◆ Express unrelated ideas in separate journaling blocks.
◆ Create a pensive mood with soft-colored paper.

"Wisteria in Spring"
by Susan Bascom
Birmingham, AL

For her first spring in the South, Susan took pictures of every kind of flower she could find. The wisteria lines her favorite walkway.

◆ Mount fiber with a glue pen to create stems.
◆ Set the eyelets partway to make sure they're aligned with the "stem" before finishing the mount.
◆ Finish the look by tying French knots in the center of each eyelet, using a lightweight piece of cardstock behind it as an anchor.

Supplies *Patterned paper:* Karen Foster Design; *Fiber:* From www.fibersbytheyard.com; *Computer font:* Saginaw, downloaded from the Internet; *Heart and scalloped eyelets:* From www.scrapadoodledoo.com.

"role" call

Journal your roles, from parent to friend

Figure 1. How many roles do you play on any given day? Have a little fun by creating a layout about it. *Page by Rebecca Sower.* **Supplies** *Patterned paper:* Kate's Paperie; *Alphabet stamps:* PSX Design; *Stamping ink:* StazOn, Tsukineko; *Fibers:* Adornaments, EK Success; *Computer fonts:* CK Constitution, "Fresh Fonts" CD, *Creating Keepsakes;* Mom's Typewriter, downloaded from the Internet; *Printed vellum:* Anna Griffin; *Poetry dog tag:* Chronicle Books; *Other:* Assorted charms and safety pin.

So, how many hats do you wear? Let your scrapbooks tell all about it.

WHAT DO I HOPE you'll get out of this article? I'd love to see you start thinking about all the varied roles you play in life. I hope you'll begin mentally formulating a page layout or two that recognizes some of these roles and how you can share them with people now and in the future.

Playing Your Part

One of my life's roles is that of sink scrubber. Hmm, that's not a role that ranks high on my "important roles" list. However, I'm also honored to play the role of friend, and that's a role I cherish tightly. It's the same with you.

Taxi Driver

On the stage of your world, you play many parts. Some are small and, by nature, menial. But they exist, and you can't bow out of them. For a light-hearted approach to these thankless roles, see Figure 1. Every school day for the past eight years, I've played the role of taxi driver. Not once has one of my children said, "Gee thanks, Mom! You could expect us to find our own way

Figure 2. Let the world know about the roles you take very seriously. *Page by Rebecca Sower.* **Supplies** *Paint:* Lumiere, Jacquard Products; *Photo-editing software:* Photoshop, Adobe; *Alphabet rubber stamps:* PSX Design; *Stamping ink:* StazOn (black) and VersaColor (brown), Tsukineko; *Rubber stamps:* Stampington & Company (text) and Limited Edition (pens); *Polymer clay:* Sculpey; *Fibers:* Adornaments, EK Success; *Metal tag:* Anima Designs; *Brad fastener:* Magic Scraps; *Pen:* Galaxy, American Crafts.

Figure 3. Consider scrapbooking the roles you probably haven't even considered to be roles. *Page by Rebecca Sower.* **Supplies** *Rubber stamps:* Close To My Heart (background) and Stampin' Up! (hydrangea); *Shaved ice:* Magic Scraps; *Fibers:* Adornaments, EK Success; *Computer font:* CK Gutenberg, "Fresh Fonts" CD, *Creating Keepsakes; Alphabet stamps:* Turtle Press; *Stamping ink:* StazOn, Tsukineko; *Chalk inkpad:* Colorbox, Clearsnap; *Buttons:* Making Memories; *Other:* Snaps and thread.

home from school, but you're such a great mom that you come all the way over here and pick us up. You're the best!"

I'm not holding my breath. But I'm OK with that—being a "taxi driver" is just one role that falls under the big umbrella role of mom.

On another note, other parts we play on the stage of life are much more monumental. They are roles that make us tick, keep us happy, motivate us, and on many days just make life worth living. These are our relationship roles (parent, sister, friend, daughter, grandmother and more).

Friend

Let's go back to the role of being a friend. As seriously as I take this role, it's not one that gets the attention it deserves, and that bothers me. I wish I were a more attentive friend. I wish I kept in better contact. I wish I remembered birthdays. I wish I offered a nice gesture every time I *thought* of offering a nice gesture for one of my friends.

But that isn't my reality right now. And when I start beating myself up about it, I remember that most of my friends are just like me—*extremely busy!* So there are the makings of a scrapbook page. To at least let the world know that I cherish my friends and although I'm not always the most attentive person, I'm still a good friend who will be there when needed (see Figure 2).

Mother

Another amazing and valuable role I play in life is that of mother. So many different aspects are included in this role, and I hope the pages of my scrapbooks will tell how seriously I take this position. And my roles as a parent are constantly changing. My 11-year-old daughter obviously doesn't need me to bathe and feed her anymore, but she very much needs me to be a listener when she wants to talk. Can *you* think of any reason I wouldn't tell about this privilege on a scrapbook page? Neither can I. (See Figure 3.)

The World's a Stage

Once you've mused over the many roles you play in your own life, turn your attention to other significant people. I know every wife says this, but I think my husband can do *anything*. Just this morning, he was under the house adding more floor supports to our old farmhouse. Then he showered and headed off to his treasurer duties at the company where he works (after he helped his dad via phone with some tax-return questions).

When my husband gets home, he'll most likely go out and practice baseball with Luke, run a few more electrical wires, then fall asleep reading a book on how to lay a natural stone wall around our patio-to-be. That's a typical day in the life of my husband. Pretty amazing, huh? And he's a thousand other things to our children. Do you think he deserves a page layout or two? (See Figure 4.)

As you likely know, I'm always eager to work advice for my children (and future grandchildren) into the pages of my scrapbooks. Why not create a layout focusing on different roles in which a child may find himself or herself someday? (See Figure 5.) I see it as yet another small boost in the "meaningful journaling" category for my scrapbooks.

You may not be a butcher, baker or candlestick maker, but you have many parts to play in this game called life. Set aside a little time to focus on your different roles, then work your way toward documenting them within the pages of your scrapbooks. Job well done! ❤

Figure 4. Tell someone how much you recognize and appreciate the roles he or she plays. *Page by Rebecca Sower.* **Supplies** *Alphabet stamps:* Fusion Art Stamps; *Patterned paper:* K & Company; *Stamping ink:* Nick Bantok, Ranger Industries; *Pen:* Zig Writer, EK Success; *Mesh:* Magenta; *Brad fasteners:* Making Memories; *Acrylic paints:* Delta; *Watercolor paper:* Strathmore; *Other:* Paper clip.

Figure 5. Your child's future roles—should you offer any helpful advice? *Page by Rebecca Sower.* **Supplies** *Stamping inks:* VersaColor (colors) and StazOn (black), Tsukineko; *Pen:* Zig Writer, EK Success; *Alphabet stamps:* PSX Design; *Rubber stamp:* Acey Deucy; *Tassel:* Hobby Lobby; *Craft lacquer:* Sakura; *Other:* Fabric, plus words cut from a vintage book.

april pleasures

Enjoy every moment to its fullest this month as you witness the renewing of the earth. Spend time outside in the warm, gentle sunlight, and remember to carry your camera so you can capture life's pleasures on film. Here are a few ideas:

- tall tulips waving in the breeze
- practical jokers caught in the act
- baby animals at a petting zoo
- colorful flowers at a garden center
- the tinkling sounds of wind chimes
- children clad in yellow raincoats and stomping through puddles
- cherry blossoms floating to the ground

- brightly colored Easter eggs hidden in tall grass
- the clean smell of the awakening earth
- boys and girls in fancy Sunday clothes
- birds carrying nesting materials in their beaks
- pastel-colored chalk drawings on the sidewalk

- throwing bread to the baby ducks at the pond
- colorful umbrellas moving down the sidewalk
- organizing a recycling system in honor of Earth Day

ARTICLE BY CATHERINE SCOTT

easter and spring

Nine colorful layouts to inspire you

Supplies *Patterned paper and die cuts:* All About Me; *Vellum:* PrintWorks; *Lettering template:* Kiki, ScrapPagerz.com; *Jump rings:* Darice; *Craft wire:* The Beadery; *Beads:* Zany Brainy; *Micro eyelets:* HyGlo, American Pin & Fastener; *Small flower eyelets and green eyelets:* Doodlebug Design; *Large flower eyelet:* Cut-It-Up; *Punches:* All Night Media (daisy), EK Success (leaf) and Emagination Crafts (circle); *Pen:* Sakura; *Glue dots:* Glue Dots International.

"Water"

by Stacy Hackett
Murrieta, CA

What's a mother to do when she catches her child playing contently? "Grab the camera!" says Stacy.

◆ To suspend title blocks, cut enough squares for your title (or use die cuts or punches). Cut a frame border slightly larger than the square. Attach micro eyelets to the outside corners of your squares and the inside corners of your border squares, then connect them by threading jump rings through the eyelet holes. Mount the squares with glue dots or foam tape.

◆ Add a "buzz trail" with craft wire.

◆ To create a wire antennae, fold a 4" length of craft wire in half, curve the ends, then attach a gold and black bead to each end. Adhere the fold of the antennae to the die cut with double-sided adhesive.

Supplies *Patterned paper:* Sandylion; *Buttons:* Hillcreek Designs; *Paper yarn:* Twistel, Making Memories; *Raffia:* Plaid Enterprises; *Craft wire:* Artistic Wire Ltd.; *Flannel paper:* Paper Adventures; *Lettering template:* Whimsy, Déjà Views, The C-Thru Ruler Co.; *Adhesive:* Glue Dots International; *Vellum:* Autumn Leaves (green) and The Paper Company (platinum); *Mulberry paper:* PrintWorks; *Computer font:* Girls Are Weird, downloaded from the Internet; *Embossing powder:* Stampendous!; *Eyelets:* Creative Impressions.

"Li'l Chicks"

by LauraLinda Rudy
Markham, ON, Canada

After LauraLinda's birthday breakfast, her good friend treated LauraLinda to a photo shoot with her daughters.

◆ Pop a chick out of an "egg" by cracking a button in two. Use a pair of pliers and wire cutters and make sure you wear eye protection!

◆ Heat-emboss your computer lettering for extra shimmer and dimension.
◆ To create a woven basket, fold a length of craft wire in half, then bend it into a half-circle. Weave two shades of paper yarn around the edges and through the middle.

"Innocence"

by Shelley Kilgore
Niles, MI

Shelley wanted this layout to be perfect and spent several months thinking about this favorite photo of her daughter.

◆ Dress up a laser die cut by placing cutouts (like the pink flowers in this frame) behind the die cut.
◆ What's the first word that comes to mind when you look at a layout? At times that's all you need for your title.

Supplies *Patterned paper:* Frances Meyer; *Flower eyelets:* Making Memories; *Vellum:* DMD Industries; *Laser die cut:* Laser Layouts, Provo Craft; *Computer font:* Brush Script MT, Microsoft Word.

What I Love about my
LITTLE SISTER

She keeps me company.
She watches movies with me.
She helps me build Tinker Toys.
She makes funny faces.
She watches the Hermit crabs with me.
We do puppet shows together.
I wouldn't have anyone to play with without her.

What I Love about my
BiG SiSTER

She hugs me.
She kisses me.
She puts band-aids on my boo-boos.
She plays dollhouse with me.
She dances with me.
I like her Aaron Carter music.

Supplies *Computer fonts:* ToonTime and BoysRgross, downloaded from the Internet; *Flower cutouts:* Pam's own designs.

"What I Love"
by Pam Kopka
New Galilee, PA

When Pam's two girls started bickering, she was ready to send them to their room for eternity. Instead, she turned the experience into a scrapbooking opportunity.

◆ Get design and accent inspiration from greeting cards.
◆ When kids start to fight, ask them to write down what they love about each other.
◆ Creating with an X-acto knife takes time but is worth the effort. Try using a stamp or clip art as a pattern.

"Reflections"
by Toni Holoubek
Rockford, IL

Toni's son Michael was absolutely enthralled with his reflection in the pond. Toni recorded her reflections in her journaling.

◆ Add extra "eye candy" to serendipity squares with punches, patterned paper and mesh. They help tie the elements of this layout together.
◆ For a two-toned photo mat, cut an opening from two-colored cardstock, then curl the edges outward. Attach the mat to the layout with eyelets.

Supplies *Specialty paper:* Jennifer Collection; *Maruyama paper:* Magenta; *Computer fonts:* Scriptina (title) and National Primary (journaling), downloaded from the Internet; *Leaf punches:* The Punch Bunch; *Flat-top eyelets:* The Stamp Doctor; *Other:* Embroidery floss and metal-rimmed tag.

Reflections

May 2002

I can't believe our little man is going to be starting preschool this fall. As I look back and reflect on his childhood, I realize how much joy and he has brought into our lives. Yes, he is growing up very fast, but it is exciting to see what he is going to do next as he matures into a young man. He is a loving, energetic, and very happy little boy. We love him with all our hearts and there will always be only one Michael no matter how old he gets.

Supplies
Computer font:
2Peas Architect,
downloaded
from *www.two-
peasinabucket.com*;
Chalk: Craf-T Products;
Embroidery floss: DMC;
Egg template: Frances
Meyer; *Lettering tem-
plate:* Block, EK Success.

"Decorating Eggs"
by Rhonda Pflugh
Canton, OH

Rhonda's kids and their cousins love getting together at Grandma's house for their annual egg-coloring activity.

◆ Trace your title or accent from a template and hand stitch around the letters.

◆ Chalk inside your title or accent, then blend the colors to add subtle color.

Supplies *Corrugated paper:* Tibbetts Imports; *Stickers:* Magenta; *Buttons, square eyelets, and metal shapes and letters:* Making Memories; *Computer font:* Amazone BT, Microsoft Word; *Craft wire:* Darice; *Other:* Fiber and gemstones.

"A School for Easter Bunnies"
by Sharon Whitehead
Vernon, BC, Canada

When Sharon visited her daughter at college, she went armed with film to capture photos of the rabbits that swarm the campus.

◆ Borrow elements from Becky Higgins' "One Sketch" column for a balanced layout. The March sketch inspired this design.

◆ Add simple buttons, charms, stickers or wire to a tag for a quick embellishment.

◆ Repeat accent elements in sets of three to draw your audience through the layout.

Supplies *Patterned paper:* Mustard Moon; *Eyelets:* Doodlebug Design; *Computer fonts:* Bradley Hand (journaling) and Brush Script MT (title), Microsoft Word.

"What Eggheads"
by Gwyn Calvetti
West Salem, WI

Toddlers eventually grow up, Gwyn says, adding, "Might as well give them their due." She couldn't resist taking pictures of her teenage boys coloring Easter eggs.

◆ Don't limit your Easter layout to tradi-tional hues if a pastel palette contradicts your subjects.

◆ Create your own egg-patterned vellum by scanning, cropping, resizing and print-ing a photo of colorful eggs.

"There's Still You and Me"
by Pam Nafziger
McDonald, PA

When Pam and her husband get away from life's daily demands, Pam says, "It reminds us just how much we like each other!"

◆ Manipulate your journaling in Microsoft's WordArt to create a shadowed effect. Here, the repetition represents life's daily chores.

◆ To hide a sentiment or photo, create a vellum-lined window as a top sheet, showing a peek of the photo or journaling underneath.

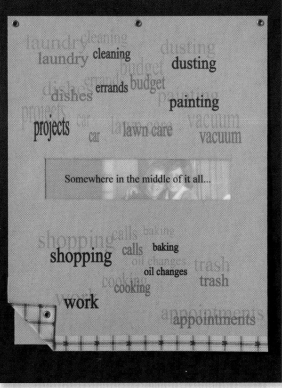

Supplies *Patterned paper:* Over The Moon Press, EK Success; *Eyelets:* Making Memories; *Vellum:* Colorbök; *Computer font:* Times New Roman, Microsoft Word.

A Circle of friends

inspire (in spir) v. 1. to stimulate or impel, as to some creative effort 2. to motivate as by divine influence 3. to activate a thought or feeling in someone

Celebrate creativity and each other with a book exchange

♥ ♥ ♥

Sure, scrapbooking is about preserving memories, but that's not the only thing that motivates me. I love to be inspired. I look for inspiration everywhere— in magazines, in anthropology, in store windows. I get a big kick out of discovering a great idea, doing something wonderful with it, and passing the idea on. It's also fun to see what other scrapbookers do with the same concept.

That's where a circle journal comes in. A circle journal is a book that's circulated among friends, each adding his or her own pages. It's not a new concept—you may have heard it called a "round robin" before.

Circle journals are especially alluring because they're springboards for creativity. Anything goes! I can explore new ideas or techniques before they find their way onto my scrapbook pages. I can see other scrapbookers' creations up close, plus it's fun to have lovely, tangible treasures from some of my dearest friends.

BY HEIDI SWAPP

Secrets

This accordion-folded book is one exchanged between Stephanie McAtee and me. I created this using two 4" x 6" pieces of heavyweight chipboard for the front and back and cardstock for the pages. I wanted it small and interactive. As you can see, it's not polished or perfect but raw and experimental. To keep the circle journal closed, I just stick a thick rubber band around it!

How to Get Started

Circle journals are artistic, introspective, and a great way to learn more about others and yourself. To get started:

1 Involve a friend or group of friends. I share circle journals with the following:

- *A girlfriend who lives in a different state.* We each created a book with 12 spots so that as we exchange the journal each month, at the end of a year we'll each have a completed journal. Half of the entries will be mine, and half will be hers.

- *My "regular" scrapbook group.* Three of us get together regularly for dinner and a scrapbook night. We're all facing different joys and challenges, yet we've found that we all benefit from the lessons we're learning individually. We chose to have our circle journals go around three times before we were finished, so we made books that accommodated 12 entries.

- *My scrapbooking friends I've met online.* These are women who inspire me deeply with their creations. The journals will travel in a big circle to three different countries and five different states. Over the course of a year, imagine the growth and change that will happen to each woman involved. (This is also a fun idea for family members.)

For this circle journal, I decided to take "circle" literally! I wanted the book to stand up and not have a beginning or an end.

To create the book, I cut twelve 6" x 6" squares of cardstock (from three pieces of 12" x 12" cardstock) and folded them in half. Next, I put all the folded edges together, then rubber-banded them. I wanted them to all fan out in a circle. Entries are folded in half and tucked into the rubber-band binding.

When the book is complete, I'm sure it will inspire others as it travels in a gallon paint can. Note how the label on the outside is created with a magnet sheet.

In a Can

2 Choose a book that will fit specific needs. It can be anything from a beautiful blank journal purchased from a bookstore to a creation all your own! Be sure to consider:
• the number of entries (or pages) needed
• the size of each entry
• how the journal will be transported
• how durable the journal is
• whether the journal can be expanded

3 Outline a time frame or schedule. To keep the journals circulating, it's a good idea to set up a schedule. A circle journal does not need to span the globe or take an entire year to complete! Plan a night with a group of friends. Invite each person to bring a little book and spend the evening creating something for each book.

Another option is to ask each participant to create multiple "entries" that are identical. Simply exchange entries and compile them into books the evening you and your friends get together!

Whenever you're sharing your circle journal over long distances, add in extra time for shipping and stick to those deadlines. No one likes them, but they can help you get your circle journals completed!

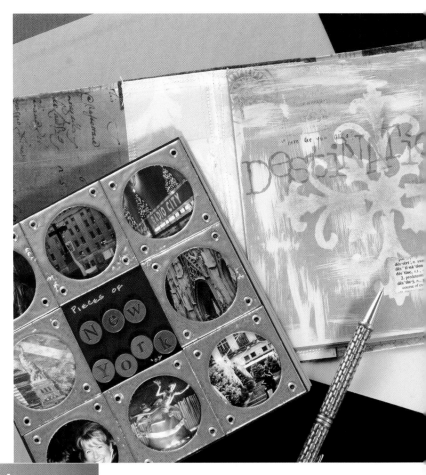

destinations

I sewed my "Destinations" journal together with my sewing machine, so the assembly was pretty quick. The album is covered with wrapping paper and handmade paper. The theme was inspired by the song "Where Are You Going?" by the Dave Matthews Band.

I am so excited to see how the theme is interpreted by each participant!

choose *your approach*

Before you begin your book, consider the approach, whether simple or crazy. What you choose is up to you. Consider these possibilities:

• an accordion fold book
• a re-covered sketch book
• a chipboard/cardstock book bound with wire
• envelopes bound together, with journaling entries tucked inside
• a book bound with screw posts, nuts and bolts, rings
• a plain book that's been decorated
• a book of pockets
• a "junque" book
• elastic binding

Once you've created your circle journal, come up with fun "housing" for it. Some ideas? A paint can, a cigar box or a tin container.

a circle journey of your own

The idea of circulating small journals among family and friends isn't new—in fact, Circle Journey has promoted this concept for years and offers several correspondence kits.

"At Circle Journey, we help keep you connected with those who matter most in your life—whether a friend, child, romantic partner or grandparent," says owner Paul Westrick. "We've developed blank books for communicating your thoughts and expressing yourself creatively with family and friends. Each Circle Journey book comes with everything you need to get started—envelope mailers, photo corners, stickers and labels, an Idea Starter, a keepsake box and more. You simply record your thoughts and mail the book back and forth with loved ones. The result is a treasured keepsake."

Each 4" x 6" book is sturdy, archival quality and sports a distinctive cover. Current themes include:

- Wishing You Close
- Baby Wings
- Hot-Dots
- Parkbench Waiting
- Road to Horizon
- Mailbox Skies
- Flowers for Friday
- Forever Beach
- MetroLines
- Cup of Conversation
- Winter Window
- Scenic Route
- Wonder Clouds
- Stars at Dusk
- Quiet Light

For more information or to find the location of a store near you, visit *www.circlejourney.com*.

theme ideas *for circle journals*

A circle journal can cover any theme. Here's a quick sampling:

- simple pleasures
- technique of the week
- what you like best about being a girl
- positive affirmations
- dream destinations
- inspirations
- recipes
- colors
- quotes

a girly little circle journal

Shannon Wolz crafted this circle journal from different shades of paper. She used an envelope die cut to create 12 cutout envelopes, then adhered them together by gluing the inside flap of one envelope to the bottom front of the next.

The envelopes fold like an accordion, then the flap from the back comes over the top and wraps around eyelet letters. Each entry is a card that fits one envelope. The theme is "Things you like about being a girl!"

4 Determine a theme. Choose a theme, and everyone involved in the circle journaling will breathe a little easier. A theme can be a serious contemplation about life, an admission of your "most embarrassing moment," or even a useful recipe exchange! Interpretation of the theme will be different for each participant.

The theme can also contain a challenge or focus on a particular product. For example, each time you send off the journal, ask the recipient to incorporate a certain item (such as buttons) in whatever's created.

5 Create the first entry. To help set the desired tone for your circle journal (and establish the theme), create the first entry yourself.

6 Protect your circle journal during its travels. Your journal will be on the move, so protect it well on its journey. If your journal will be mailed, place it in a sturdy box so the journal can easily be repackaged and sent on its way. Consider including a preprinted label for the next person who's to receive the journal.

Even if you're simply passing the circle journal to your next-door neighbor, take precautions to protect it. (You never know when an inquisitive toddler or a badly placed can of soda pop will appear.) Place the circle journal in anything from a heavyweight envelope to a sheer organza bag.

From the colors to the embellishments, this little book is just so "Shannon Jones." She created this simple pocket book with just two pieces of 12" x 12" cardstock. For similar results:

1 Fold 12" x 12" cardstock accordion-style into four 3" sections. These will be the vertical sections.

2 Fold the bottom third of the paper up horizontally.

3 Sew a knot at each crease, creating pockets for the journal entries to slide in.

4 Hand stitch the two pieces of card-stock together, creating eight pockets.

5 If desired, tie a knot in a thin piece of elastic (dyed with an ink pad) to help keep the journal closed.

how i feel about life

life is about...

those you Lo[ve]

This tag book was part of a swap where my friends and I showcased on tags what our lives are all about—love, art, friends, imagination, dreams, faith and family. Each page is an oversized tag decorated by a scrapbooking friend. A metal bolt holds the tags together.

happiness

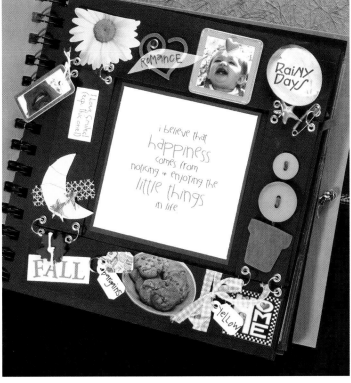

Hilary Shirley started a circle journal about the little things that make her happy—her husband's smile, cookies, bargains and daisies. Lori Houk's pages include slide holders that contain items such as screening, a game piece and a postmark. Mary Larson answers the question "What makes Mary merry?"

may

the magic of may

As May approaches, the outdoors come alive with color and motion. Take your indoor activities outside this month to enjoy the beautiful weather, bright flowers and traditional spring pleasures. Plan now to capture May activities like these on film and in your scrapbooks.

- Running through a field of wildflowers
- Reading on a park bench in the gentle sun
- Pulling a wagonload of kids around the block
- Blowing bubbles and watching them float in the breeze
- Teaching hopscotch to the next generation of children
- Watching playgrounds come alive with swarms of kids
- Hearing birds sing as they bathe in water warmed by the sun
- Marveling at the green shoots peeking through dirt in the garden
- Napping on a blanket in splashes of sunlight coming through the trees
- Moving the lunch table to the front yard for a springtime picnic
- Tasting cotton candy again at the year's first outdoor festival
- Playing Frisbee with the dog in a wide-open, grassy area
- Staring at the blue sky through leafy green treetops
- Visiting with friends and family on the front porch

ARTICLE BY CATHERINE SCOTT

mothers and more

9 layouts that celebrate love and life

Supplies *Patterned paper, stickers and border stickers:* Debbie Mumm, Creative Imaginations; *Computer fonts:* CK Handprint (journaling), "The Best of Creative Lettering" CD Combo, *Creating Keepsakes;* 2Peas Rocking Horse ("Mother's"), downloaded from *www.twopeasina-bucket.com; Eyelet:* The Happy Hammer; *Fiber:* On the Surface; *Tag:* Michelle's own design.

"Picking Flowers for Mother's Day"

by Michelle Tardie
Richmond, VA

Michelle's heart melted when her son picked a weed bouquet for her and told her how much he loves her. "It was my best Mother's Day gift ever," she says.

◆ Create a botanical tag accent with textured paper and flower cutouts.

◆ Use tiny pop dots to add dimension to flower cutouts. For even more dimension, layer additional cutouts over the mounted flowers, adhering them with pop dots.

ARTICLE BY LANNA WILSON

"Lavender Fields Forever"

by Debbie Daunis
Santee, CA

While on a family vacation, Debbie found a lavender farm in full bloom. While she and her daughter cut stems of the fragrant flower, her son snapped pictures.

◆ For gardening layouts, label the foliage with small, hanging tags. This lets you use larger images on your layout and still identify the pictures you're showcasing.

◆ Use screen (or mesh) to add texture without much bulk. Debbie used it to help ground her lavender-filled memorabilia pocket. On the left page, the screen creates the look of a fence.

◆ Sew on photo mats to add subtle texture and a sense of permanence to your layout.

Supplies *Patterned paper:* Karen Foster Design; *Screen:* Phifer Wire Products, Inc.; *Vellum tags:* Making Memories; *Memorabilia pocket:* 3L Corp.; *Vellum:* Paper Adventures; *Mounting tape:* Henkel Consumer Adhesives; *Other:* Glue dots.

"Sleep, Sweet Baby, Sleep"

by Kristen Swain
Bear, DE

Kristen learned from her first daughter that babies grow up entirely too fast. When her second daughter, Annalise, was born, Kristen took lots of pictures.

◆ Use coordinating papers, vellums and stickers for a unified, multi-level layout.

◆ Cut out embossed vellum and patterned paper for beautifully coordinated accents, overlays and photo mats.

◆ For softer journaling, use muted paper tones and colored inks.

Supplies *Patterned paper and embossed vellum:* K & Company; *Pink vellum:* The Paper Company; *Stickers and cutouts:* K & Company; *Eyelets:* Impress Rubber Stamps; *Computer fonts:* Adorable (title) and Bradley Hand ITC (poem), downloaded from the Internet; *Tags:* Kristen's own designs; *Fiber:* On the Surface.

Supplies *Embossed paper:* Club Scrap; *Paper yarn:* Twistel, Making Memories; *Pre-made tag:* Fresh Cuts, EK Success; *Eyelets:* Making Memories; *Computer fonts:* Mistral and Century Gothic, Apple.

"Mother's Day Mountain Biking"
by Suzi Gurney
Portland, OR

What could be better than scrapbooking? For Suzi, it's scrapbooking about her other favorite hobby: going mountain biking with her family.

◆ For photos in the forest, go for a woodsy, rustic motif, such as the embossed paper by Club Scrap.

◆ Short on time? Use pre-made accents, such as tags and envelopes.

◆ Add a touch of texture to your title block by mounting eyelets, then threading paper yarn through the holes and knotting the ends.

"Loren Dancing in the Rain"
by Sunny Ledford
Elkins, AR

Getting Loren to hold still for a picture is difficult, says Kim Anthony, her mom and a friend of Sunny's. "My daughter loves to stomp around in the rain puddles."

◆ Glass pebbles magnify words you want to highlight, such as the "who" and "when" on this page. You can adhere them to the layout with double-sided adhesive.

◆ A shadow box helps lessen the bulkiness of glass pebbles on your page. To create a shadow box, punch a square out of your background paper, frame the opening with foam tape, then back the opening with a complementary color of paper.

Supplies *Cardstock and patterned vellum:* DMD Inc.; *Patterned paper:* Westrim Crafts; *Nailheads:* Westrim Crafts; *Glass pebbles:* JudiKins; *Pen:* Zig Writer, EK Success; *Computer font:* Angelica, downloaded from the Internet.

Supplies *Patterned paper:* Kim's own design; *Vellum:* Paper Adventures; *Embroidery floss:* DMC; *Other:* Brads.

"The Love of a Mommy"

**by Kimberly Bailey
Twin Falls, ID**

As a new mom, Kim was excited for her first Mother's Day with her daughter, Emma. This layout is a tribute to their special day.

◆ If you have a special-occasion card, consider preserving it in a pocket on your layout. Add journaling to the front of the pocket.

◆ Looking for a new patterned paper? Scan a tissue box (or any other patterned surface), then print it on vellum. For more dimension, randomly fold, then flatten, the box before you scan it.

"What I Can Do"

**by MaryRuth Francks
Spokane, WA**

When she was feeling down about not having children, MaryRuth created this layout about the characteristics that could make her a better mother someday (and a better person).

◆ Add a hint of dimension by texturing accent and title blocks, then layer the blocks with stickers.

◆ Not every layout needs a photo, especially if the page includes a lot of journaling.

◆ Vertical lines, such as those in the title block, patterned paper strips and sticker blocks, help move the viewer's eye across the page.

Supplies *Stickers:* Watercolors, Provo Craft; *Computer fonts:* CK Handprint, "The Best of Creative Lettering" CD Combo; CK Fun, "The Art of Creative Lettering" CD, *Creating Keepsakes*; Doodle Script and Sheerelegance, downloaded from the Internet; 2Peas Arizona, downloaded from *www.twopeasinabucket.com*; *Other:* Mini brads.

Supplies *Handmade paper:* Jennifer Collection; *Computer font:* StarbabeHMK, Hallmark Scrapbook Studio; *Snaps:* Making Memories; *Mesh:* WireForm, Paragona; *Chalk:* Craf-T Products; *Fibers:* DMC and Rubba Dub Dub, Art Sanctum; *Rubber stamps:* Hero Arts (flowers) and PSX Design (letters); *Stamping ink:* Tsukineko; *Embossing enamel:* Suze Weinberg; *Microbeads:* Magic Scraps; *Formica chips:* WilsonArt; *Circle tags:* OfficeMax.

"Perfectly Imperfect"
by Lisa Russo
Woodstock, GA

Kids don't come with instructions, so Lisa and her husband, Vic, want their son to know they'll do their best to be good parents.

◆ To decorate a Formica tag, stamp a flower image onto the tag with pigment ink, then heat-set it. Next, coat the entire surface with clear embossing ink, sprinkle embossing enamel over the surface, and heat-set it. Sprinkle another layer of embossing enamel and reheat. Add micro beads to the warm enamel and reheat again. Add a final coat of enamel, heat it, then let it cool.

"Eyes"
by Amy Stultz
Mooresville, IN

When Amy looks at this photo of her daughter, she can't help but notice her eyes. "They show me that even at her young age, my daughter has gained a great depth of knowledge."

◆ A photo software program, such as Adobe Photoshop, will let you manipulate photos. Note the distressed edges and sepia tones here.

◆ Sand patterned paper to create a faded and timeworn appearance.

◆ Create an aged patina look on white mesh paper by stippling the mesh with black ink.

Supplies *Patterned paper:* Scrap-Ease; *Tag:* Amy's own design; *Fiber:* Rubba Dub Dub, Art Sanctum; *Eyelet:* The Stamp Doctor; *Photo corners:* Canson; *Computer font:* Scriptina ("Eyes"), downloaded from the Internet; Monotype Corsiva (journaling), Microsoft Word; *Mesh:* Magenta; *Decorative scissors:* Fiskars; *Stamping ink:* Ancient Page, Clearsnap; *Pen:* Memories Le Plume, Marvy Uchida; *Metallic paper:* Peterson Arne; *Nailhead:* Source unknown.

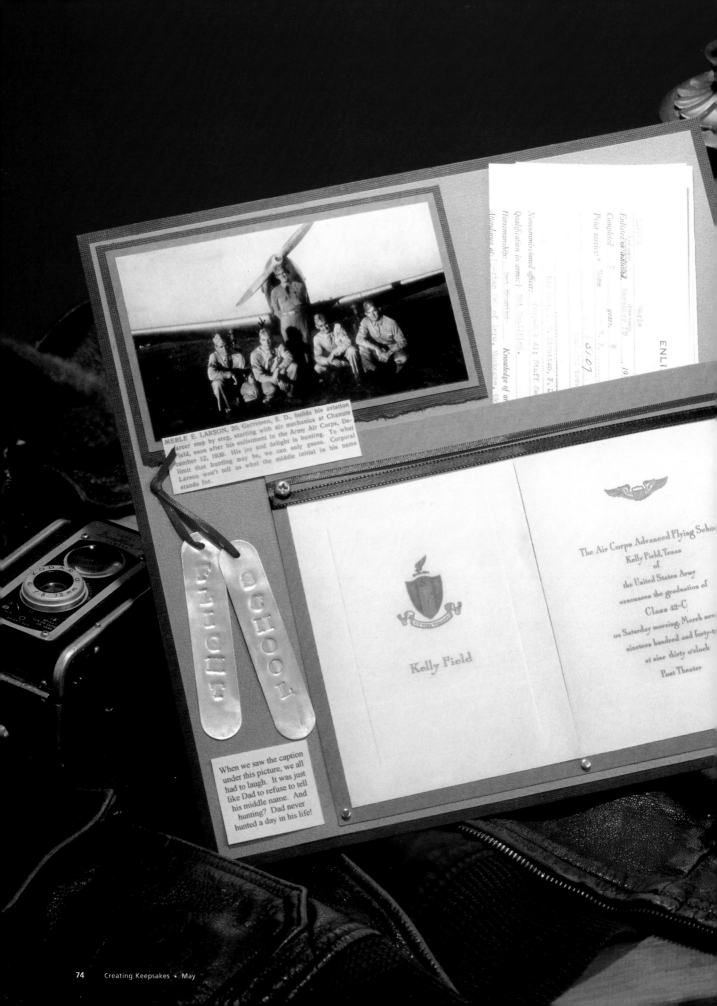

MERLE E. LARSON, 20, Garretson, S. D., builds his aviation career step by step, starting with air mechanics at Chanute Field, soon after his enlistment in the Army Air Corps, December 12, 1930. His joy and delight is hunting. To what limit that hunting may be, we can only guess. Corporal Larson won't tell us what the middle initial in his name stands for.

When we saw the caption under this picture, we all had to laugh. It was just like Dad to refuse to tell his middle name. And hunting? Dad never hunted a day in his life!

Kelly Field

The Air Corps Advanced Flying School
of
Kelly Field, Texas
the United States Army
announces the graduation of
Class 42-C
on Saturday morning, March next
nineteen hundred and forty-two
at nine thirty o'clock
Post Theater

Tribute to a War Hero

CREATE AN ALBUM WITH THESE INSPIRING IDEAS

M y father-in-law was a war hero; I've always known that. A quiet man, he rarely talked about it. Occasionally he would open up when men from that generation gathered together. He also talked about his experiences when a Frenchman found pieces of his airplane, shot down 50 years earlier, in 1944. But those times were rare and totally unexpected.

When he passed away in 1997, an important story died with him. After his death we discovered a vast amount of documents from his 30-year career in the United States Army Air Corps and the United States Air Force. Many documents were newspaper clippings saved since World War II. They detailed the highs (becoming an "Ace") and the lows (being a prisoner of war in Buchenwald, Germany) of his military career.

BY MARY LARSON

The Goal and Challenges

I decided to take on the daunting task of organizing my father-in-law's history into a tribute album. I began my venture with three goals. First, I wanted to preserve historical information. Second, I wanted to provide a visual legacy for my husband and his siblings. Third, I wanted this tribute to be as complete as possible so we wouldn't have to handle the original documents, which are now deteriorating.

I had a few obstacles from the outset. The 60-year-old newspaper clippings were firmly adhered to old scrapbook pages, so I couldn't remove the clippings without destroying them. My father-in-law and mother-in-law had both passed away. And, although my father-in-law had saved large quantities of information, it was in unorganized pieces—clippings, letters, certificates, telegrams and more.

But, I also had a couple of advantages. My father-in-law's family was diligent in saving articles about his experiences, making the fact gathering much easier. The documents included numerous newspaper interviews. Even more informative was the book in which his World War II squadron wrote in 1978 about their experiences. Sadly, they didn't know where my father-in-law lived at the time, so his personal accounts aren't included. However, they still included wonderful information about him.

Figure 1. Create dual functionality by using a copy of an announcement as a pocket for documents. *Page by Mary Larson.* **Supplies** *Screw eyelets:* Making Memories; *Ribbon:* C.M. Offray & Son; *Metal alphabet stamps:* The Leather Factory; *Other:* Metal sheets.

Managing the Project

To make this tribute album a more manageable undertaking, I concentrated on just his World War II experiences. This marks the beginning of my father-in-law's career and incorporates the oldest documents. (I felt the most urgency to preserve this information.) The rest of his career will come later.

Because the newspaper clippings are crumbling, it was more important to me to preserve the information on the clippings than the actual clippings. Instead of trying to remove the clippings from the old scrapbook pages, I copied the clippings onto colored cardstock. This maintained the vintage look and eliminated the

need for expensive color copies.

I grouped the documents into the following categories (remember that these categories work for current as well as historic albums):

• Enlistment and training. We had his enlistment forms, plus the invitation to his fly school's commencement (see Figure 1).

• Main accomplishments. The layouts in Figures 2 and 3 include information about becoming an operations officer and Flying Ace. I used newspaper articles, photographs and recollections from the squadron book.

• Ribbons and medals. I scanned my father-in-law's medals and tried to find information on each. The United States National Archives *(www.archives.gov)* has wonderful information about

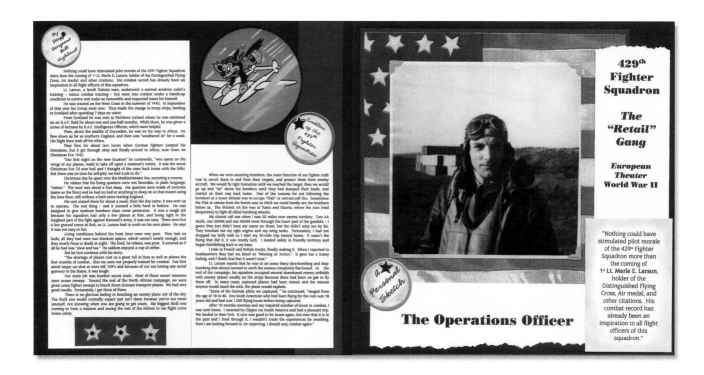

The layout image contains:

429th Fighter Squadron

The "Retail" Gang

European Theater World War II

The Operations Officer

"Nothing could have stimulated pilot morale of the 429th Fighter Squadron more than the coming of 1st Lt. Merle E. Larson, holder of the Distinguished Flying Cross, Air medal, and other citations. His combat record has already been an inspiration to all flight officers of this squadron."

Figure 2. Color-copied emblems, subtitled tags and a remarkable story make an interesting layout. *Pages by Mary Larson.* **Supplies** *Patterned paper:* K & Company; *Tags and star brads:* Making Memories; *Punch:* Nankong; *Brads:* American Tag Company.

the meanings of achievement awards, medals and ribbons. You can also request important military personnel records, such as a DD214 form, which details service stations, awards, medals, certificates, promotions and more.

• Events. I have many newspaper articles and letters about when my father-in-law was shot down over France and taken prisoner by the Nazis (Figure 4). We were fortunate to also have his prisoner of war documentation (written in German), plus some very fragile, folded pieces of paper. These fragile papers are my father-in-law's handwritten list of military personnel by name and serial number. We believe he wrote this list while at Buchenwald as a way of keeping track of the other American prisoners.

• Recent events. Several years before my father-in-law died, a man in France found pieces of the plane when he was shot down. The pieces had enough information that the man could find my father-in-law and send him the pieces, 50 years later. I have pictures of these relics and wanted to document that story.

• Other. This includes anything else not already included. For example, we had an aerial photograph of one of my father-in-law's first dive bombs.

Figure 3. Quotes and a map draw attention to the story on the layout. *Pages by Mary Larson.* **Supplies** *Patterned paper:* Karen Foster Design; *Mesh paper:* Maruyama, Magenta; *Metal letters:* Making Memories; *Lettering template:* ScrapPagerz.com; *Other:* Star brads and fibers.

Requesting Military Documents

The National Personnel Records Center in St. Louis, Missouri, stores military records dating back to the mid-1800s. Records originating prior to that time are at the National Archives Building in Washington, D.C. You can learn more about both facilities by visiting *ww.archives.gov*.

For a complete list of dates for the records stored by the National Archives and Records Administration (NARA), visit *www.archives.gov/publications/prologue/fall_2002_military_records_overview.html*.

More than 5,000 requests are received daily by the NARA for military personnel records. The average wait time to receive information is between 14 and 16 weeks. You can download the standard request form at *www.archives.gov/research_room/obtain_copies/standard_form_180.pdf*. The Standard Form 180 is for veterans and next-of-kin, a relationship you may have to prove in order to receive the records.

Mail or fax your request to the National Personnel Records Center at:

Military Personnel Records
9700 Page Avenue
St. Louis, MO 63132-5100

314/801-9195 (fax)

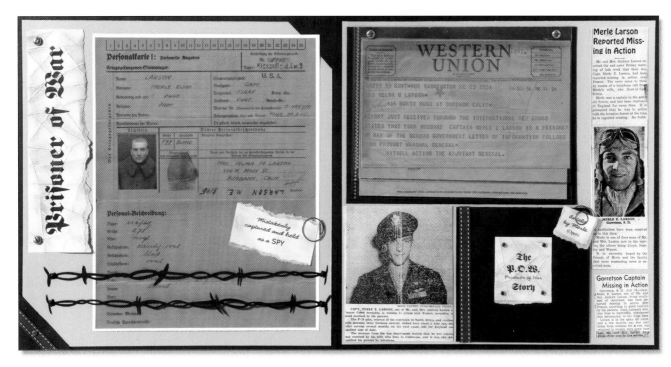

Figure 4. Use a small book to include more of the story for your page. *Pages by Mary Larson.* **Supplies:** *Die cuts:* Deluxe Designs; *Screw eyelets:* Making Memories; *Chalk:* Craf-T Products; *Other:* Ribbon, brads and spiral clips.

Putting It Together

After gathering the information and making copies of everything, I typed the squadron book information about my father-in-law. Next, I scanned the photographs and printed them. At this point, I was ready to start scrapbooking. Although I did not use the same papers throughout the album, I did stick to a version of the patriotic red, white and blue colors.

The pages are filled with informational reading. To help facilitate the album's flow, I garnered interesting tidbits from the newspaper clippings or articles, such as key phrases or quotes, and highlighted them on the page. This way, the reader can quickly get a feel for each page's theme. Some pages are interactive and involved—this is not an album for the casual reader. I want the reader to pull out the pages and read the whole story.

On an emotional level, this was not an easy album to create. So many times I wanted my father-in-law to explain a detail or tell me his story. I got caught up in the history as I stared at the pictures of my father-in-law and read the accounts of his experiences.

With the current world situation, I want this album to be a very special and patriotic tribute to a very special and patriotic man. During the Persian Gulf War, I observed my father-in-law as he watched the war unfold on TV. He was amazed at the way planes were flown and all the progress that had been made in aviation technology. I could tell if given the chance, he would have been up there with all those pilots, fighting for his country once again. ♥

Figure 1. Create a casual look on a layout by hanging tags from a photo mat with safety pins. *Page by Katrina Lawrence.* **Supplies** *Photo frame and stitched title letters:* Forget Me Not Designs; *Rubber stamps:* PSX Design and Hero Arts; *Stamping ink:* Stampa Rosa; *Chalk:* Craf-T Products; *Star eyelet and metal-rimmed tag:* Making Memories; *Computer fonts:* 2Peas Hot Chocolate and 2Peas Evergreen, downloaded from *www.twopeasinabucket.com; Pen:* American Crafts; *Other:* Safety pins. *Idea to note:* Katrina sanded the photo frame to give it a rustic look

Safety Pin Hangers

While looking for a fun way to hang tags from a photo mat, I reached for something everyone has in their home—safety pins! I simply poked the pins through the frame and then the tags, making sure to keep the pins' "heads" on top. The look is the perfect finishing touch for this rustic page.

—*Katrina Lawrence, Provo, UT*

june

the joys of june

The skies are blue, the sun is bright, and everyone is heading for the pool. Summer has finally arrived! The slow, relaxed days this month bring numerous photo opportunities, from floating in an innertube on a lazy river to finding refreshment in a tart glass of lemonade. Find a comfy rocking chair on the porch, get your camera ready, and enjoy the grand pleasures of summer:

- Children spilling out of school on the last day of class
- Cheerful music from a passing ice-cream truck
- Patio barbecues with family and friends
- Kids out after dark playing flashlight tag
- Yards lit with the glow of lightning bugs
- Fruity, frozen drinks with paper umbrellas
- A child soaring on a tree swing in the backyard
- Sleeping in mild temperatures under the stars

- Serving fresh-squeezed lemonade on the front porch
- Bike rides around the neighborhood at dusk
- The car all packed for the first family vacation of the season
- Watching the sun rise on an early-morning walk
- Staying up late during summertime slumber parties
- Wearing wide-brimmed hats and colorful sunglasses to protect from the sun

ARTICLE BY CATHERINE SCOTT

dads, school and everyday things

11 ways to scrapbook the best moments

Supplies *Letter stamps:* Stampers Anonymous; *Stamping ink:* Archival Ink, Ranger Industries; *Computer font:* 2Peas Hot Chocolate, downloaded from *www.twopeasina-bucket.com; Other:* Denim, corduroy and thread.

"Safe and Secure"

by Cathy Blackstone
Columbus, OH

Ellie is a daddy's girl, says Cathy. She couldn't resist taking this touching photo of her daughter at the petting zoo.

◆ Add a touch of texture to a layout with fabric.

◆ One strong focal point is all you may need in a single-page layout. To keep the focus on your photo, use few if any accents.

ARTICLE BY LANNA WILSON

"Kendra"

by Tamara Morrison
Trabuco Canyon, CA

Tamara wants her daughter to remember her younger years—what's important to her daughter, her memories, her school marks and more.

◆ Emphasize certain colors in your layout by adding accent fiber in a coordinating color.

◆ Create a corner pocket with cardstock or other heavy paper to hold items such as report cards, progress reports, awards and teacher comments.

◆ Include a fact sheet in your end-of-school layout. By printing it on vellum, you can still see what's behind it.

Supplies *Vellum:* Making Memories; *Tag:* Fresh Cuts, EK Success; *Alphabet and number stamps:* Jive Alphabet, Stampcraft; *Eyelets:* Creative Impressions (small) and unknown (large); *Computer font:* Annifont, downloaded from the Internet.

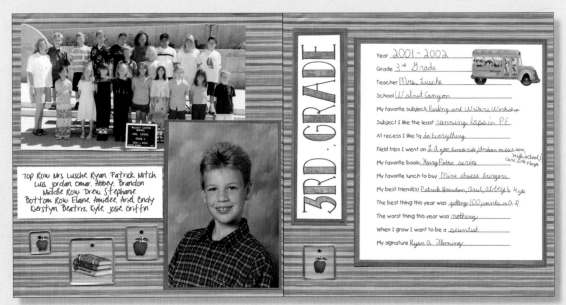

NOTE: CLASS PHOTO WAS BLURRED ELECTRONICALLY TO MEET LEGAL REQUIREMENTS.

"3rd Grade"

by Michelle Flemming
Moorpark, CA

Each year, Michelle asks her children to fill out information about their school classes, favorite things, friends and goals.

◆ Have your child fill out a questionnaire (in his or her own handwriting) at the end of each school year. Include your child's answers on a layout.

◆ Include names of classmates with a class photo. Over the years, your child will probably forget names.

◆ Mount cutouts on vellum tags for quick embellishments.

Supplies *Patterned paper and tags:* Making Memories; *Stickers:* Debbie Mumm, Creative Imaginations; *Computer fonts:* CK Fill In (title), "The Best of Creative Lettering" CD Combo, *Creating Keepsakes*; First Grader (questionnaire), downloaded from the Internet; 2Peas Little Buddy, downloaded from *www.twopeasinabucket.com*; *Other:* Brads.

Supplies *Vellum:* Bazzill Basics; *Computer font:* American Typewriter, downloaded from the Internet; CB Classic, source unknown; *Square punch:* Marvy Uchida; *Alphabet stamps:* PSX Design; *Number stamps:* Stampers Anonymous; *Stamping inks:* Anita's, Stampin Up, Hero Arts, Tsukineko, Crystal; *Rubber stamps:* Anita's (coffee mug), All Night Media (handprints), Stampcraft (footprints), The Rubbernecker Stamp Co. (coffee beans), Inkadinkadoo (script background); *Stickers:* Jolee's Boutique, Stickopotamus; *Circle punch:* McGill; *Rectangle hand punch:* Fiskars; *Tags:* Donna's own designs; *Jewelry tags:* Avery; *Eyelets:* Making Memories; *Date stamp:* 2000 Plus; *Other:* Jump rings and circle clip.

"Morning Routine"

**by Donna Downey
Huntersville, NC**

Donna's morning routine is a big part of her day. She wanted to remember it in her scrapbook album.

◆ Consider putting sequential photos on tags in vellum envelopes. This provides visual separation but maintains the flow of your layout.

◆ Create your own patterned vellum by stamping on it with white stamping ink.

◆ Don't forget to take pictures of even the mundane things in life. Fifty years from now, they may not be so mundane.

"I Can Only Imagine"

**by Mary Ramsaver
Spring, TX**

Mary loved the expression on her son's face as Sean watched his daddy and brothers play outside during a family reunion last summer.

◆ Looking for an innovative way to use metal words? Incorporate them in your journaling.

◆ If you prefer scrapbooking 12" x 12" pages, ask your photo developer to print a favorite photo 12" deep. This generally doesn't cost more than the smaller 8" x 10" size, and the results provide a beautiful focal point.

◆ Experiment with black-and-white film. If you can adjust your camera settings, play with shutter speeds, aperture openings, lenses and filters.

Supplies *Vellum:* Paper Adventures; *Silver and platinum cardstock:* National Cardstock Supply; *Computer font:* Times New Roman, Microsoft Word; *Metal words:* Making Memories.

Supplies *Vellum:* The Paper Company; *Eyelets:* Doodlebug Design; *Foot punch:* Family Treasures; *Computer font:* SlashHmk, Print Shop.

"Walk a Little Slower, Daddy"
by Cynthia Anning
Virginia Beach, VA

These photos are special to Cynthia because they were taken the day before her husband left on an extended overseas naval assignment.

◆ If you already know how you want your finished layout to look, take an additional photo—such as these footprints—to complement the layout's other photos and journaling.

◆ Use a favorite poem on a layout. Adapt the words to fit your special circumstances.

◆ Don't have the right color of vellum? Type your text and add a colored background before you output your title on vellum.

"Unconditional"
by Jackie Bonette
Taber, AB, Canada

Jackie thought of a favorite greeting card when she took these photos of her husband and their children. "The quote actually inspired the layout," she says.

◆ Do you have a greeting card saved from years ago? Consider using its message as part of your journaling.

◆ Band the lower third of a layout to keep the focus on the largest picture while still including other memorable pictures.

◆ Get perfectly cropped photos with a square punch.

Supplies *Brads:* Lost Art Treasures; *Square punch:* Marvy Uchida; *Heart button:* Hillcreek Designs; *Letter stamps:* Stampcraft; *Computer fonts:* Unknown, downloaded from the Internet; *Round button and letter beads:* Michael's; *Other:* Tag.

"Surrounded by Women"

by Tracy Miller
Fallston, MD

When friends challenged Tracy to create a masculine layout, it wasn't easy. "I ended up scrapbooking about how my husband is always surrounded by women," says Tracy.

◆ When a paper design is prominent like the SEI paper here, avoid breaking up the continuity. Tracy cut slivers in the paper so the photo corners would tuck into the circle bands.

◆ Cut circle accents from complementary patterned paper to add visual appeal to your layout.

◆ Want journaling continuity on 12" x 12" paper? Print your journaling on matching cardstock and mount it on the layout. Once you place your page in a sheet protector, most people won't notice the separate journaling piece.

"A Boy Is a Joy"

by Krista Austin
Chicago, IL

Krista's son discovered that dirt and sunscreen make great body art. "I had trouble holding the camera steady through my laughter," she says.

◆ You can never have too many pictures of a funny moment! The expressions will last a lifetime.

◆ Monochromatic colors help draw viewers to your focal point, especially if the layout has few embellishments.

◆ Note how the patterned paper in this layout blends with the photo background. It helps the focal point "pop."

creative marriage proposals

How eight women
were asked the
big question

It's the phrase every girl dreams of: "Will you marry me?"
Although my husband's proposal wasn't as romantic as those
in my dreams—the open ring box was sitting on my office
desk when I returned from lunch and he was hiding behind
the door—it was meant for me. We discussed it together,
decided together and planned together. The only thing I
didn't do was help choose the ring—Brian did that by himself. And, to his credit, he did a great job!

Whether your proposal was the stuff dreams are made of
or nothing more than a casual question and answer, getting
engaged is a special time. Here's to the guys who got up the
nerve to propose. And here's to eight talented women who
captured proposals memorably for a scrapbook!

by Lanna Wilson   Illustration by Betsy Everitt

"Anything for a Yes"
by Heidi Gnadke • Centerville, MN

Journaling excerpt: "Although I found Randy's wedding proposal a bit unusual and less than utterly romantic, I couldn't help but be impressed at his attempt to woo me! On February 7, 1995, Randy got up in front of all of our college classmates during the chapel service to 'make an announcement.' I was highly suspicious when he walked up to the front....

"As Randy began his little speech he pulled out three items and began juggling. One of the items was a ring box. He went on to ask me for my hand in marriage. He didn't have to do much coaxing because despite Randy's interesting attempt at proposing, I had already decided months before that Randy was definitely the one I would spend my life with."

Supplies *Patterned paper:* Carolee's Creations; *Computer fonts:* Butterbrotpapier (journaling) and Brush455 BT (title), downloaded from the Internet; *Eyelets:* Making Memories; *Fiber:* Filiatura Di Crosa; *Flower buttons:* Blumenthal Lansing; *Jump ring and rhinestone:* Westrim Crafts; *Ribbon:* C.M. Offray & Son; *Stamping ink:* Rubber Stampede; *Vellum:* Paper Adventures; *Metal-rimmed tag:* Making Memories; *Oval eyelet:* The Stamp Doctor; *Keys:* Rusty Tin Tiques, DC & C; *Photo corners:* Canson; *Embroidery floss:* DMC.

"A Proposal Story"
by Cathryn Zielske • St. Paul, MN

Journaling excerpt: "It was the day when President Bush had drawn a line in the sand, marking the start of Desert Storm. We were miles from home on a beach in Ocho Rios, Jamaica. Maybe it was the sudden awareness of our vulnerability during a time of war that made it the perfect time to commit our lives together. Maybe it was the pristine beaches and tropical breezes. Maybe, in such an idyllic setting, it was just too good an opportunity to pass up.

"Whatever the case, it happened like this: while jealousy had never been a part of our relationship, for some bizarre reason I was jealous that he had been hanging around a fellow female manager. (When my dander is up, I have been known to be a bit punchy.) So, I called him on it, to which, of course, he replied, 'What are you talking about?' It was a good question. What *was* I talking about?

"I apologized for being crabby and generally unpleasant to be around that day, then I threw out my standard line for making sincere apologies: 'You know, I still want to marry you someday.'

"His reply: 'How about October?' "

Supplies *Patterned paper frames:* Anna Griffin; *Small frame charms:* Impress Rubber Stamps; *Computer font:* Goudy, Adobe Systems; *Pop dots:* All Night Media; *Other:* Ribbon. *Idea to note:* Cathryn converted a color photo to black and white on the Kodak Picture Maker system to give the picture a more timeless look.

"Just Try It"

by Vivian Smith • Calgary, AB, Canada

Journaling excerpt: "Dal thought it would be fun to hide the ring [box] in a piece of cake and propose when I found it. We went out for dinner at a great restaurant, then went up to a parking area that overlooked the city.

"Although I knew Dal had brought dessert to save money, I ate so much at dinner, I turned down his first offer to have a piece of cake. He asked again.

"Really, Dal, it looks great, but I'm full."

"C'mon, just try a piece."

"No really, I'm not hungry."

"Just try the center, you'll love it!"

"No Dal, I really don't want any!"

"Please, just try some for me."

"Oh, alright." I took a tiny piece off the edge and told him it was good. After more convincing, I eventually tried the center. I stuck my fork in and it was the hardest center I've ever felt. As I was uncovering the case, Dal hopped out of the car, came around to my side, and went down on one knee. The cake was the best I'd ever had and the rest is history."

Supplies *Patterned paper:* Making Memories; *Specialty paper:* Treehouse Designs; *Computer fonts:* CK Constitution (journaling) and CK Elegant (title), "Fresh Fonts" CD, *Creating Keepsakes; Letter eyelets:* Making Memories; *Embossing powder:* Creative Zoo; *Embossing pen:* Tsukineko; *Brads:* Provo Craft; *Paper-pieced cake:* Vivian's own design. *Idea to note:* Vivian used an embossing pen to apply ink to the letter eyelets, then heat-embossed them several times for full coverage.

"Did You Ask Her Yet?"

by Cindy Knowles • Milwaukie, OR

Journaling excerpt: "Right after our third date, Quinn's friends constantly questioned, 'Did you ask her yet?' It didn't matter if I was with him or not, they still would pester him about his intentions....

"I guess people started asking him THAT question because we were both hovering around 30 and had not dated anyone else steadily.

"After going out to dinner one night, we went back to my basement apartment. We were sitting on the couch talking and laughing. Out of the blue, Quinn blurted, 'Will you marry me?' I was taken completely by surprise. 'Do you mean it?' I asked. 'You're serious?' Quinn thought about it for a minute. "Yeah, I mean it."

"I happily gave him my answer, 'YES!'

"When Quinn got home that night, his roommates again asked, 'Did you ask her yet?' He was able to reply in the affirmative."

Supplies *Patterned paper:* K & Company; *Vellum:* Hot Off The Press; *Letter stickers:* Flavia, Colorbök; *Computer font:* Lilith, downloaded from the Internet; *Ribbon:* C.M. Offray & Son; *Pearls, craft wire, embroidery floss and cording:* Westrim Crafts; *Tags:* Making Memories; *Photo corners:* 3L Corp.; *Embossing powder and embossing ink:* Stampendous!; *Dried flowers:* JS Designs. *Idea to note:* Cindy heat-embossed the tag with white embossing powder for a subtle yet elegant embellishment.

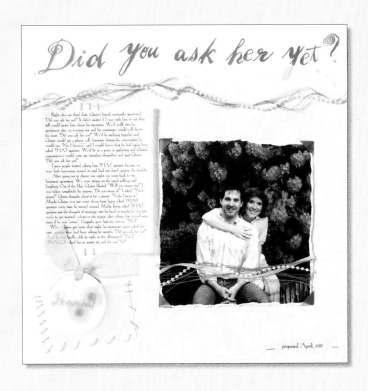

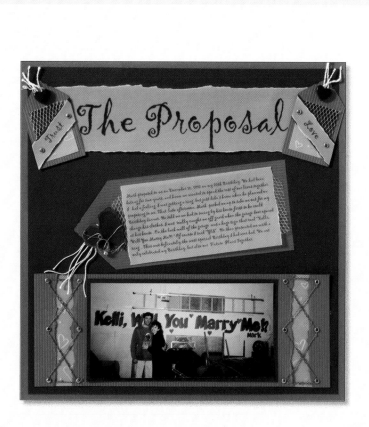

"The Puppy Proposal"

by Felicia Voss • Temple, AZ

Journaling excerpt: "Dave totally had me fooled this night when he proposed! We headed out to Mesa, arrived at Freestone Park, and fed the ducks. We then took a walk, and as we headed over the hill there was the cutest picnic set up!

"A lady with a chocolate Labrador walked by (turns out David knew her from work). As we all talked, she gave the dog some treats from the pouch around its neck. The next thing I knew, I saw Dave digging in the pouch for a treat. But, instead of a treat, he pulled out a ring. Then he got down on one knee, and said the most beautiful words as I could only laugh in shock and say, 'Yes!'"

Supplies *Dog stickers:* Dog House; *Rubber stamps:* PSX Design; *Ring:* Jolee's Boutique, Stickopotamus; *Computer font:* Two Peas Beautiful, downloaded from *www.twopeasinabucket.com.*

CK's Wedding Idea Book
Whether your sweetheart's just proposed or your dad's crying because he's "giving" his little girl away, be sure to scrapbook your big day. Look to *The Big Idea Book of Wedding Memories* for page-layout ideas, preservation tips, and information on classic products perfect for wedding albums. Whether it's photographing your bouquet or preserving his love letters, this book is sure to help you celebrate your new life together. 164 pages. $14.95.

"The Proposal"

by Kelli Gamble • Austintown, OH

Journaling excerpt: "Mark proposed to me on my 20th birthday. I had a feeling I was getting a ring, but didn't know when he planned on proposing to me. Late that afternoon, Mark picked me up to take me out for my birthday dinner. He told me we had to swing by his house first so he could change his clothes.

"I was really caught off-guard when the garage door opened. On the back wall of the garage was a huge sign that said, 'Kelli, Will You Marry Me?' Of course I said, 'YES.' He then presented me with a ring. This was definitely the most special birthday I had ever had. We not only celebrated my birthday, but also our future plans together."

Supplies *Vellum:* Paper Adventures; *Embossed vellum:* Source unknown; *Mini brads:* Making Memories; *Fiber:* On the Surface; *Heart buttons:* Westwater Enterprises; *Ring charm:* www.giraffecrafts.com; *Craft wire:* Artistic Wire Ltd.; *Wire mesh:* Activa.

"An Engaging Choice"
by Jennifer Borowski • Princeton, NJ

Journaling excerpt: "In November of 1995, Brett and I decided we would get married. Brett warned me that he would not be able to afford a ring for me by Christmas, but I remained hopeful.

"On Christmas Day, Brett handed me a gift bag that held a Boyd's teddy bear snowman ornament wearing TWO engagement rings, one on each paw.... Brett couldn't decide which one he liked better, so he bought them both so I could make the final decision.

"While my parents toasted us with champagne, I was faced with the daunting task of choosing which of the two rings to keep. When Brett returned the other one, he assured me that the clerk was very sympathetic and asked him no questions. We're sure the clerk thought Brett had proposed and been turned down. After all, who would suspect that a prospective groom would buy his future bride TWO engagement rings?!"

Supplies *Patterned Paper:* Making Memories; *Patterned vellum:* Embossing Arts Co.; *Computer fonts:* Team Spirit (title) and I Souvenir Light Italic (journaling), downloaded from the Internet; *Fiber:* Making Memories.

"Will You Marry Me?"
by Heather Lancaster • Calgary, AB, Canada

Journaling excerpt: "Brian was (of course) star-struck when we met, but instead of the romantic proposal every girl dreams of, we just one day started looking for rings and picking dates for a wedding. I never received a 'formal' marriage proposal, and so, for four years of marriage, I never let Brian live it down!

"One summer I was so surprised when out of the blue (or should I say gray bucket), Brian painted his way back into grace with a HUGE proposal of marriage on our backyard fence. Naturally at this point I said yes!"

Supplies *Textured paper and patterned paper:* Provo Craft; *Fiber:* Rubba Dub Dub, Art Sanctum; *Brads:* PC Bradletz, Provo Craft; *Computer font:* PC Ratatat, "A Gathering of Friends" HugWare CD, Provo Craft; *Vellum:* Provo Craft and Paper Adventures. *Idea to note:* The journaling block at bottom right opens to reveal the story.

How about You?
Your marriage proposal was undoubtedly memorable, for what it was or wasn't. Scrapbook it! This is one of life's milestones that should be recorded, especially when it involves fun stories to pass down. Or, be a gatherer of family stories and record how other family members, past and present, proposed.—*Jana Lillie*

july

JENNA EASTON

july moments

The heat of summer is here! With July's warm weather and clear skies, you'll find several opportunities to make memories with loved ones. Plan a few extra-special activities this month—and tell family members often how much they mean to you. Here are some July moments to savor:

- Watching a double feature at the drive-in
- Climbing as high as you can in the tallest tree
- Tracing your name in the air with holiday sparklers
- Screaming and giggling on a giant roller coaster
- Bathing the dog with a hose in the back yard
- Breakfasting on fresh berries and cream
- Spending the whole day in your swimsuit
- Building sandcastles and filling the moats with water

- Listening to music and nighttime noises at outdoor concerts
- Waiting in line to get slathered with sunscreen before heading outside
- Letting fruity Popsicles drip on your hand in the heat
- Creating a strategic breeze through the house with fans
- Lying on your back, watching clouds drift through the sky
- Tossing a multicolored beach ball through the air
- Waking up with no "to-do" list

ARTICLE BY CATHERINE SCOTT

july celebrations

10 layouts with summer festivities

Supplies *Rubber stamp:* Pledge of Allegiance stamp, Stampabilities; *Alphabet stamps:* Hero Arts; *Watermark ink:* VersaMark, Tsukineko; *Stamping ink:* Impress Rubber Stamps; *Paper yarn:* Twistel, Making Memories; *Eyelets:* Making Memories (tag) and Happy Hammer (stars); *Stickers:* Jolee's Boutique, Stickopotamus; *Letter stickers:* Sonnets, Creative Imaginations; *Photo corners:* Canson; *Mesh:* Magic Mesh, Avant Card; *Computer font:* CK Constitution, "Fresh Fonts" CD, Creating Keepsakes; *Other:* Bookplate.

"Our Patriotic Little Guy"

by Amber Crosby
Houston, TX

After September 11, 2001, Amber would sing "God Bless America" to her son as she rocked him to sleep. Now, it's his favorite song.

◆ Need to reduce the image size of your stamp? Stamp it onto a neutral background, then scan and reduce the image on your computer.

◆ Untwist paper yarn and line it behind an accent or journaling. Or, use it to add color to a tag.

◆ Want to create custom patterned paper for your layout's theme? Use a stamp!

A few days before Canada Day, we were given some flag tattoos at Zellers. On July 1st we carefully applied them to our cheeks. At the end of the day, when it was time to clean up and wash off the tattoos, Tristan absolutely refused. "I can't take it off, it is like my label that shows that I am made in Canada!" He proudly wore his "label" until it wore off. He is the cutest little Canadian boy that I know!

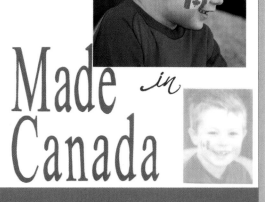

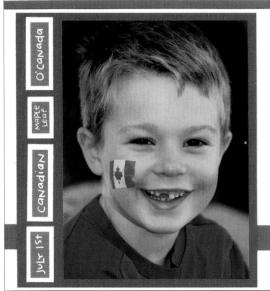

Made *in* **Canada**

TRISTAN JULY 2002

Supplies *Vellum:* Paper Adventures; *Button:* Better Button Company; *Computer fonts:* Times New Roman, Microsoft Word; 2Peas Canada Blocks, downloaded from *www.twopeasin-abucket.com.*

"Made in Canada"

by Tracy Kyle
Coquitlam, BC,
Canada

If anyone has any doubts, Tracy's son, Tristan, is made in Canada. He was proud of the removable tattoo he wore on his cheek for Canada Day (July 1).

◆ To accent just one part of a special photo (see the picture at lower right), scan the photo, change the image to black and white, then fade the image to a percentage of its full exposure (saturation). Output the image on vellum. Tracy kept the color on the flag tattoo to draw attention to it.

◆ Instead of using a non-descript black, customize your font color to make it match your background color.

◆ If your vellum doesn't work well on the default printer setting, try setting your printer to a "transparency" setting.

"Summer Days"

by Lonnie Seriosa
Victoria, BC, Canada

Lonnie was a little nervous about how her son, Jesse, would react to his first camping trip. To her relief, he had a blast!

◆ To add extra room to your layout, create a side flap. Here, Lonnie cut two window openings in a wide strip of cardstock, punched holes along the side of the flap and the layout, then threaded the two sides together with jute.

◆ Make square screen frame accents for subtle dimension. Use two square punches to create the frame. Mount screen behind it. Embellish it with smaller shapes mounted with eyelets through the screen.

Supplies *Eyelets:* Making Memories; *Jute:* Ace Hardware; *Punches:* Creative Memories (square), Emagination Crafts (star) and Fiskars (circle); *Computer font:* CK Hustle, "Fresh Fonts" CD, *Creating Keepsakes*; *Pop dots:* Therm O Web; *Other:* Wire mesh.

Supplies *Vellum:* Stampin' Up!; *Computer fonts:* Rage Italic (title) and Papyrus (journaling), downloaded from the Internet; *Craft wire:* Artistic Wire Ltd.; *Chalk:* Stampin' Up!; *Beads:* Westrim Crafts.

"Strength"
by Heather Hillman
Meridian, ID

Heather and her family enjoyed a vacation to Bumgardners near Anderson Dam in Idaho. While there, they marveled at the grandeur of this forest.

◆ Look for different angles when you take pictures. To get this shot, Heather lay on the ground near the base of the tree and shot up.

◆ To make a strong vertical photo stand out even more, "lengthen" the photo with a long mat. Add wire and beads at the bottom or side of the mat for decoration.

◆ If the subjects in your photo are too small to serve as focal points, tear the photo and use it as an accent.

◆ Highlight important words in your journaling with a little chalk.

"Bungalow"
by Wendy Woodby
Russellville, AR

Wendy remembers with delight her son Ty building sandcastles and chasing white sand crabs every night during his family's vacation in Alabama.

◆ Age a tag by liberally applying a metallic finish.

◆ To create this rustic photo mat, mount your picture on black cardstock. Cut another mat roughly ¼" wider on the sides and ½" longer on the top and bottom. Mount eight eyelets to the top and bottom. Weave jute through the eyelet holes.

◆ Use a touch of glaze to attach fragile items, such as the sand dollars and starfish.

◆ Don't have vellum tape? Attach vellum to your layout with eyelets.

Supplies *Patterned paper:* Mustard Moon; *Vellum:* DMD Inc.; *Eyelets:* Making Memories; *Sandcastle die cut:* QuicKutz; *Sticky paper, sand, sand dollars and starfish:* Magic Scraps; *Tags:* Avery; *Paint:* Spanish Copper, Rub 'n Buff; *Chalk and pop dots:* Stampin' Up!; *Computer fonts:* Darling and Bernie, downloaded from the Internet; *Other:* Diamond Glaze, JudiKins.

Supplies *Pen:* The Ultimate Gel Pen, American Craft; *Mesh:* Magic Mesh, Avant Card; *Buttons:* Hillcreek Designs; *Embroidery floss:* Making Memories; *Small star punch:* Emagination Crafts; *Computer font:* Deseryl, downloaded from the Internet; *Star template:* Provo Craft; *Flag:* Renée's own design; *Color-blocking template:* Close To My Heart.

"Fourth of July 2002"

by Renée Foss
Seven Fields, PA

The Fourth of July holiday is extra special for Renée's family because they get to celebrate her daughter's birthday as well as the birth of the nation.

◆ Dress up your die cuts by layering them with other embellishments. Here, Renée matted her stars with cardstock and mesh, then topped them with stitched buttons.

◆ Add dimension to your title by tracing one side with a pen. Determine the direction of your "light" source, then trace the opposite side of each letter to create a "shadow."

◆ Visually "ground" your accents and photos to the layout by matting and double-matting them.

"Untitled"

by Angie Cramer
Redcliff, AB, Canada

Supplies *Patterned paper:* Scrap-Ease; *Daisy punch:* Marvy Uchida; *Square punch:* Fiskars; *Circle punch:* EK Success; *Computer font:* CK Sketch, "The Art of Creative Lettering" CD, *Creating Keepsakes.*

Angie wasn't convinced she'd enjoy her family's trip to Disneyland. When she got home, she could hardly wait to go to Disney World!

◆ Do your pictures have colors that clash? Combine solid and textured papers to help them blend together.

◆ To create an extra-full daisy, punch the image in two different colors, then overlap them.

◆ Add knotted accent strips to your layout. To create them, cut thin strips of cardstock, then carefully tie them, creasing the final knot.

◆ You don't always need a title for your layout, especially if it's part of a theme album, such as this Disneyland album.

Supplies *Brads:* Midwestern Home Products; *Twine:* Wal-Mart; *Mulberry paper:* PrintWorks; *Mini beads:* Magic Scraps; *Chalk:* Close To My Heart; *Computer fonts:* CK Script (on photo) and CK Bella, "The Best of Creative Lettering" CD Combo, *Creating Keepsakes*; *Other:* Charm.

"By the Sea"

by Marnae Buchanan
Tucson, AZ

The day Marnae took her kids to Mission Beach in California was chilly. The cold water and breeze didn't stop the kids from enjoying a beautiful day, however!

◆ Tear pieces of neutral-colored mulberry paper, then mount them in a shaker box filled with microbeads for a sandy look.

◆ To print on your photo, scan the image into your computer, then write on it with photo-editing software. Print on photo-quality paper.

◆ Don't rule out printing journaling on 12" x 12" paper. Here, Marnae changed the print orientation to landscape in Microsoft Word for her text, then printed it on a 12" strip of cardstock.

◆ Knot your jute or fiber before mounting it to your layout. The knots will stick better to mini pop dots.

Supplies *Patterned paper:* Chatterbox; *Ribbon:* C.M. Offray & Son; *Fibers:* Creative Scrapping Accents; *Beads:* Darice; *Chalk:* Craf-T Products; *Mulberry paper:* PrintWorks; *Vellum:* Making Memories; *Adhesive:* Scrappy Glue, Magic Scraps; *Computer fonts:* CK Jot, CK Script, CK Sketch, CK Fun, CK Toggle, CK Journaling and CK Cursive, "The Best of Creative Lettering" CD Combo, *Creating Keepsakes*; Gigi and Curlz MT, Microsoft Word.

"Daddies Are a Girl's Best Friend"

**by Christy Tomlinson
Shelley, ID**

As the only girl in a family of boys, Allie Belle is certainly a daddy's girl, says Christy. "My husband spoils her silly!"

◆ Capture and preserve fun family sayings in your layouts.

◆ Edge your punched shapes with beads. Just rub glue along the edges, then dip the shapes into a bowl of beads. Let the shapes dry for 3–5 minutes.

◆ To create a puffy look, mount the tallest pop dot in the center on the back of your accent. Mount smaller pop dots around the edges.

◆ Chalk your words to add emphasis and visual warmth.

Supplies
Pre-made tags and accents: Mini Fresh Cuts, EK Success; *Starfish:* Michael's; *Vellum:* Paper Adventures; *Computer font:* Joplin, downloaded from the Internet.

"Kodak Moment"

**by Stacy Ford
Pt. Mugu, CA**

Stacy's daughter, Daniana, loves family trips to the beach. This trip was extra special because she got to take pretend pictures with a broken camera.

◆ For an elegant title, print it on vellum, then frame the title with cardstock, patterned paper, textured paper or a metal frame.

◆ For a large portrait, such as the photo at left, set your camera to the portrait setting. This will keep the focus on your subject while slightly blurring the photo background.

◆ Prefer flat pages? Consider pre-made tags and accents, such as Rebecca Sower's Fresh Cuts by EK Success.

one good reason

Offer a
glimpse
inside
you or
someone
else

im a
Night
person
because...

Caffeine addict =
night person

It's the only time I get
to watch television
that's not Noggin, Nick
Jr., Disney or ESPN.

That's when Cheetos,
Dr. Pepper and
Peanut Butter M&Ms
taste the best.

Art
Imagine
Create

11 p.m. to 3 a.m. is
prime scrapping time!

The kids are sound asleep.

Use journaling to present the reasons
behind your trademark habits.

WHEN YOU THINK ABOUT IT, we have a reason, an excuse or a rationalization for everything. Whatever the question, there's an answer. Why did we move? Because we outgrew our old house. Why do I love summer? Because the days are warm and I love to wear shorts. Why did I eat an entire pint of Ben & Jerry's? Because it tasted good—and because my diet doesn't start until tomorrow. See?

Whether whimsical or reflective, filled with love or humor, reasons offer a glimpse into our lives. Each reveals a feeling, a motivation, an interest or an aspect of our personality. For this reason, reasons also make great subjects for "all about me" layouts. They're a clever way to put you back into your family album.

Simply think of a subject (something you love or don't, something you do or want to do), then highlight the reasons why through photos, accents or journaling. For a little inspiration, check out the following layouts that demonstrate a wide variety of subjects and styles.

ARTICLE BY DENISE PAULEY

"I'm a Night Person Because . . ." (See layout on page 101)

by Denise Pauley
La Palma, CA

SUPPLIES
Patterned papers: Club Scrap (Java) and
Sharon Ann Collection, Déjà Views
(woodgrain), The C-Thru Ruler Co.
Handmade paper: ArtisticScrapper.com
Vellum: Paper Adventures
Rubber stamps: Club Scrap (coffee cup

and coffee ring), Impress Rubber Stamps
(Thank you) and Limited Edition (art col-
lage and Art/Imagine/Create)
Stamping inks: VersaMark and Dauber
Duo, Tsukineko
Computer fonts: CK Twilight, CK
Constitution, CK Newsprint and CK
Tipsy, "Fresh Fonts" CD, *Creating
Keepsakes*
Beads, jump rings and wire ring: Blue

Moon Beads
Chalk and metallic rub-ons:
Craf-T Products
Metallic paint: Silk, Stampa Rosa
Letter stickers: Flavia, Colorbök
Brad: American Pin & Fastener
Alphabet stamps: PSX Design
Sticker: K & Company
Other: Book pocket, clock face sticker
and conchos

Use journaling to present the reasons behind your trademark habits.

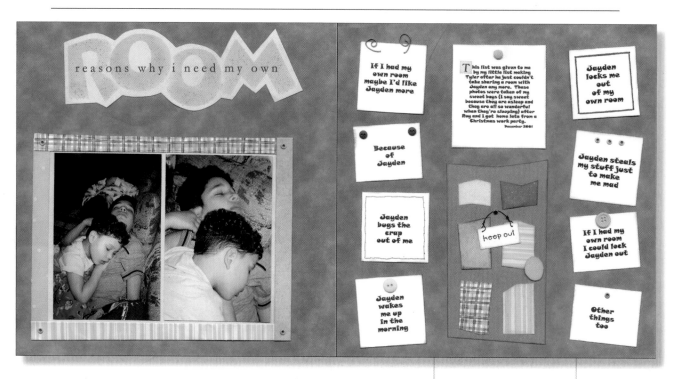

"Why I Need My Own Room"

by Kristy Banks
Highland, UT

SUPPLIES
Patterned papers: Karen Foster Design
and Making Memories
Spritzer: Color Workshop

Lettering template: Déjà Views,
The C-Thru Ruler Co.
*Eyelets, paper yarn, buttons and
embroidery floss:* Making Memories
Craft wire: Artistic Wire Ltd.
Stamping ink: Stampin' Up!

Include accents
to extend—and
play up—your
page theme.

"What I Love about Being a Mom"

by Cheryl McMurray
Cardston, AB, Canada

SUPPLIES

Vellum: Paper Reflections, DMD Industries

Computer font: Garamouche, Impress Rubber Stamps

Eyelet letters, eyelets and tag: Making Memories

Envelope die cut: Ellison

Fibers: On the Surface

Sticker: Provo Craft

Mini pockets can hold and showcase the "reasons" you relish being a mother.

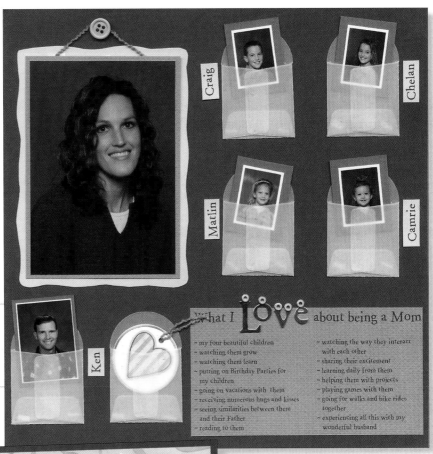

What I Love about being a Mom

– my four beautiful children
– watching them grow
– watching them learn
– putting on Birthday Parties for my children
– going on vacations with them
– receiving numerous hugs and kisses
– seeing similarities between them and their Father
– reading to them

– watching the way they interact with each other
– sharing their excitement
– learning daily from them
– helping them with projects
– playing games with them
– going for walks and bike rides together
– experiencing all this with my wonderful husband

"Reasons 4 Change"

by Janet MacLeod
Dundas, ON, Canada

SUPPLIES

Patterned paper: K & Company

Computer font: Bad Hair Day, downloaded from *www.twopeasinabucket.com*

Eyelets: Creative Imaginations (extreme) and Impress Rubber Stamps (small)

Tags and letter/number charms: Making Memories

Paper yarn: Twistel, Making Memories

Letter stickers: Flavia, Colorbök

Other: Paper clips

Use "before" and "after" photos to illustrate the reasons for—and results of—changes you've made in your life.

Reasons 4 Change

to live
to love
to savor
to move

In May of this year, I started to work on losing the weight I'd gradually gained since having the girls. I started teaching at a new gym and began following Weight Watchers. By November, I've lost 44 pounds and am on my way to a healthier me!

I have lots of reasons to motivate me to take the time to live healthier. First and foremost, I want to be a healthy mom for my children. I want to enjoy my food more (not just eating in a rush, but making healthy recipes and trying new foods!) I want to feel stronger and have more energy for life. I want to look and feel better and fit in my clothes, too! I want to enjoy my fitness classes– having fun with creating new moves and grooving to the music (and having everyone else grooving with me!) I want to take the time to be good to ME!

"My Sophie"

by Twyla Koop
Surrey, BC, Canada

SUPPLIES

Patterned paper: The Scrapbook Wizard
Computer font: Kidprint, AppleWorks 6
Embossing powder: Stampendous!
Stamping ink: ColorBox, Clearsnap
Letter stickers: Flavia, Colorbök
Alphabet stamps: Hero Arts
Other: Mini brads and ball chain

Design faux tags to help illustrate the reasons your pet is a beloved member of your family.

I love Sophie because she gives the best snuggles day and night. She gives wet nose kisses when I do something nice for her. She is always excited to see me. I love Sophie because she loves to play even more than I do. She loves to play chase. Sophie is getting great at catching her frisbee and ball. I love Sophie because she lets me dress her up in bandanas. She likes to lay beside me the grass outside, or on the floor inside. She likes watching movies with me. Sophie can play with me even when I am sick. Sophie is one of my very best friends! Shelby and Sophie '02

my Sophie

"Why I'm a Teacher"

by Darcee Thompson
Preston, ID

SUPPLIES

Handmade paper: ArtisticScrapper.com
Computer fonts: AucoinLight, package unknown; CK Stenography, "Fresh Fonts" CD, *Creating Keepsakes*; Artsy and Wedding Day, downloaded from www.twopeasinabucket.com
Flowers: Pressed Flower Gallery
Transparency: Pockets on a Roll
Tag: Making Memories
Other: Buttons

Document the way you chose your path in life, and the reasons you're thankful you did.

why I'm a

teacher

I started out in college as an Elementary Education major but I had SO many people make comments like, "Half the campus is in that major," or "Everyone and their dog is majoring in that." It bothered me that I was doing what everyone else was, so I changed my major. Nothing else interested me, though, because I had wanted to be a teacher for as long as I could remember. So my first two years my major was undeclared. Then during one of my classes a professor talked about becoming something our egos could handle. He gave the example of a UPS man. Even though everyone *loves* the UPS man because he delivers packages, our self esteem might not be able handle that job. I thought about that a lot. My ego could handle (love!) being a teacher, it just didn't like the comments from peers. So I decided that my ego would just *have* to handle being an Education major. I have not had a minute of regret. (I've also learned to not worry so much about what others think!) I often reflect on this experience and wonder what my other reasons were for becoming a teacher. The following are probably not the reasons I started out with, but they fit my way of thinking in my 9th year of teaching. This picture reminds me of a position I'm in a lot at school. Photo taken by Cache, November 9, 2002

- I still get to go to school.
- Kids are funny. I get many good laughs a day.
- I get to be loved by 23 second graders every year.
- I love to teach kids how to read.
- Summer vacation.
- I love to plan fun activities for the kids.
- I have an excuse for buying a year supply of Skittles and Starburst Jellybeans.
- I get to share my favorite books over and over.
- I don't want my kids to have to ride the bus to school. (Or so *they* think!)
- I get to make an impression on young minds.

"I Need A Pony"

by Allison Strine
Atlanta, GA

SUPPLIES

Patterned papers: Flavia, Colorbök (green); Sonnets by Sharon Soneff, Creative Imaginations (teal); Karen Foster Design (yellowish green)

Computer font for title: Bubblegum Superstar, downloaded from the Internet

Computer fonts for journaling: Calvin & Hobbes, Extraflexidisc, Pupcat, Sedillo, Onsuko, Napkin Script and OCRB, all downloaded from the Internet; CK Hustle, "Fresh Fonts" CD, *Creating Keepsakes*

Rubber stamps: Above the Mark (numbers "6" and "7"), Hero Arts (subtitle alphabet), Postmodern Design (numbers "3" and "5") and Wordsworth (number "2")

Stamping ink: Brilliance, Tsukineko

Pens: Milky Gel Roller (white), Pentel; Zig Writer (teal), EK Success

Numbers "1" and "4": Making Memories

Tin embellishments: Scrapyard 329

Embossing powder: Stampendous!

Glue dots: Glue Dots International

Mosaic squares: The Bee Hive

Watercolors: Niji

Idea to note: Allison downloaded the horse image from Microsoft's Design Gallery Live, printed the image onto a transparency, then transferred the image to canvas (coated with Acrylic Glazing Liquid from Golden Artist Colors, Inc.).

Children have a lot of "needs." Capture the reasons behind your child's most whimsical needs in his or her own words.

More Ideas for Reason Pages

Need additional ideas to help you get started on a reasons layout? Try building on one of the following topics to create a page that will help your loved ones learn more about you.

◆ **"Why I Cherish You."** Whether it's your husband, child, other family member or friend, illustrate the reasons they mean the world to you.

◆ **"I Scrapbook Because . . ."** Show what motivates you to spend so much time with adhesive and cardstock—you can even use this page as a "dedication" for your album. Or, if you also love other crafts, include those as well.

◆ **"I Love to Travel to . . ."** Do you have a favorite vacation spot? Reveal why it's your perfect getaway.

◆ **"My Favorite Holiday."** Use photos and journaling to discuss why one holiday is the most special to you.

◆ **"How You Make Me Smile."** Detail the reasons, such as quirky habits or silly inside jokes, that someone can always bring a smile to your face.

◆ **"I Love Summer Because . . ."** Highlight the activities, weather, holidays or feelings that make you look forward to one particular season each year.

◆ **"Why This Is Home."** What makes you take comfort and pride in your home? What helps you feel love there?

◆ **"Why I Love . . ."** Create a cool pop culture layout that will be a fun reminder years from now. Journal about your favorite shows, movies, music, gadgets and fashions and why they entertain you. ♥

august

august delights

Enjoy these last few weeks of summer—the sweltering heat will fade into cooler weather before you know it! If you haven't

captured the carefree days of summer on film yet, make plans to live life to its fullest in the next few days. Bring your camera

along, and immortalize what you and your family cherish about the summertime. Here's a list to get you started:

- Half-moon slices of juicy watermelon
- Sun-kissed skin against cool white sheets
- Bright sunflower blossoms next to beaming faces
- Travels to new destinations to escape the everyday
- Kids (and kids at heart) in round innertubes, floating down a lazy river
- School visits to see who next year's teachers will be
- Dirt tracked into the house by your "little explorers"
- Groups playing street hockey outside your home

- Ladybugs, dragonflies and other exotic bugs around the house
- Club meetings in the treehouse or a secret fort
- Nothing but blue skies as far as you can see
- Shopping the local malls for school clothes
- Sailboats drifting through the water
- School outfits laid out days in advance
- Exciting new animals at the zoo
- Frisbees sailing through the air

ARTICLE BY CATHERINE SCOTT

glimpses, canoes and chalk art

Nine layouts to inspire you on hot summer days

Supplies *Pen:* Zig Writer, EK Success; *Paper yarn:* Wraphia, Target; *Eyelets:* Emagination Crafts; *Other:* Mini brads.

"Let Creativity Run Wild"

by Shelley Sullivan
Abbeville, SC

Shelley isn't the only artistic member of her family. Joshua and Chandler also enjoy creating art with sidewalk chalk.

◆ Shelley changed the color of the gold brads by painting them with fingernail polish. (You can also use metallic rub-ons and embossing powder.)

◆ Note how the asphalt in the pictures adds a touch of texture and dimension to the layout.

◆ Show macros of an art project or other special project by cutting (or punching) small photos to line the bottom of the layout.

ARTICLE BY LANNA WILSON

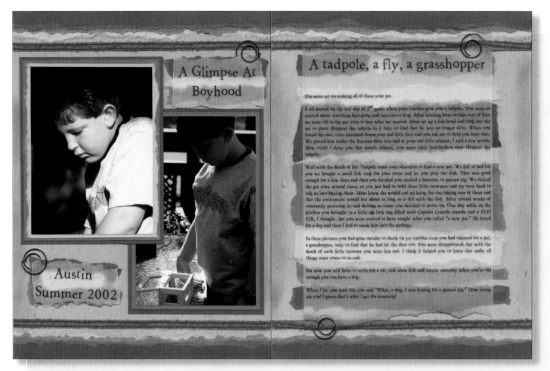

Supplies *Vellum:* Paper Adventures; *Computer font:* P22 Garamouche, downloaded from the Internet; *Fibers:* On the Surface; *Stamping ink:* Stampin' Up!; *Other:* Round paper clips.

"A Glimpse at Boyhood"

by Yvonne Schultz
South Jordan, UT

What's a mother to do when her son's pet tadpole dies? For Yvonne, it involved several trips to the pet store. Austin had his own pet ideas when he came home with a fly and then a grasshopper.

◆ Mount torn cardstock behind each paragraph in vellum-printed journaling blocks. Note how it helps carry the color theme, adds texture and emphasizes each paragraph.

◆ Rub dark stamping ink along the bottom torn edges of your journaling blocks. This will help "ground" them visually.

◆ Capture your child's moments of growth. Someday, Yvonne's journaling will tell her son how he began to understand an important fact of life.

"A Crisp Blue Shirt"

by Nia Reddy
Brooklyn, NY

Her son's first vacation was an outing that needed to be documented, says Nia. Her choice of blues helps bring attention to her son's colorful shirt and hat.

◆ Rummage up some origami paper for a quick patterned accent. Note how this paper complements the boy's color-blocked shirt.

◆ The inspiration for these clean lines came from a magazine ad.

◆ Nia took her pictures to a photo developer and asked that several be converted into panoramic photos. Remember that the sides will be cropped to get the 4" x 13" dimensions.

Supplies *Letter stamps:* Stampers Anonymous; *White pigment ink:* ColorBox, Clearsnap; *Computer font:* Copperplate Light, Microsoft Word; *Other:* Origami paper.

"Why Kansas?"

**by Sunny Milleson
McPherson, KS**

Before deciding to create this layout, Sunny spent five summers snapping pictures of sunflowers and telling people why she moved to Kansas.

◆ Sunny wrote her journaling, then created this layout to match the poignancy of her journaling. Note how the pictures visually support Sunny's journaling.

◆ Make your journaling a part of the picture instead of just an overlay. After strategically lining her journaling, Sunny used a craft knife to cut the sunflower petals, then slipped the torn vellum journaling between the cut layer and the rest of the photo.

Supplies *Vellum:* Bazzill Basics; *String:* Hillcreek Design; *Square punch:* Whale of a Punch, EK Success; *Computer font:* CK Cracked (title), "The Art of Creative Lettering" CD, *Creating Keepsakes;* Itasca ITC (journaling), Microsoft Word.

"Wonder"

**by Gayla Feachen
Irving, TX**

Gayla found the baby pool's serenity a perfect contrast to the crashing waves on the barrier rocks. This layout of her daughter Chelsea is one of many in her family's Hawaiian vacation album.

◆ To secure a large, bulky item like this netting, wrap adhesive tape (such as Scrappy Tape by Magic Scraps) around the back of your layout. Glue dots work well to secure shells and starfish.

◆ Consider adding your title directly to a duplicate photo with permanent ink.

Supplies *Patterned paper:* Club Scrap; *Net and shells:* Crafts, Etc.; *Tag:* Avery; *Chalk:* Craf-T Products; *Spiral clips:* Target; *Rubber stamps:* Hero Arts; *Stamping ink:* StazOn, Tsukineko; *Picture pebbles:* Making Memories; *Computer font:* P22 Garamouche, downloaded from the Internet.

Supplies *Vellum:* Paper Adventures; *Mesh:* Magenta; *Glitter mulberry paper:* Scrap-Ease; *Lettering template:* Déjà Views, The C-Thru Ruler Co.; *Paper yarn:* Twistel, Making Memories; *Eyelets:* Box Scrapbooks; *Beads:* Blue Moon Beads; *Craft wire:* Artistic Wire Ltd.; *Other:* Foam dots.

"Our Ladies' Man Jake"

by Sandy Brown
Forest Grove, OR

W hen friends visited the Browns, their pet iguana Jake donned his photogenic charm and posed for some shots.

He's quite the ladies' man, says Sandy.

◆ Sandy used beads and mesh to accent Jake's coloring and the texture of his skin.

◆ Looking for a unique and textured title look? Unroll pieces of paper yarn, layer various colors, then use a lettering template to cut the title out.

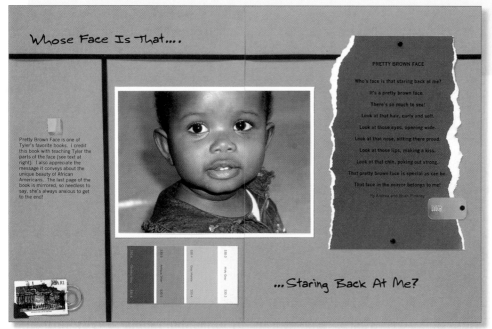

"Whose Face Is That?"

by Faye Morrow Bell
Charlotte, NC

Supplies *Metallic paper:* Accu-Cut Systems; *Computer fonts:* Ralph's Hand and News Gothic, downloaded from the Internet; *Brads:* American Pin & Fastener; *Dog tag:* Chronicle Books; *Circle clip:* Target; *Postage stamp:* Stampa Rosa; *Photo corner:* Canson; *Other:* Paint chip and mirror tile.

F aye's little girl learned the parts of the face from a beloved children's story. The mirror at the end of the story is her favorite page.

◆ Does your child have a favorite bedtime story? Record the text in a journaling block.

If you can, match the font. Even out of context, your child can often recognize it.

◆ Have a large focal-point photo? Keep your layout cohesive by carefully splicing your photo and extending it across two pages.

◆ Check out your local hardware or paint store for paint chips. You can use the colors for small, coordinated punches (or use them for an entire accent strip like that shown here).

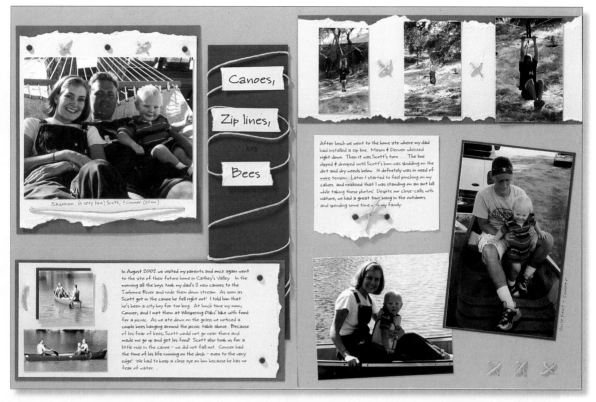

Supplies
Computer font: CK Sketch, "The Art of Creative Lettering" CD, *Creating Keepsakes; Pen:* Zig Millennium, EK Success; *Other:* Jute and brads.

"Canoes, Zip Lines and Bees"

**by Shannon Brown
St. Helens, OR**

S hannon's family enjoyed a day with extended family at the lake. She found out too late that she was standing in an anthill to get some of these pictures!

◆ Shannon wrapped the jute around her title block to complement her journaling about zip lines.

◆ Stitched jute lines and X marks call attention to important points and help ground the layout visually.

◆ Mix clean and torn lines for visual appeal and texture.

"Dirty Hands, Pure Fun"

**by Sunny Kohler
Midway, UT**

W hen Sunny's boys returned from their camping trip, she knew they'd had a good time. The telltale sign? Just look at their hands!

◆ Turn your journaling into a rustic scroll. After journaling your thoughts on a torn strip, roll both ends, then secure the scroll to the layout with brads.

◆ "Dirty" up your layout safely by tearing, crinkling and chalking your frame and layout edges.

Supplies *Patterned paper:* Scrap in a Snap; *Chalk:* Leaving Prints; *Lettering template:* ScrapPagerz.com; *Pen:* Zig Writer, EK Success; *Brads:* American Pin & Fastener.

A Family Reunion with Flair

Do something different

EVER BEEN TO A FAMILY REUNION? If not, attend one and you'll find everything from favorite family recipes to friendly contests. You'll find youngsters frolicking with cousins, adults gathering to reminisce and reconnect. Family reunions are known for their good company, good food, and the feeling of belonging to something bigger.

Afraid you'll be bored? No need to be! We've gathered ideas for pages, photographs and activities that'll help you hold a family reunion with flair.   →

© AFLO FOTO AGENCY

You Are Family . . . Scrapbook It!

Whether you're young or old, married or not, you belong to a family. Savor it. Celebrate it. Scrapbook it. Following are six fresh ideas.

✳ "Our Family Line"

by Mikelle Foster
Birmingham, AL

◆ While you've got everyone together, take pictures for a "generations" page. Note how Mikelle's daughter, Kennedy, appears with four generations of relatives. Mikelle included their names and ages as well.

◆ Sew skeletal leaf accents to your page for a timeless touch.

Supplies *Patterned and solid sage paper:* Anna Griffin; *Patterned ivory paper:* Provo Craft; *Eyelets:* Making Memories; *Computer font:* Graphite Light, Microsoft Word; *Leaves:* Black Ink.

Supplies *Alphabet snaps, heart snaps and metal-rimmed circle tags:* Making Memories; *Computer font:* CK Easy Going, "Fresh Fonts" CD, *Creating Keepsakes.*

✳ "Reunion"

by Hilary Shirley
Idaho Falls, ID

◆ To convey a sense of closeness, "group" photos of family spending time together.

◆ Use heart snaps to help signify the love family members feel for each other.

Supplies *Chalk:* Craf-T Products; *Pen:* Marvy Uchida; *Eyelets:* Creative Imaginations; *Flower petals and pen lines:* Inspired by Eva Flake in *Rags to Riches*; *Mesh:* Maruyama, Magenta; *Computer fonts:* CK Letter Home and CK Artisan, Becky Higgins' "Creative Clips & Fonts" CD, *Creating Keepsakes; Other:* Watch faces and hemp.

"Blossoms on the Family Tree"

by Sarah Ackerman-Hale
Spring Hill, KS

◆ Show how your family has "blossomed" over time. Include scanned photos from different generations, as well as strips containing names and dates.

◆ Convert photo scans to black and white in photo-editing software, print them on white cardstock, then tear and chalk them to match the layout.

◆ Incorporate clock faces in your design to help convey the impression of passing time.

Supplies *Patterned papers and accents:* Chatterbox.

"Our Family"

by Melody Ross
for Chatterbox

◆ Gather your family—whether immediate or extended—and create a layout that includes "words to describe us," "what we are known for," "our favorite place" and "favorite activities." Celebrate what makes you strong!

"Family Face"

by Alisa Bangerter
Centerville, UT

◆ Spotlight how a family member looks like an ancestor.
◆ Use brown tones, buttons and stitching to communicate a sense of heritage.

JOURNALING TO NOTE:
"What a face! My cousin Zeb won the ancestor look-alike contest hands down (or would that be face down) at our Edwards Family Reunion. It was amazing the resemblance Zeb had to our Great-Great-Grandfather Easias Edwards. I'm sure the beard helped a little, but the similarities are definitely there. We had a great time looking at old family photos and comparing the traits and features we all inherited. Generations may separate us, but we will forever be family!"

Supplies *Patterned paper:* K & Company; *Computer fonts:* Arial Black (title), Microsoft Word; CK Newsprint, "Fresh Fonts" CD, *Creating Keepsakes; Letter stickers:* Provo Craft; *Photo corners:* Dennison; *Embroidery floss:* DMC; *Sewing thread:* Coats & Clark; *Buttons:* Making Memories; *Chalk:* Craf-T Products. *Ideas to note:* Alisa used a sewing machine to sew her side border to the background cardstock. She also sewed around the photo mat.

Supplies *Patterned paper:* Bryce & Madeline, Creative Imaginations; *Eyelets and metal-rimmed tags:* Making Memories; *Ball chain:* Nicole, Jewelry Connection; *Heart charm:* Hirschberg Schutz & Co.; *Chalk:* Craf-T Products; *Flower nailheads:* Bedazzled; *Computer fonts:* 2Peas Unforgettable (title) and 2Peas Bad Hair Day (journaling), downloaded from *www.twopeasinabucket.com*.

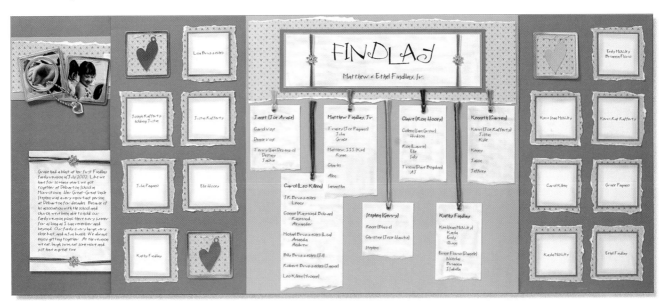

The image above shows the layout once the right-hand page is opened up.

 **"We Are Family"**

by Tracey Pagano
North Caldwell, NJ

◆ Include a collection of photos (Tracey used 19) from the reunion.

◆ Open up the right-hand page for boxes with identifying information for the people pictured, plus a family tree!

◆ Create a family tree with software such as FamilyTreeMaker.

september

savor september

September is a month of contradictions—hot summer days followed by chilly fall ones. As the school year starts and the excited activity of summertime ends, savor the still, silent moments that remind you life is good. Here are a few "snapshots" to capture this month:

- Buying and opening fresh boxes of crayons
- Watching your favorite TV show's season premiere
- Escaping to the beach one last time while the water is still warm
- Watching squirrels scurry as they gather their winter stores of acorns
- Smoothing blankets on the beds so you can sleep with the windows open

- Seeing children step off buses with fresh artwork in their hands
- Feeling the faintest hint of fall weather in the early evening air
- Going to the country for the evening to watch the harvest moon rise
- Observing the outlines of leaves turning shades of yellow and red
- Noticing how silent the house is after the kids leave for school

- Enjoying one last picnic before the ground turns cold
- Watching the afternoon light turn golden as the sun sets
- Biting into crisp, sweet-tart apples fresh from the tree
- Harvesting the last fruits from your outdoor garden
- Finding patches of soft sunlight to nap in

ARTICLE BY CATHERINE SCOTT

grandparents and fall

Nine layouts that celebrate changing seasons

Supplies
Patterned paper:
Michelle Anderson,
Provo Craft; *Stamping
ink:* ColorBox,
Clearsnap; *Chalk:* Craf-T
Products; *Metal-rimmed
tag:* Making Memories;
Charms: Embellish It!;
Square punch: Family
Treasures; *Eyelets:*
Creative Impressions;
Computer font:
Staccato 322,
Micrografx; *Fibers:*
Brown Bag Fibers;
Pen: Zig Writer,
EK Success; *Craft wire:*
Artistic Wire Ltd.

"The Brilliance of Fall"

**by Michelle Hubbartt
Grand Junction, CO**

The mountains behind Grand Junction, Colorado, are on fire with color each fall, and Michelle's family took full advantage of the autumn splendor.

◆ Fit more photos on your layout (this one has 23) by including an album as part of the design.

◆ Add dimension and color variety by chalking and rubbing stamping ink along torn and rolled corners (see photo at upper left).

ARTICLE BY LANNA WILSON

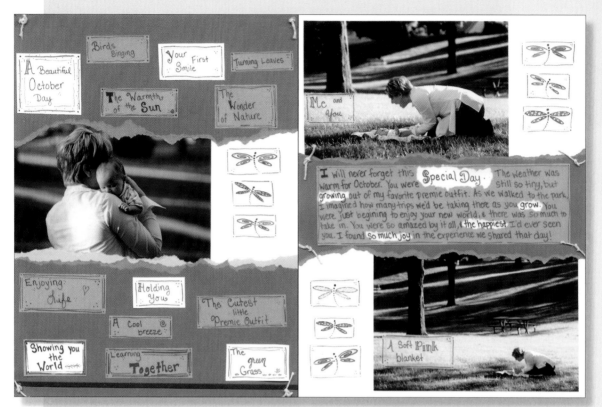

Supplies *Vellum:* DMD, Inc.; *Patterned vellum:* Source unknown; *Pens:* Zig Memory System, EK Success; *Other:* Hemp.

"A Beautiful October Day"

by Mandy Henry
Beloit, WI

Mandy will never forget bonding with her newborn daughter on this beautiful October afternoon.

◆ Looking for a way to accentuate your patterned vellum? Trace the pattern with a dark pen. Here, Mandy drew over the dragonflies in black, then shaded the wings in various colors.

◆ Use shadows to add interest and depth to your photos. These were taken with a telephoto lens while the sun was low in the sky.

◆ Highlight key words on vellum-printed journaling by layering colored cardstock strips behind them.

"And There Was Love"

by Jana Millen
Batavia, OH

Only recently when she found this picture of her grandparents did Jana begin to understand their love for each other.

◆ Lace your layout with organza ribbon for a soft accent. Here, Jana used an anywhere hole punch, then laced the ribbon through the holes.

◆ To create a beaded cross-stitch, attach graph paper to your layout, then use it as a guide to poke holes through the layout. Remove the graph paper, then thread floss through a hole. String a bead onto it, then thread the floss through the diagonal hole. Repeat the process with the other two holes, threading the floss through the bead and centering it in the "X".

Supplies *Ribbon:* C.M. Offray & Son; *Embroidery floss:* DMC; *Beads:* Mill Hill; *Computer fonts:* Voluta Script (title) and Amazone BT (journaling), downloaded from the Internet; *Anywhere hole punch:* Making Memories; *Other:* Charms.

old·er (ōld'ər), adj., having lived or existed as specified with relation to younger or newer ones: our oldest child

broth·er (brŭth'ər), n., a male offspring having both parents in common with another offspring; male sibling

friend, confidant, playmate, buddy, pal, chum, companion, and sometimes known as...

con Artist

Nathan: That yellow leaf looks nice. I wonder if I can get Shane to trade.

Shane: Nice orange leaf.

Nathan: If I act real charmmy, maybe he won't notice I have his leaf.

Shane: Hey, that yellow leaf looks very familiar.

Nathan: Ha! I think it worked.

Shane: Hmmm...I think I've been had!

Shane: Out of my way older brother, now I have to find a new yellow leaf!

Supplies
Rubber stamps, chalk and blender pen: Stampin' Up!; *Stamping ink:* Memories; *Pen:* Zig Writer, EK Success; *Lettering template:* Wordsworth.

"Con Artist"
by Debbie DeMars
Overland Park, KS

Debbie's fall photo shoot turned into a friendly competition between older and younger brothers as they battled for the colorful leaves.

◆ Use strips of solid-colored cardstock to help move your reader's eye through the layout.

◆ Use a rolling border stamp on various matted blocks to add continuity to your layout.

"Great Grandma Great"
by Ashley Gull
Salt Lake City, UT

great great grandma

Supplies *Chalk:* Stampin' Up!; *Embroidery floss:* DMC; *Circle punch:* EK Success; *Computer font:* Calligraph421 BT, downloaded from the Internet; *Fabric studs:* Dritz; *Buckles:* JHB International; *Trunk pocket:* Ashley's own design; *Other:* Crocheted doilies.

Ashley calls her grandmother Grandma Great. So, for her children, she's Great Grandma Great. The elderly woman was delighted to spend time with her great-grandson.

◆ Do you have handwork from a special relative? Why not include it in a layout honoring that person? Include a hand-stitched title for an extra homemade look.

◆ Handwriting is an important part of history. Include a letter from a grandparent or other special person on a layout for your child. If you are a grandparent or great-grandparent, take time to write a letter to your posterity.

◆ Age your layout with crumpled paper, chalk and olden accents, such as this trunk pocket, complete with studs, buckles, paper lock and hinges.

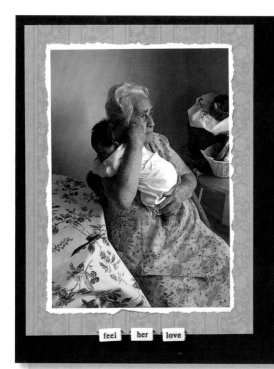

I was playing around with my new digital camera one morning, and I shot a few pictures of Mami with Baby Devyn. It was their usual pose. Mami was comforting her after she woke up crying for some reason. When I downloaded the pictures, I was amazed at how well this picture came out, and how well it captured the special relationship my Grandmother has with my girls. For as long as I can remember, Mami has been there. She has cared for me, raised me when my parents couldn't. She has been a pillar of strength, always standing tall. Even when things have been hard, I can never repay her for all the good things she has done for me. She is so much a part of what I am today. When I was little she told me that she found me in a trashcan, and that I was crying so hard that she felt sorry for me. I believed her for the longest time. But the truth is that she took me in when my parents were overwhelmed with their own problems. I stayed with her and have always been like her youngest daughter. She drives me crazy sometimes. And even though she is no longer living with us, every room of this house has something that reminds us of her. and that's how it will always be. Mami raised 8 children of her own, cared for all of the grandchildren and loved her great-grandchildren even more. Chloe, Zoe and Devyn are so lucky to have spent time with her and always remember their 'buelita. I hope that they always will.

Picture taken May, 2002

feel her love

Supplies *Patterned paper:* Close To My Heart; *Vellum:* Paper Adventures; *Computer font:* CK Scriпт, "The Best of Creative Lettering" CD Combo, *Creating Keepsakes;* *Other:* Word beads.

"Feel Her Love"
by Ari Macias
Staten Island, NY

Ari was crushed when her computer crashed and she lost all of her digital images. Imagine her delight when she discovered a printed copy of this precious moment.
◆ If you have a very powerful or emotive picture, consider including your journaling on an opposing page so it doesn't distract.
◆ Try matting your focal-point photo with torn glossy paper instead of cardstock or patterned paper.

"More Alike Than We Seem"
by Amber Ries
Munich, Germany

When people ask Amber where she gets her curly red hair, her response usually requires an extensive family history. This picture helped Amber see how much like her mom she really is.
◆ Do you have family similarities in personality, expression or physical attributes? Scrapbook them!
◆ To create the overlapped title in Microsoft Word, select WordArt and type in the chunky background font. Change the solid black lines to dotted gray. Overlap the image with a text box with the smaller script words, then select "No Line" in the formatting option.

Supplies *Computer fonts:* CK Cursive, "The Best of Creating Lettering" CD Combo, *Creating Keepsakes;* Garamouche, Impress Rubber Stamps; *Pens:* Uniball, Sanford; VersaMark, Tsukineko; *Watch stickers:* Jolee's Boutique, Sticko.

more alike
than we seem

When I was young, and ignorant people said "where does she get that hair?" you would answer "the milkman" and leave their bemused faces behind. As I got older I would wish to use that comment myself instead of going through the whole complicated process of...my mother's father's sister and my father's mother...I would often wonder, "who do I look like?" I have your chin, your brown near-sighted eyes, your curls. That's not much I often thought, what about my build, the nose, my height, my fair, fair skin? This whole picture doesn't make another you, it makes a single me. And though I sometimes wonder, "Were did that come from?" when I see a picture like this, I realize, you and me, we are more alike than we seem.

strasbourg 7/62

"Shopping Napa Style"

by Lisa Soares
Alisa Viejo, CA

Supplies *Patterned paper:* Chatterbox by Melody Ross, EK Success; *Vellum:* DMD, Inc.; *Diamond punch:* Emagination Crafts; *Flat-top eyelets:* The Stamp Doctor; *Computer fonts:* Agate Normal ("Napa Style"), Bickley Script Letraset ITC ("Shopping") and Melanie BT (journaling), downloaded from the Internet.

On a trip to Napa Valley for her wedding anniversary, Lisa couldn't resist snapping shots inside a culinary store.

◆ Get inspiration from non-conventional places. Lisa used the business card from an epicurean shop as inspiration for this layout. She scanned the card, electronically removed the address, enlarged the image and added her journaling on vellum.

◆ Do shapes and colors trigger a certain theme? To create this harlequin look, use a diamond punch to cut patterns along the bottom of the layout. (Turn the punch upside-down so you can line up the lines.) Add flat-top eyelets at the intersecting points. Use the punch "positives" to continue the line onto the next page.

"Little Engineer"

by Margaret Scarbrough
S. Lancaster, MA

Matthew dressed the part for his long-awaited trip to see Thomas the Tank Engine. Clad in overalls and a red bandana, he was quite the little engineer.

◆ Hang the words of your title after stitching them together with jute or hemp.

◆ Working with a large, focal-point photo? Consider overlapping your title on part of the picture.

◆ Use existing elements in your surroundings, such as the round wood opening in the top photo, as a natural frame in your photos.

Supplies *Computer fonts:* Garamouche, downloaded from the Internet; 2Peas Evergreen, downloaded from *www.two-peasinabucket.com*; *Other:* Hemp.

Showcase school pictures in an
easy-to-maintain format

BY MARY LARSON

Ever since I was in grade school, I've seen those 13-slotted frames where you can put a school picture every year. Great idea! When my sons started school, I wanted to do something similar, but more flexible.

I decided to create a 6" x 6" mini-album to showcase school photos and keep track of my sons' changing looks. After designing a school-themed cover, I included a library card and pocket inside to keep track of the school years.

I made the inside pages very simple, with just a place for photos and the grade. The pages are large enough to add a child's signature, teacher information and more. Because I started the project after my oldest son had started school, I couldn't have him sign each page. I plan to go through my son's school papers from previous years to find the signatures I need.

At the back of the book, I included a place for the list of schools attended. *Note:* Leave enough lines for elementary, junior and high schools, plus extras spaces if you think your family could move or your child might change schools.

These books are easy to make and keep up with. Best of all, when they're completed your child will have a wonderful keepsake!

Back-to-School Forms

Assign your favorite student some extra-credit homework

BY LANNA WILSON

Once school has started and your kids come home, buzzing with energy as they face a new school year, capture their interest on paper. Ask them to fill out a form like that shown here.

eLemenТary ☕ SCHOOL

Your Name .... Month & Year ....

School, City and State ....

What grade are you in? ....

Who is your teacher? ....

What do you like best about your teacher? ....

What is your favorite subject? ....

What is your least favorite subject? ....

What are you studying in school this year? ....

How do you get to school? ....

Who are your best friends at school? ....

What do you like to do at recess? ....

What are your favorite school activities? ....

Are you in chorus or band? ....

Do you play sports? ....

What field trips have you been on? ....

october

LISA WINZELER

JANNA SAEGER

october splendor

Prepare for sensory overload this month as the earth transforms again into a fall paradise. October ushers in brilliant colors, nostalgic smells and comforting traditions, then leaves as quickly as it came. Don't miss a minute—keep your camera ready to immortalize the splendor of fall moments like these:

- seeing leaves turn a thousand different shades
- cooking a hearty stew while the wind whistles outside
- savoring the smell of wood smoke floating on the air
- heading outdoors to get energized by the cool, crisp weather
- relishing almost-forgotten warm days during Indian Summer

- noting how morning frost now covers your lawn and windows
- enjoying carved pumpkins that flicker with candlelight on the front porch
- hearing crunchy leaves rustle as you make your way down the sidewalk
- feeling sheltered and protected as you relax by the warm fireplace
- pausing unexpectedly to wonder at the beauty surrounding you

- donning cozy knit scarves and hats to keep away the chill
- seeing clusters of trick-or-treaters traipse down your street
- brainstorming creative ideas for Halloween costumes
- simmering cider on the stove for all-day enjoyment
- filling the house with the smell of warm pumpkin pie

ARTICLE BY CATHERINE SCOTT

a patch full of pumpkins

Gear up for fall and Halloween pages

Supplies *Patterned paper:* Carolee's Creations and Scrap-Ease; *Vellum:* The Paper Co.; *Mulberry paper:* PrintWorks; *Pumpkin accents:* Kim's own design; *Craft wire:* Darice; *Leaf punch:* Marvy Uchida; *Other:* Brads, raffia and mesh ribbon.

"Punkin Patch"

by Kim Bailey
Twin Falls, ID

Kim watched her daughter's sleepy frown turn into a smile as she discovered and explored the mounds of pumpkins at a local patch. Some tips to "harvest" from this fall-themed layout:

◆ Match homemade accents to your background paper. Here, Kim tore her patterned paper scraps into pumpkin shapes that complement the paper on the right-hand page.

◆ To help maintain control, dampen your paper or cardstock before tearing it. Kim crumpled the paper to add more texture to her pumpkin accents.

◆ Remember to rotate your camera angle when you take multiple photos of an event.

ARTICLE BY LANNA WILSON

Supplies *Leaf punch:* Emagination Crafts; *Pumpkin border:* Flip-Over Borders, My Mind's Eye; *Pen:* Creative Memories; *Computer fonts:* Junebug (title), downloaded from the Internet; ScrapBrother ("October"), downloaded from *www.letteringdelights.com*; *Chalk:* Craf-T Products; *Paper wire:* DMD, Inc.; *Raffia:* Raffia Accents, Plaid Enterprises; *Paper yarn:* Twistel, Making Memories.

"Pumpkins"
by Susan Clausen Paquin
Freeland, MD

October is pumpkin season for Susan's family. "My son had a ball climbing over the mountains of pumpkins," she says.

◆ Add "hay" to your layout by cutting up natural-colored raffia. Adhere it with clear-drying glue.

◆ For perfect printing on an accent, scan it, type the text in a photo-editing program, then output the text. Cut and adhere the text on top of the original accent.

◆ Add texture to your punches by using unraveled paper yarn.

◆ Adhere paper wire to your layout by stitching it with matching or transparent thread.

"Dream"
by Wendy Malichio
Bethel, CT

Wendy took this picture the day she brought her new son home from the hospital. Notice who *isn't* sleeping . . . Wendy.

◆ Create your own patterned paper by randomly typing words in various fonts and colors.

◆ Wrap or tie fibers around key elements to represent the bonds that exist in your relationships.

◆ Use the capital letters in the CK Wanted font to frame letters in your text.

Supplies *Patterned paper:* Provo Craft; *Corrugated paper:* DMD, Inc.; *Letter stickers:* Sonnets, Creative Imaginations; *Computer fonts:* CK Wanted, CK Tipsy and CK Sassy, "Fresh Fonts" CD, *Creating Keepsakes*; Times New Roman, Microsoft Word; Bernie and Adler, downloaded from the Internet; *Fibers:* Plymouth Cocktail; *Frame and charms:* The Card Connection; *Star brads:* Making Memories; *Chalk:* Craf-T Products.

"Pieces of the Whole"

by Carol Wingert
Gilbert, AZ

Ashley learned a lot about adult responsibility while working with horses. Her mother, Carol, says it's a great character-building activity.

◆ Spray puzzle pieces with an acid-neutralizing spray before you use them on your layout.

◆ Stipple your puzzle pieces with ink, then stamp your title letters on them for a distinctive title approach.

◆ Create "holders" for your journaling blocks by wrapping card-stock strips around the edges. Mount the strips to the layout with eyelets.

"A Day at the Patch"

by Yvonne Schultz
South Jordan, UT

A pumpkin patch offers more than just pumpkins. Yvonne snapped this photo while her son played near a window.

◆ Add a hint of color to wood squares with shadow ink. Stamp your words in black.

◆ Let your color choices help carry your theme. Note how the rustic colors here lend a naturalistic and contemplative mood.

◆ Print your journaling on a transparency sheet, then layer it over a picture.

Supplies *Patterned paper:* Itty Bitty Pad, Provo Craft; *Alphabet stamps:* PSX Design (small) and Hero Arts (large); *Date stamp:* Office Depot; *Stamping ink:* Fiskars (black) and Stampin' Up! (brown); *Gold shadow ink:* Hero Arts; *Rivets:* Scrapbook Interiors, Chatterbox; *Wood squares:* Forster Craft; *Computer font:* Problem Secretary Normal, downloaded from the Internet; *Transparency sheet:* Kinko's; *Transparency squares:* 3L Corp.: *Other:* Twine and skeleton leaves.

Supplies *Puzzle pieces:* Hasbro; *Stamping ink:* Nick Bantock, Ranger Industries; *Pen:* Zig Millennium, EK Success; *Letter stamps:* Stampers Anonymous; *Eyelets:* Making Memories; *Computer font:* CK Newsprint, "Fresh Fonts" CD, *Creating Keepsakes.*

Supplies *Lettering template:* Spunky, Déjà Views, The C-Thru Ruler Co.; *Chalk:* Craf-T Products; *Embossing enamel:* Ultra Thick Embossing Enamel, Suze Weinberg; *Stamping ink:* VersaMark, Tsukineko; *Computer font:* Comic Sans, Microsoft Word; *Cat sketch:* Shannon's own design; *Other:* Wig fibers.

"It's a Seuss Thing"

by Shannon Taylor
Bristol, TN

After reading Dr. Seuss books in class, Shannon's little boy had a character dress-up day at school.

◆ Add extra shine and dimension to your accents and title with embossing enamel.

◆ Sketch a favorite cartoon character on cardstock, then cut it out with a craft knife. Shannon cut the character out to look like an outline, then lined the openings with white and colored cardstock.

◆ For a fresh twist, mat your accent or photo with fibers.

"My Closet"

by Jordan Stone
Omaha, NE

Supplies *Patterned paper:* Making Memories; *Vellum:* Paper Adventures; *Computer fonts:* 2Peas Sleigh Ride, downloaded from *www.two-peasinabucket.com*; Klinkomite and Sunshine, downloaded from the Internet; *Fibers:* Fibers By The Yard; *Shrink plastic and bookplate:* Two Peas in a Bucket; *Clothing stickers and hangers:* The Card Connection; *Eyelets:* Eyelet Queen; *Letter eyelets:* Making Memories; *Gem stickers:* Mrs. Grossman's; *Other:* Brads and jute.

Admits Jordan, "I hope I won't look at these pictures in 10 years with the same disdain as I do pictures from 1985!"

◆ Think you have a classic wardrobe? Take pictures of your favorite outfits and scrapbook them, then look back in 10 years.

◆ Hangers are meant to be hung. Create a clothesline on your layout and hang small hangers from it.

◆ For sequence shots or photos with individual journaling, number the photos and the corresponding journaling. Jordan used shrink plastic to get this effect.

"There's Your Trouble"

by Miley Johnson
Omaha, NE

With two boys about two years apart in age, there's bound to be mischief. Little did Miley know it would involve a 2 a.m. haircut!

◆ Mount conchos and nailheads by pushing them through the layout and into a mousepad. It saves fingers from getting poked and protects your table!

◆ Fill the inside of a small concho or nailhead with a meaningful accent. Miley used her sons' initials, a tip she got from Ali Edwards.

Supplies Patterned papers: 7 Gypsies (newsprint), Magenta (green); Sharon Ann Collection, Déjà Views, The C-Thru Ruler Co.; *Letter cutouts:* Typabets, FoofaLa; *Rubber stamps:* Hero Arts ("There's") and Stampers Anonymous ("Your Trouble"); *Metal tags and stamps:* FoofaLa; *Stamping ink:* Clearsnap (brown) and Close To My Heart (black); *Raffia:* Raffia Accents; *Ribbon:* Michaels; *Computer fonts:* 2Peas Distressed, downloaded from *www.twopeasinabucket.com*; CK Constitution, "Fresh Fonts" CD, *Creating Keepsakes. Idea to note:* Miley's stamp set didn't include punctuation marks, so she left the apostrophe out of her title.

"Macey & Mark"

by Jennifer Lamb
Rolesville, NC

October's weather is still nice enough that a trip to the park is a treat for Macey and her dad.

◆ Form a visual triangle with your photos. This will help draw viewers through the layout.

◆ Run prominent journaling along the entire length of your page.

◆ Note how Jennifer repeats the red highlights in the photos, mats, fibers, journaling and accent blocks.

Supplies Computer fonts: 2Peas Sunflower (quote) and 2Peas Wonderful, downloaded from *www.twopeasinabucket.com*; *Fibers:* Making Memories; *Leaf punch:* Impress Rubber Stamps; *Buttons:* Hillcreek Designs.

A HAUNTING WE WILL GO

IDEAS FOR COSTUME PAGES

As a child, Halloween was always one of my favorite holidays. Was it the candy? No. Was it the spooky stories or the Charlie Brown TV special "Search for the Great Pumpkin"? Maybe a little, but for me, Halloween was mostly about the costumes.

The idea of dressing up in disguise, pretending for one brief night to be someone else, fascinated me. I could be a fairy princess, Little Red Riding Hood, or a character from a favorite book. I could dress up in beautiful ethnic costumes from countries I wanted to visit someday, or fashion my outfit after a famous historical figure. Or, I could be a wild child like Pippi Longstocking or cackle like the Wicked Witch of the West.

From the Halloween costumes I've seen lately, I'd say this enthusiasm for make-believe still thrives. How many Spiderman or Harry Potter figures will show up on your doorstep this year? Whether the costumes in your photos are hauntingly scary or whimsical, be sure to capture the magic of make-believe in your scrapbooks. The following layouts offer great ideas for Halloween pages. *by* LORI FAIRBANKS

"THE LION, THE WITCH AND THE WARDROBE"

by Dece Gherardini

Mesa, AZ

>> Twist fibers to fashion textured borders for photos, accents and journaling blocks.

SUPPLIES
Computer fonts: CK Journaling, "The Best of Creative Lettering" CD Combo; CK Flair, "The Art of Creative Lettering" CD, *Creating Keepsakes*
Colored pencils: Memory Pencils, EK Success
Fibers: On the Fringe
Accents: Dece's own designs

"ALEC'S FIRST HALLOWEEN"

by Alannah Jurgensmeyer
Rogers, AR

SUPPLIES
Patterned paper: Magenta (blocks) and Mustard Moon (solid orange)
Computer font: Garamouche, Impress Rubber Stamps
Vellum: DMD Industries
Eyelets: The Stamp Doctor
Embroidery floss: DMC
Dog tags: Poetry Dog Tags, Chronicle Books

>> Customize dog tags with a Halloween message such as "trick or treat."

"Dragon Duos"
by Mary Larson
Chandler, AZ

SUPPLIES
Webbing spray: Krylon
Square punch: McGill
Black brads: American Tag
Fibers: Rub-a-Dub-Dub, Art Sanctum
Computer font: McBooHmk, Hallmark
Card Studio, Sierra Home

"Halloween, three Amigo Style"
by Hilary Shirley
Idaho Falls, ID

SUPPLIES
Computer font: Okrien, "Hallmark
Card Studio 2" CD, Sierra Home
Grommets: Dritz

≫ Give your layout the "kiss"
of style with grommets and
torn paper squares.

"TRICK OR TREAT"
by Lauralee Sorensen
for Stampin' Up!

SUPPLIES
Rubber stamps: Haunts & Howls set
and alphabet stamps
*Black hemp, tags, vellum, chalk and
black eyelets:* Stampin' Up!
Stamping ink: ColorBox, Clearsnap
Circles: AlphaAccents, Stampin' Up!

» Brew up Halloween charm with black hemp, black eyelets, and the ghostly application of chalk and vellum.

This Halloween, Madalyn was finally old enough to understand that people were giving her candy for just for saying "trick-or-treat"! Mom took the girls just around our block, but then Dad took them out around the neighborhood. It was really cold outside but it was definitely worth getting lots of candy!

october 2001

"Halloween"
by Teresa Snyder
Orem, UT

>> Use a tole-painting book for inspiration when designing and decorating page accents.

SUPPLIES
Pumpkin, ghost, bat and star: From the *Pitter Patter Pigtail Girls* tole-painting book by Stacy West
Computer font: CK Handprint, "The Best of Creative Lettering" CD, *Creating Keepsakes*
Lettering template: Whimsy, ScrapPagerz.com
Craft wire: Artistic Wire Ltd.
Linen thread: Twice as Nice
Pen: Pigma Micron, Sakura
Thread: Coats and Clark
Star punch: EK Success
Chalk: Craf-T Products

PAGE STARTER IDEAS

Fingering through those Halloween pictures but just can't come up with a page idea? Here are suggestions to get you started.

• **Tell about your favorite childhood Halloween costume.** What was it? Why did you want to wear it for Halloween? Was it handmade or purchased from a store? What made the costume meaningful to you?
• **Ask your parents about their favorite childhood Halloween costumes.** Do they have pictures of themselves wearing the costumes? Do they have any stories to tell about their favorite past Halloweens?
• **Record your Halloween mishaps.** Did your temporary, spray-on black haircolor leave your golden tresses gray for a week? Did your child absolutely hate the darling costume you spent hours creating?
• **Share your family's Halloween traditions.** Do you go trick-or-treating? Do you have a family or neighborhood costume party? Does Mom or Dad always make homemade chili and cornbread for the kids before they go trick-or-treating?

try our slime alphabet

Add spook-tacular goop to title letters

ICE CREAM, CHOCOLATE, MUD, POPSICLES, paint—if there's anything messy, my boys will find it. I'm never short of goopy topics to scrapbook at my house. And now, with Halloween approaching, it's time for slime, ghosts and creepy potions (see Figure 1).

I've found the Slime Alphabet in Figure 2 to be gloriously versatile. You can, too. Grab a pencil, some pens and paper, and let's have fun!

5 Steps to Guide You

The following steps (illustrated in Figure 3) can help you create your own slimy lettering:

❶ Lightly pencil in your letters.

❷ Expand your letters on each side of your pencil lines to create block-style lettering. A lettering template is a quick, easy tool and will eliminate the first step.

❸ Keeping in mind how thick you want your goop, round the edges of your letters and add drips with light pencil strokes. As liquid slides, it will drip and cascade, so you'll want to make part of your letters thick or thin in various parts (see Figure 2).

Keep in mind that thicker goop will have wide drips (Figure 4), while thinner sub-

Figure 1. Slime lettering can add a creepy touch to Halloween layouts. *Pages by Laura Bowden.* **Supplies** *Computer font:* Frankendork, downloaded from the Internet; *Iridescent string:* May's Arts; *Black buttons and paper yarn:* Making Memories; *Chalk:* Craf-T Products; *Pens:* Milky Gel Roller and Hybrid Gel Roller, Pentel; J-Roller Medium, Zebra; *Gray marker:* Tombow; *Colored pencils:* Crayola; *Acrylic paints:* Apple Barrel Colors and FolkArt Waterbase Varnish, Plaid; *Paper clay:* Creative Paperclay Company; *Mulberry paper:* PrintWorks; *Vellum:* Paper Adventures; *Other:* Googly eyes and a cotton ball; *Treat bag, bats, spider, cat, tombstone, ghost, pumpkin, eyes and cauldron:* Laura's own designs.

ARTICLE BY LAURA BOWDEN

Slime Alphabet

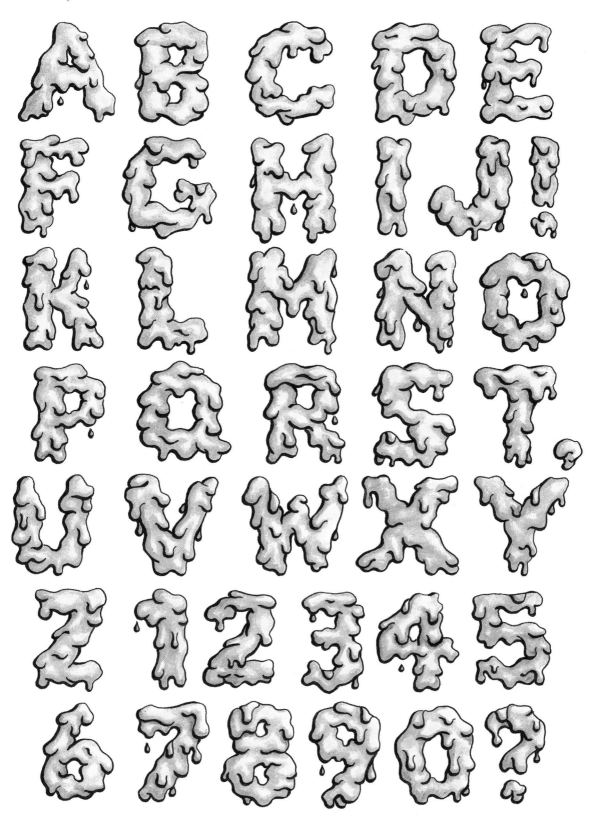

Figure 2. The Slime Alphabet gives letters a gooey touch. *Alphabet by Laura Bowden.* **Supplies** *Pens:* Hybrid Gel Rollers, Pentel; *Chalk:* Craf-T Products; *Colored pencils:* Crayola.

STEP BY STEP

❶ Lightly pencil in your letter.

❷ Expand your lines to create a block letter.

❸ Create smooth edges and drips.

❹ Use a pen to darken your design, then erase any leftover lines.

❺ Add color, then shade your letter with a darker color.

Figure 3. Follow these steps for your creepy creation. *Steps by Laura Bowden.* **Supplies** *Pen:* Hybrid Gel Roller, Pentel; *Chalk:* Craf-T Products; *Colored pencils:* Crayola.

stances like paint or water will have long, thin drips (Figure 5). Also, gravity pulls straight down, so if you decide to place your letters at an angle on your page, create the drips on your letters so they'll drip directly toward the bottom of your page.

❹ Next, trace over your pencil lines with a permanent, acid-free pen. Erase your pencil marks. If you want a more realistic look, use a colored pen that matches the

color of the substance you're trying to re-create.

To add dimension, thicken some of your pen lines. Decide where your "imaginary" light source would be and thicken those lines that would be in the shade (see Figure 2).

❺ Color in your letters using chalk, pens or paint. Add a greater sense of dimension by using a darker shade of color in the shaded areas.

Tricks and Treats

The Slime Alphabet is fun for kids and adults alike. Here are five quick tips:

• **Create unique looks with a variety of scrapbook supplies.** I used acrylic paint in Figure 5, colored pencils in Figure 6, an embossing pen and thick embossing powder in Figure 7, and vellum in Figure 8. How about liquid appliqué and glitter? You've got lots of possibilities to choose from!

Figure 4. You don't have to slime your entire letters. Try topping them instead. *Pages by Laura Bowden.* **Supplies** *Pens:* Hybrid Gel Roller, Pentel; Zig Writer, EK Success; *Computer fonts:* Girls Are Weird and Background Font 2, downloaded from the Internet; *Craft wire:* Artistic Wire Ltd.; *Beads:* Blue Moon; *Title:* Laura's own design; *Other:* Beaded dragonfly, bumblebee and flowers created by Laura's sister, Linda Maughan.

Figure 5. To make a liquid look thinner or more watery, make your drips thinner and longer. *Title by Laura Bowden.* **Supplies** *Pen:* Zig Writer, EK Success; *Chalk:* Craf-T Products; *Paint:* Apple Barrel Colors, Plaid; *Craft wire:* Artistic Wire Ltd.; *Eyelets:* Impress Rubber Stamps.

• **Don't worry about always covering your entire letter or word in slime.** Consider topping your letters instead (Figures 4 and 5). Or, use a slimy letter on the initial cap only. It's much simpler!

• **Add fun items to your letters.** I added beaded flowers to the mud in Figure 4. How about some spiders in the spooky slime or mock cobwebs?

• **Come up with a variation.** For Figure 7, I switched my look from slimy letters to some that looked like they were melting in the sun. To create this variation, make letter sections dip and the bottom of the letters sag.

• **Create the letters by layering cardstock or vellum at different parts.** If you're using cardstock, it's a good idea to chalk the edges so the layers can be seen better. This will also add a sense of dimension. Vellum creates a unique look because it becomes more colorful as your layers thicken. It's great for a ghostly look (Figure 8).

Ready to dive into this slimy lettering style? Get ready to wiggle, jiggle and grin your way to looks that'll be "spooktacular" for your scrapbook pages! ❤

Figure 6. The versatile Slime Alphabet can be used for goopy topics like ketchup, ice cream and mud. *Page by Laura Bowden.* **Supplies** *Pens:* Hybrid Gel Roller, Pentel; *Computer fonts:* Andy, Microsoft Word; CK Handprint, "The Best of Creative Lettering" CD Combo, *Creating Keepsakes; Colored pencils:* Crayola; *Paper yarn:* Making Memories; *Embroidery floss:* DMC.

Figure 7. The Slime Alphabet is perfect for summer layouts. It can look like it's melting away under the hot sun! *Title by Laura Bowden.* **Supplies** *Patterned paper:* Karen Foster Design; *Pens:* Tombow; Wet Looks Embossing Marker, Marvy Uchida; *Computer font:* Gigi, Microsoft Word; *Vellum and raffia:* Paper Adventures; *Chalk:* Craf-T Products; *Other:* Thick embossing powder.

Figure 8. Layer your paper for a different look and added dimension. The vellum and slime lettering style combine for a ghostly image. *Title by Laura Bowden.* **Supplies** *Pens:* Zig Writer, EK Success; Tombow (gray); *Chalk:* Craf-T Products; *Vellum:* Paper Adventures.

november

november nuances

Although November can be dreary and cold, it also brings a strange, gloomy beauty and a renewed awareness of our homes' warmth and comfort. Discover a rough beauty outdoors in the stark landscape and threatening storms, then turn your sights indoors and capture the coziness therein. Following are ideas for moments to record this month:

◆ Placing scented candles around the house to generate warmth

◆ Wrapping soft, wool scarves tighter to protect against the bitter wind

◆ Slipping into soft flannel pajamas and slippers after a warm bath

◆ Admiring the stark silhouettes of bare trees standing against the horizon

◆ Getting a head start on holiday cards while listening to your favorite carols

◆ Gathering with family and friends around an aromatic feast to give thanks

◆ Feeling encouraged by warm lights glowing from kitchen windows in the darkness

◆ Watching children celebrate the first snowfall of the season

◆ Looking up at gray skies that warn of coming snowstorms

◆ Taking hot pies out of the oven

◆ Listening to freezing rain make music on the windows

◆ Snuggling up in a downy comforter with a good book

◆ Getting a family picture taken with loved ones

◆ Sipping hot chocolate at a football game when it's cold outside

ARTICLE BY CATHERINE SCOTT

family ties and veterans

Celebrate the season of families

Supplies *Patterned paper and vellum:* Shotz, Creative Imaginations; *Fibers:* Fibers By The Yard; *Clock parts:* All the Extras; *Tag:* This & That, My Mind's Eye; *Computer font:* Budhand, downloaded from the Internet; *Skeleton leaves:* Club Scrap; *Corrugated paper:* DMD, Inc.; *Butterfly pebble:* Michaels; *Other:* Dried flower, cardboard, transparency and wine charm.

"Some Hopes I Have"

by Martha Crowther
Salem, NH

A poem inspired Martha to create this layout for her son.

◆ Want to create the look of journaling printed on 12" x 12" paper? Print the journaling on a transparency, then adhere the transparency to your layout.

◆ Put packing boxes to good use by peeling off a layer to expose the corrugated core, then using the layer as part of a collage.

◆ Add meaning with your embellishments. These clock pieces represent the lifetime of Martha's son.

ARTICLE BY LANNA WILSON

Supplies *Patterned paper:* Scrap-Ease (gold marble) and Provo Craft (wood); *Computer fonts:* Problem Secretary (on small tags), Papyrus (journaling and quote), Angelica, Acadian, CurlzMT, Crushed Out Girl and Stonehedge, all downloaded from the Internet; *Rubber stamps:* Stamp Craft (dragonfly), Rubber Stampede (leaf), All Night Media (compass), Stampendous! (cube) and unknown (primitive house); *Stamping ink:* Crystal (gold) and Brilliance (coffee), Tsukineko; *Pens:* Gelly Roll (gold), Sakura; Le Plume (green and red), Marvy Uchida; *Mesh:* Maruyama, Magenta; *Tags:* Avery; *Craft wire:* Making Memories; *Chalk:* Craf-T Products; *Flat-top eyelets:* All the Extras; *Other:* Skeleton leaf, raffia, jute, buttons, stamps, dictionary pages, bleach and tea bags.

"Sweet Childish Days"

by Madeline Fox
River Ridge, LA

While the adults watched TV after a hearty Thanksgiving dinner, Madeline snapped photos of her son playing in the backyard.

◆ Use bleach as a stamping medium (see the dragonfly tag) if archival safety is not a concern or you're working with duplicate photos. Fold an absorbent paper towel into a rectangle.

Saturate the towel with bleach. Tap your stamp into the bleach pad, then onto dark cardstock. (Wash your stamp as soon as you finish!)

◆ Create a collage on a mesh base. The background paper will show through, and the mesh will add texture to your collage.

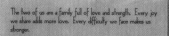

"Family Is a Bond"

by Jocelyne Hayes
Ladera Ranch, CA

Who are you most thankful for? For Jocelyne, it's her husband, Ken.

◆ Think outside the box. Try your hand at a horizontal, 8½" x 11" layout.

◆ Mute your patterned paper (or accent) by layering a sheet of vellum-printed journaling over it.

◆ Emphasize a knot or tie on your layout by framing it with a concho.

Supplies *Patterned paper:* Karen Foster Design; *Vellum:* Accent Designs; *Concho:* ScrapWorks; *Ribbon:* Close To My Heart; *Computer fonts:* 2Peas Sailboat (journaling), downloaded from *www.twopeasinabucket.com*; Hannibal Lecter (quote), downloaded from the Internet.

"Honoring Those Who Served"

by Lana Rickabaugh
Maryville, MO

After September 11, 2001, Lana took her family to an all-inclusive Veteran's Day parade that honored veterans, law enforcement officers, firefighters and ambulance crews.

◆ Look for different perspectives when you take pictures. Lana photographed the reflection of a U.S. flag in the mirror on a fire truck.

◆ Print your journaling on vellum, then adhere it on top of your photo. This helps conserve space, especially if you have a lot of photos.

"Dad, Would You Have Done It?"

by Sara Tumpane
Grayslake, IL

While watching a war documentary with her dad, Sara asked him about his thoughts as a World War II pilot.

◆ For a shiny title cutout, cut your title from a lettering template, then coat it with crystal lacquer to add sheen. You can also use shiny paper.

◆ Create a title strip with paper clay. Roll the clay ⅛" thick, stamp your title, then let the clay dry. Paint it with rub-ons, metallic craft paint or pigment powder that you've mixed with gum Arabic.

Supplies *Patterned paper:* NRN Designs (military) and Scrap in a Snap (mottled); *Vellum and photo corners:* K & Company; *Computer fonts:* Marydale and Sheer Grace, downloaded from the Internet; *Sticker:* Stamping Station; *Chalk:* Craf-T Products; *Other:* Eyelets.

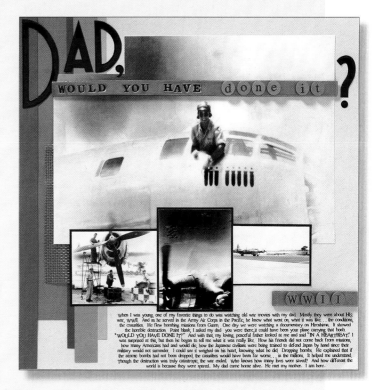

Supplies *Clay:* Creative Paperclay; *Crystal lacquer:* Diamond Glaze, JudiKins; *Pigment powder:* Pearl-Ex, Jacquard Products; *Mesh:* ScrapYard 329; *Metal letters:* Making Memories; *Alphabet stamps:* The Leather Factory; *Stamping ink:* Rubber Stampede; *Computer font:* Times, Microsoft Word; *Other:* Gum Arabic.

Each of our girls got an older car to drive when they got their licenses. It was easier than trying to take each of them to their jobs and activities, since we didn't live in town. They had to pay for their gas and insurance, but we paid for the cars and the upkeep until they were out of college. Having this many cars meant that Jim spent lots of time fixing one or another of them, changing the oil, or getting tires and mufflers replaced!

Nicole: '87 Dodge Colt AND '96 VW Jetta
- muffler
- fender & grill (from accident)
- axle & wheel bearings
- tires

Stacey: '89 Ford Probe
- headlights, hood, fender (accident)
- alternator
- windshield wiper motor
- muffler

Jessica: '91 Nissan Sentra
- starter
- emergency hand brake
- battery
- brakes

Laura: '93 Ford Tempo
- brakes
- clutch X 2
- tires
- muffler

Supplies *Computer fonts:* CK Print and CK Script, "The Best of Creative Lettering" CD Combo, *Creating Keepsakes;* Mom's Typewriter, Teletype and Hans Hand, downloaded from the Internet; *Eyelets:* Impress Rubber Stamps; *Other:* Toy car and tool pieces.

"Dad, Help!"
by Pam Nafziger
McDonald, PA

With four teenage drivers and four used cars, automotive repairs are inevitable, says Pam.

◆ If your children (or grandchildren) have similar experiences, chronicle the events in a side-by-side format.

◆ Browse the dollar store for non-traditional accents like the toy tools here.

◆ Use text boxes to create a catchy title box. Pam used three different boxes and fonts in this title. See Computer Corner in the October 2002 issue for step-by-step instructions.

"Got Math?"
by Colette Stucki
Glen Allen, VA

Colette's son Brad has plastered his bedroom with "Got Milk?" ads. When he got the assignment to create an ad to promote math, he had just the campaign!

◆ To play upon the math theme, Colette created the layout with straight lines and right angles.

◆ Add shine to embellishments (or any layout element) with a layer of crystal lacquer or a cropped transparency sheet.

Supplies *Transparency:* Avery; *Square punch:* Family Treasures; *Pen:* Zig Writer, EK Success; *Computer font:* Borzoi, downloaded from the Internet; *Crystal lacquer:* Diamond Glaze, JudiKins.

Supplies *Patterned and embossed paper:* Both by 7 Gypsies; *Corrugated paper:* All Night Media; *Mesh:* Maruyama, Magenta; *Rub-ons:* Bradwear, Creative Imaginations; *Page pebbles:* Making Memories; *Decoupage medium:* Mod Podge, Plaid Enterprises; *Computer font:* 2Peas Rain (journaling), downloaded from *www.twopeasinabucket.com*; *Brads:* Creative Imaginations and Lost Art Treasures; *Alphabet stamps:* PSX Design; *Ribbon:* Michaels; *Stamping ink:* StazOn, Tsukineko; *Other:* Walnut ink, watch crystals and charm.

"Yemenite Love"

by Lilac Chang
San Mateo, CA

Notes Lilac, "Sometimes pictures say more than words. I was overwhelmed by the love that shone in these pictures of my son with my parents."

◆ For a 3-D title block, stamp your lettering on watch crystals. (Letter rub-ons will also work.) Next, adhere the crystals over embossed, patterned-paper circles.

◆ Want to "age" your layout? Lightly rub stamping or walnut ink on vintage patterned paper. Smear a decoupage medium over your journaling.

◆ Mix textures on your layout. Note how Lilac used fabric and corrugated, mesh and embossed papers on this layout.

"Directly Linked"

by Delanie Matheson
Mesa, AZ

Supplies *Patterned paper:* Frances Meyer; *Patterned vellum:* Autumn Leaves; *Computer font:* A Yummy Apology, downloaded from the Internet; *Pen:* Zig Millennium, EK Success; *Chalk and metallic rub-ons:* Craf-T Products; *Watch crystals:* Deluxe; *Paper crimper:* Fiskars; *Screen:* ScrapYard 329; *Cutouts:* Mini Fresh Cuts, EK Success; *Adhesive:* Terrifically Tacky Tape, Art Accents; *Paper clips:* Clipiola; *Tag:* American Tag Company; *Other:* Concho.

With some research, Delanie learned about her rich family heritage and the legacy her third great-grandfather left his posterity.

◆ Create a picture pedigree. Crop the photos to fit inside watch crystals. Adhere the photos to your page, then attach the crystals over them with crystal lacquer.

◆ Add a little history to heritage layouts by adding your family tree or family crest. Visit *www.names.com* or *www.coatofarms-shop.com* to research and download your crest.

AUTUMN GOLD

Strike it rich with these spectacular fall layouts

WHEN I ASKED MEMBERS OF THE EDITORIAL TEAM TO NAME THEIR FAVORITE SEASON, I was surprised to find that most favor fall. I'm almost the lone dissenter—autumn runs a distant third for me! Still, I can see why people love this season with its deep-blue skies, milder temperatures, brilliantly colored leaves and comfy sweaters.

Fall layouts? They're as gorgeous as the season. I love the rich use of color, the delicate accents with nature themes, and the pictures of people frolicking in the leaves and enjoying the season. Read on for layouts and ideas you're sure to love—you've struck autumn "gold"!

BY LORI FAIRBANKS

"BEAUTY SEEN IS NEVER LOST"
by Twyla Koop
Surrey, BC, Canada

Supplies
Lettering template: Scrapbook
Designer, Provo Craft
Deacidification spray: Archival
Mist, EK Success
Buttons: Favorite Findings,
Blumenthal Lansing
Letter stamps: Printer's Type,
Hero Arts
Stamping ink: Rubber Stampede
Quote: John Greenleaf Whittier
Shrink plastic: Shrinky Dinks
Metal tag: Making Memories
Chalk: Craf-T Products
Fibers: On The Surface
Other: Mini brads, jump rings,
jute and deacidified newspaper
from 1966

Shrink Title Letters

Here's how to use your lettering templates and
shrink plastic to create cool dimensional titles:

❶ Use a lettering template to trace each letter
of the title onto shrink plastic. *Remember:* Each
letter will end up a third of the original size. Cut
out each letter (or use a die-cutting machine).

❷ Make a hole at the top of each letter with
an ⅛" hole punch.

❸ Gently press each letter into a pigment ink
pad. Or, color the letters with colored pencils.

❹ Follow the manufacturer's directions for
shrinking the plastic. I used my daughter's
Shrinky Dink oven, although a standard oven
or a heat gun can also be used.

❺ Attach jump rings to each letter. String the
letters on fiber, ribbon or wire and adhere
them to your layout.

~ Twyla Koop

"MINNESOTA SPECTACULAR"
by Christine Brown
Hanover, MN

Supplies
Patterned paper: Karen Foster Design
Computer font: 2Peas Chestnuts, downloaded
from *www.twopeasinabucket.com*
Eyelet and charm letters: Making Memories
Photo-editing software: Adobe Photoshop
Acrylic paint: Delta Technical Coatings

Stamping ink: VersaMark, Tsukineko
Leaf stamp: Hampton Arts
Skeleton leaves: Nature's Pressed
Copper tags: Lee Valley
Chalk: Craf-T Products
Rusty leaves: Darice
Other: Brads, mesh ribbon and copper sheet

Faux Stamped Watermark
To create a fake stamped watermark:
❶ Stamp the leaf image with black ink on a scrap of paper. Scan the image into your photo-editing software. (I used Adobe Photoshop.)
❷ Use the magic wand tool to delete all the background areas, including between the lines within the image.
❸ Type in your journaling and add the transparent stamped image over it. Change the color of the image to match your layout, then enlarge it to better fit the journaling block. Set the opacity to 85% so the image doesn't overpower the journaling. Print the block and chalk the leaf image.

Copper Frame
To create a copper frame:
❶ Cut a piece of copper sheeting approximately 1½" wider and taller than your journaling block.
❷ Using a ruler and pen, mark cutting lines on the back to indicate where to remove the center of the frame.
❸ Pierce the center with a craft knife. Use sharp scissors to cut along the pen lines and carefully remove the center.
❹ Measure ⅛" from the center opening, then use an embossing stylus to impress a line all the way around the inside edge. Use this line as a guide when folding back the inside edges to create a finished edge. To give the copper an aged, weathered look, sand it and apply black acrylic paint. Quickly wipe the paint off, leaving a slight residue.

~ Christine Brown

"MOMENT IN TIME"
by Brenée Williams
Boise, ID

Supplies
Leaves: Sizzix
Patterned paper: Michelle Anderson, Provo Craft
Computer font: PC Stone Script, "Little Images" HugWare CD, Provo Craft
Embossing powder: Close To My Heart
Vellum: Paper Adventures
Aluminum mesh: Amaco
Foam tape: 3M Corp.
Other: Fiber and clock charm

Metal Mesh Leaves
To create a unique leaf accent for an autumn page:
❶ Punch the shape from wire mesh.
❷ Bend the form slightly to give it a little dimension.
❸ Apply glue liberally, with more glue in some areas and less in others. Sprinkle on embossing powder, coating all areas. Heat the powder with an embossing tool.
❹ Bend and shape the mesh to add even more dimension.

~ Brenée Williams

"AUTUMN HARVEST"
by Pam Easley
Bentonia, MS

Supplies
Patterned papers: EK Success and Karen Foster Design
Computer fonts: JSL Ancient, downloaded from the Internet;
2Peas Essential, downloaded from *www.twopeasinabucket.com*
Definition stickers and buttons: Making Memories
Pumpkin photos: Shotz, Creative Imaginations
Embroidery floss: DMC
Chalk: Craf-T Products
Transparency: Royal

Fast Fall Accents
Want to create fast, colorful accents for your fall pages? You can with a square punch and pumpkin photos! Here's how:
❶ Strategically place the punch in areas where you'll get the most color and the best sense of the pumpkins. Punch out your squares.
❷ Place the squares side by side and randomly adhere definition stickers over them.
❸ Cut the squares apart and "age" them with a quick brush of chalk.

~ Pam Easley

"PUMPKIN PATCH"
by Tracy Kyle
Coquitlam, BC, Canada

Supplies
Vellum: Karen Foster Design
Computer font: Cezanne, P22 Type Foundry
Embossing enamel: Suze Weinberg
Brads: Impress Rubber Stamps
Buttons: Better Button Company

Subtle Embossed Title
Before printing on vellum, change your printer settings to "transparency." Select a font color that will match or be slightly lighter than your colored vellum. Print out your title, then immediately sprinkle it with clear embossing powder and heat it. *Note:* Avoid placing the heat source too close to the vellum or it will warp.

~ Tracy Kyle

december

december treats

December is packed with holiday pleasures, whether you're savoring the sweet smells wafting from the kitchen or watching shoppers tote mysterious packages around town. Grab your camera and scrapbooking supplies, then capture treasured traditions, sights and moments like these:

- Homes glowing with candles in every window
- Children catching snowflakes on their tongues
- Horse-drawn sleighs carrying bundled-up passengers
- Lit luminarias lining front walks and sidewalks
- Neighbors visiting to wish you happy holidays
- Eager hands holding brightly wrapped boxes
- Evergreen branches sporting bright-red berries
- Shiny bells greeting guests at the front door

- Family singing carols together around the piano
- Children building a snow family in the front yard
- Snowshoers stepping gingerly through a winter wonderland
- Guests wearing their finest to formal holiday parties
- Decorative wreaths hanging festively on the front door
- Family and friends reminiscing during a holiday feast
- The fresh smell of pine welcoming guests to a home

ARTICLE BY CATHERINE SCOTT

'tis the season

9 "merry and bright" layouts

Photo taken at Picasso, Inc.
Supplies *Embossed paper:* K & Company; *Embossed metal frame:* Timeless Tins, Artistic Expressions; *Vellum:* The Paper Company; *Flat-head eyelets:* Making Memories; *Computer font:* Santa's Sleigh, downloaded from the Internet; *Santa and sleigh ornaments:* Provo Craft; *Metallic finish:* Rub 'n Buff, Amaco; *Other:* Glue dots, velvet paper, ribbon and bows.

" 'Twas the Month Before Christmas"

by Jeniece Higgins
Northbrook, IL

Each Thanksgiving, Jeniece wraps the family's collection of Christmas books. Her children unwrap one book to read each night until Christmas Eve.

◆ Incorporate flat Christmas ornaments on your layout. Jeniece embellished hers with a metallic finish.

◆ Alter a metal frame with metallic finish or rub-ons. Mix and match colors for a more dimensional look.

ARTICLE BY LANNA CARTER

"'Tis the Season"
by Tracy Miller
Fallston, MD

Supplies *Paper and stickers:* Simple Sets, SEI; *Computer font:* Bookman Old Style, Microsoft Word.

Tracy inherited her decorating flare (and decorations) from her grandmothers.

◆ Did you notice the strong lines and shapes in Tracy's pictures? She repeats them throughout her layout.

◆ Does your journaling refer to specific pictures? Label your pictures with letter stickers.

◆ Don't forget to take pictures, including close-ups, of your favorite decorations.

"For Allie"
by Christy Tomlinson
Shelley, ID

Supplies *Patterned paper:* Magenta; *Vellum:* Provo Craft; *Ribbon:* C.M. Offray & Son; *Metal charms:* Making Memories; *Embossing powder:* Ranger Industries; *Fibers:* Adornaments, EK Success; *Rubber stamps:* Hero Arts; *Chalk:* Craf-T Products; *Computer font:* CK Jot, "The Best of Creative Lettering" CD Combo, *Creating Keepsakes; Other:* Tissue paper.

Little girls in Christmas dresses are almost as traditional as Christmas trees and presents.

◆ Use the holidays as a time to reflect on how much a loved one has grown. Christy included hidden journaling for her daughter.

◆ Alter the color of a metal charm with embossing powder.

◆ Chalk your vellum and turn it into a shabby chic frame.

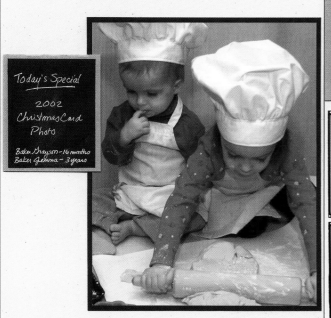

"Little Knight's Bakery"

by Jill Knight
Centerville, OH

Before the flour is even measured, Jill's children have chairs pushed up to the counter. They love helping with the annual holiday baking.

◆ Set up your own photo shoot. Jill hung white sheets from her cupboard to create a "studio."

◆ Use photo-shoot proofs on your layout. Jill used an online company to add a filmstrip border to her photos.

◆ Create an interactive flap to hide additional journaling. Jill hid her text under the chalkboards.

Supplies *Photo border:* Downloaded from *www.Shutterfly.com; Pen:* Ultimate Gel Pen, American Crafts; *Computer font:* Adorable, downloaded from the Internet; *Other:* Chalk. *Idea to note:* Jill based her layout on a sketch in Becky Higgins' *Creative Sketches for Scrapbooking* idea book.

"Erin the Red-Nosed Reindeer"

by Christiane Wilson-Grove
Kirkland, WA

A picture can communicate so much. Note how the expression and Rudolph nose say much about Christiane's daughter.

◆ Adapt this design easily for traditional hands-on or computer-generated scrapbooking.

◆ Repeat a prominent shape throughout your layout. Isolate it with bold color, such as the red nose and circle punches.

◆ To highlight the red nose, Christiane altered it in Adobe Photoshop. She selected the nose from the color photo, then layered it over a black-and-white version of the photo.

Supplies *Circle punches:* McGill; *Computer fonts:* 2Peas Beautiful, downloaded from *www.twopeasinabucket.com;* Secret Service Typewriter, downloaded from the Internet; *Watercolor pencil:* Prismacolor, Sanford.

Supplies *Embossed paper:* K & Company; *Mesh:* Maruyama, Magenta; *Patterned paper:* 7 Gypsies; *Computer fonts:* Mechanical Fun and Attic, downloaded from the Internet; *Stamping ink:* Stampin' Up!; *Letter stamps:* Hero Arts; *Tag:* Fresh Cuts, EK Success; *Stickers:* EK Success; *Letter stickers:* Sonnets and Shotz, Creative Imaginations; *Brads:* Impress Rubber Stamps; *Charms:* Embellish It!; *Dog tag:* Clare Ultimo; *Other:* Handmade paper, mini Scrabble phrases, button and thread.

"Memories of Our Home"
by Melissa Villalobos
Loves Park, IL

Melissa created this layout to help her remember her daughter's unique reaction to opening Christmas presents.

◆ Experiment with fonts and letter stickers in a word. Add a clear 3-D sticker on top.

◆ Label your photos with one-word captions. Melissa used miniature Scrabble tiles.

◆ Use mesh as a photo or layout corner.

"Dad's Christmas Lottery Prize"
by Linda De Los Reyes
Los Gatos, CA

Linda's father lobbied for a TV for Christmas, but he didn't dream he'd get it. Thanks to Linda's generous brother, her dad got the ultimate surprise gift!

◆ If your journaling runs longer than your layout will allow, present the journaling in a book format. Linda typed her journaling on nine 3" x 3" pages. She threaded the pages together with jute.

◆ Thread bulky fibers through eyelets, then knot the fibers on the back of your layout.

◆ Journal about Christmas traditions (such as swapping names for gift giving).

Supplies *Patterned paper:* Stitches, SEI; *Fibers:* On The Surface; *Yarn:* Lion Brand Company; *Charms:* Making Memories; *Jute:* Michaels; *Buttons:* Buttons Galore; *Computer fonts:* CK Journaling, "The Best of Creative Lettering" CD Combo; CK Elusive, "Fresh Fonts" CD, *Creating Keepsakes*.

"An Early Present"

by Ruth De Fauw
Woodstock, ON, Canada

Ruth exchanged pictures with her friend Jessi in an online layout swap. She chose her colors based on Jessi's Christmas card.

◆ Don't limit your scrapbook "canvas" to just one direction. Ruth rotated two 8½" x 11" pages and stacked them horizontally.

◆ Work a subtitle into your journaling with text boxes. (See Computer Corner in the October 2002 issue for details.)

◆ Wrap mesh around a holiday layout to create the look of a gift.

◆ Instead of discarding Christmas cards, use them on a layout.

Photos by Jessi Stringham. **Supplies** *Patterned paper:* Magenta; *Plaque and snowflake eyelets:* Making Memories; *Embossing ink:* VersaColor, Tsukineko; *Embossing powder:* Stampendous!; *Mesh:* Danson Décor; *Letter stamps:* PSX Design (Antique and Classic); *Computer fonts:* CK Journaling, "The Best of Creative Lettering" CD Combo, *Creating Keepsakes*; Stamp Act, Bookworm and Typewriter, downloaded from the Internet; 2Peas Evergreen, downloaded from *www.twopeasinabucket.com*; Cezanne, P22 Type Foundry.

"Dance"

by Jennifer Gallacher
Savannah, GA

Jennifer couldn't resist snapping pictures as her husband and daughter danced to Mariah Carey's "All I Want for Christmas Is You."

• Create your own musical patterned paper by scanning music and printing it on cream paper. Jennifer chalked and tore her paper for an aged look.

• If you don't have a scanner, use a photo machine at your local photo lab to change color pictures to black and white or sepia.

• Instead of cutting out the centers of template letters, use brads or eyelets to create visual "space."

Supplies *Patterned papers:* K & Company (floral) and Jennifer's own design (music); *Vellum:* Provo Craft; *Wire, snaps, heart brads, definition stickers, clear 3-D stickers and buttons:* Making Memories; *Lettering template:* Script, ScrapPagerz.com; *Computer font:* CK Typeset, "Creative Clips & Fonts" CD, *Creating Keepsakes*; *Die cuts:* Li'l Davis Designs; *Chalk:* Craf-T Products; *Other:* Ribbon.

December
on Display

Get inspired by these spectacular holiday layouts

I love big celebrations! Give me a reason to decorate, dress up, shop and plan fun get-togethers, and I'm a happy girl. The best things about December are all the celebrations— Christmas, Chanukah, Kwanzaa and New Year's Eve. What more could a girl want?

Whether you're attending or hosting holiday festivities this season, make sure you gather your loved ones together and take oodles of pictures. Then, look at the inspiring and artistic ideas on the following layouts. They're sure to give you festive scrapbooking (and card) ideas.

by LORI FAIRBANKS

"New Year Traditions"
by Allison Landy
Phoenix, AZ

Supplies
Patterned paper: Magenta
Vellum: DMD, Inc.
Letter stamps: All Night Media (large) and PSX Design (small)
Stamping ink: VersaMark, Tsukineko
Chalk: Craf-T Products
Eyelets: Making Memories
Tag and colored staples: Avery
Date stamp: OfficeMax
Computer font: CK Elusive, "Fresh Fonts" CD, *Creating Keepsakes*
Other: Ribbon and rickrack

Chalked VersaMark Letters
To create this title, first stamp your letters using embossing ink, then heat-set the ink slightly. Use a make-up applicator or cotton ball to lightly dust the area with chalk. The more chalk you add, the darker the image will be.

—Allison Landy > Phoenix, AZ

"Confessions of a Christmas Sneak"
by Erin Lincoln
Frederick, MD

Supplies
Patterned paper: Provo Craft
Computer fonts: 2Peas Nevermind, downloaded from *www.twopeasinabucket.com*; Rubberstamp, downloaded from the Internet; CK Constitution, "Fresh Fonts" CD, *Creating Keepsakes*
Punch: EK Success
Rubber stamps: Impress Rubber Stamps

Stamping ink: All Night Media
Snaps and stitched tin squares: Making Memories
Embroidery floss: DMC
Stitching on trees: Inspired by Mini Fresh Cuts by EK Success
Idea to note: Erin used shadow ink and shape stamps behind her tree accents to create a quick, double-matted look.

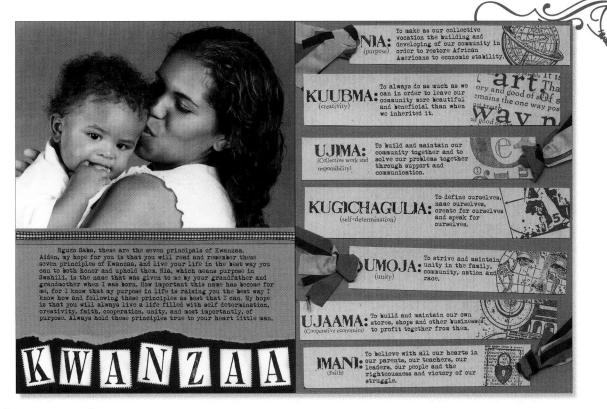

"Kwanzaa"
by Nia Reddy
Brooklyn, NY

Supplies
Ribbon: C.M. Offray & Son (gingham and black), Stamping Grounds (red and green)
Computer fonts: Fulton Artistamp (each principle) and Mom's Typewriter (journaling and definitions), downloaded from the Internet; Garamouche, P22 Type Foundry (English translation of principles)
Rubber stamps: Inkadinkadoo (globe), Stampers Anonymous (art text and architecture design), Eclectic Omnibus (jumbled letters), Stampington & Co. (antique "A" and key with script) and Stamp Francisco (face image)
Stamping ink: VersaColor, Tsukineko
Title letters: FoofaLa
Chalk: Craf-T Products

Fast Accent Tip
Use rubber stamps to add decorative accents to a page or to highlight journaling words or phrases.

I created tags for each principle of Kwanzaa and used stamps to correspond with each one. This was an easy way to emphasize the principles on my layout.
—*Nia Reddy > Brooklyn, NY*

"The Festival of Lights"

by Lilac Chang
San Mateo, CA

Supplies

Patterned papers: K & Company (maroon),
Karen Foster Design (journaling)
Rub-ons: Simply Stated, Making Memories
("The" and "of")
*Definition sticker, date stamp and
alphabet page pebbles:* Making Memories
Letter stickers: Sonnets, Creative Imaginations
Number stamps: PSX Design
Menorah stamp: Stamp Francisco
Stamping ink: Nick Bantock,
Ranger Industries
Other: Script patterned paper, ribbon
and tassels
Idea to note: Lilac downloaded the
Hebrew blessing from the Internet.
The number stamps represent the eight
days of Chanukah.

"Sharing the Magic"

by Nicole Gartland
Portland, OR

Supplies
Rubber stamp: Hero Arts
Stamping ink: Fresco, Stampa Rosa
Craft wire: Artistic Wire Ltd.
Pens: The Ultimate Glitter Gel Pen,
American Crafts; LePlume, Marvy Uchida

Computer fonts: Burr Oak (titles), BD
Renaissance (block letters), Mechanical Fun
(lined letters and numbers) and Pupcat
(journaling), downloaded from the
Internet

"Is Santa Allergic to Cow Milk?"

by Renee Villalobos-Campa
Winnebago, IL

Supplies
Patterned papers: Anna Griffin (flowered),
Daisy D's Paper Co. (striped)
Vellum and metallic paper: Paper Pizazz
Letter stickers: Sonnets, Creative
Imaginations ("to"); Nostalgiques, EK
Success ("Is" and "Cow")
Computer font: 2Peas Flea Market, down-
loaded from *www.twopeasinabucket.com*
Brads: Making Memories
Other: Scrabble tiles
Ideas to note: Renee sanded the pat-
terned paper. She covered the brads with
striped patterned paper, then sealed them
with a decoupage medium.

Andrew is our little flirt. He laughs at
anything and everything. He always
has a bright smile for anyone who's
passing by, and he greets me each
morning with a big grin. He's also a bit

July '99

This December I had the opportunity
to observe one of Alyssa's ballet
classes for the first time in a couple
years. Even though I have been a
dancer myself throughout my life

Red Wings

Tim Damon Orthodontics

P o r t e r

YE8TERDAY

Playing
neighb
Skatsboa

through the years

A SCOUT IS....
Trustworthy
LOYAL
Helpful
Friendly
Cheerful
Courteous
Kind
BRAVE
Clean
AND REVERENT

—THE SCOUT LAW

STRAW
market

Table of Contents

Portrait Pedigree Charts

Grandparents

Great-grandparents

Great-great-grandparents

Miscellaneous Photos

becky's
babypages

by **becky higgins**

Eight layouts that'll make you ooh and aah

I was recently introduced to the world of motherhood. It's also known as the world of sleep deprivation, spit-up, diaper changes and interpreting a baby's different cries. It's a world of a new kind of love I've not experienced before. To say that my new responsibility as a mother is an amazing and rewarding gift is an understatement. Porter has changed our lives forever.

Like most parents, my husband David and I do our best to preserve Porter's earliest days so he can reflect on them later. We've made molds of his tiny feet and hands. We've videotaped him sleeping, hiccupping, crying and cooing. And, of course—we've taken about a thousand pictures! Well, almost. ››

flash cards

Did you know that babies prefer contrasting colors and designs while their sight is still developing in the earliest weeks and months? Why not use the cardstock you have on hand to create flash cards for your baby? I have these flash cards in Porter's crib and at his changing area.

Supplies *Circle punches:* EK Success (small), Family Treasures (medium) and McGill (large).

Figure 1. Create a stunning first page to help set the tone in your baby album. **Supplies** *Patterned paper:* Family Archives; *Red textured paper:* Provo Craft; *Vellum envelope:* Scrap-Ease; *Computer fonts:* CK Evolution and CK Constitution, "Fresh Fonts" CD, *Creating Keepsakes; Other:* Ribbon.

As a scrapbooker who strives for organization, I spent a lot of time thinking about the scrapbooking "system" I wanted to maintain when children joined our family. I can't tell you how many times well-wishers said, "Oh, just wait! Your first kid will have a million pictures and gorgeous scrapbooks and the rest of your kids won't." I think I heard this more than all the other baby advice combined.

I'm up for the challenge. For me, scrapbooking isn't just a fun hobby; it's about preserving memories. A meaningful scrapbook is one of the greatest gifts you can give a child (or anyone!). Having said that, I am not going to skimp on my picture-taking or scrapbooking for Porter just because I'm worried his life will be better preserved than that of future siblings.

To make sure I stay caught up, I do two things: I scrapbook while Porter sleeps, and I live by the motto "Keep it simple." In fact, these words are engraved on a sign that hangs in my office. While some of my extra-important pages are more elaborate, most are clean and quick.

Whether you've just had a baby, you're working on your teenager's baby book or your own childhood album, here are some page ideas to get you started!

make a statement

First, begin your baby's scrapbook with a classy introduction page that includes a dedication or letter from you (see Figure 1). This first page sets the tone for the rest of the scrapbook. Keep this in mind as you determine the style.

Figure 2. Document your pregnancy, including monthly belly shots, cravings, doctor appointments and more. **Supplies** *Letters:* Making Memories ("Expecting") and Pioneer ("Porter"); *Brads:* American Pin & Fastener; *Vellum:* PrintWorks; *Computer fonts:* Century Gothic (journaling), Microsoft Word; CK Typewriter (bold font), "Fresh Fonts" CD, *Creating Keepsakes; Pen:* Pigma Micron, Sakura.

before baby

Preparations for your bundle of joy begin long before a trip to the hospital. Here are a few layout ideas to help you remember this busy and anxious time.

- **Include memories** and pictures from your pregnancy (see Figure 2). Don't forget to tell all about your cravings, your growing belly, sharing the news, preparations and expectations. *Note:* I created this layout for our family album and have a different layout with the same theme in Porter's book.

- **Preparing the baby's room** is worth preserving, too. Include the progress (if you make a lot of changes) and show the finished room with all the little details. Be sure to point out significant pieces of furniture or decorating touches that have a story.

- **Babies need a lot of stuff,** and the cost adds up. Consider creating a layout about the cost of having a baby. Gather receipts, clothing tags and pictures of getting ready for your new family addition.

- **Take pictures of the gifts** you received, including presents from your baby shower. If possible, include a list of the items and who gave them.

- **Be sure to save** your baby's first pictures from the ultrasound.

Stack them in a pocket attached to a page, or display them on a layout.

a history lesson

Every baby has a history. Before your baby arrives, set the tone for your child's life by including some important "history."

- **Create a family tree.** In Figure 3, I've shown one side of a two-page layout that includes my family and my husband's family. You can keep it as simple as just including names, or you can give more information, such as birthdays, marriage dates and more.

- **Who's part of your family** and where did they live when your baby was born? This is a great →

idea if you have family members who live far away (like mine). Include a map and show where the baby's aunts, uncles, cousins and grandparents live. Don't forget to show current pictures of your loved ones.

- **Showcase baby pictures** of the baby's parents and siblings (see Figure 4). This is a fun way to compare baby looks and birth statistics of each family member. *Note:* This layout has a few pictures also seen in Figure 7. That's because this layout is in our family album, not Porter's scrapbook.

- **Mom and Dad's story** is something every child will cherish. Share how you met, dated, fell in love, got engaged, married and what life has been like since then. Share your feelings about one another and what it means to have this child in your family.

- **Include a layout about you and your husband** outside of your role as parents. Share your individual strengths, weaknesses, hobbies and personal characteristics. This idea can also work well for highlighting the baby's siblings.

the big day

You've thought about it, dreamed about it, worried about it and the day finally arrives. For some it's a blur. Others remember every detail. Here are some ideas to think about as you scrapbook the "big day."

- **Be sure to include pictures** of the hospital and tell about your stay. Did you eat the hospital food or have food delivered?

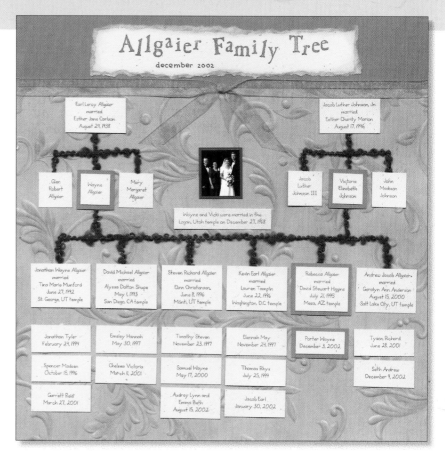

Figure 3. Create a family tree so your baby has a record of your posterity and extended family. **Supplies** *Patterned paper:* K & Company; *Letter stamps:* The Missing Link Stamp Co.; *Stamping ink:* Stampin' Up!; *Fiber:* Adornaments, EK Success; *Computer font:* CK Simple, "The Art of Creative Lettering" CD, *Creating Keepsakes; Pen:* Zig Writer, EK Success.

Who was your favorite nurse and why?

- **How was the weather?** What were some of the news headlines on that day's front page? Document a little about the world outside your own miracle.

- **Share the *entire* story**—little details and all—about your labor and delivery. Your child will want to hear it over and over again when he or she is older. After all, it's the story of how your child entered the world! I still love to hear my mom tell me how she lost a bet to her doctor that I was a boy. Even though she lost the bet, the doctor still paid up with the chocolate milkshake they wagered.

- **If friends and family came** to see you and the baby in the hospital,

be sure to include pictures of these first visitors (see Figure 5).

- **The birth certificate** makes it all official (see Figure 6). Don't forget to also preserve the hospital bracelets and other mementos from the blessed event.

after baby's arrival

In the whirlwind of events and adjustments that happen within days of going home with your new baby, take a few minutes to reflect on this precious new life. Following are some things to think about:

- **First impressions** are everlasting. What did you discover about your newborn in those first days? Did he or she already have distinct characteristics?

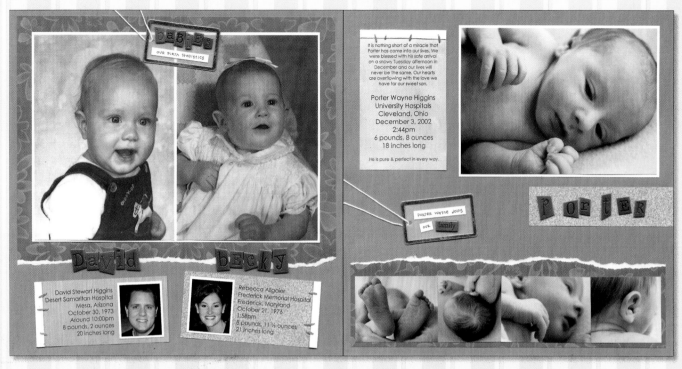

Figure 4. Compare your baby's pictures with those from your own infancy. **Supplies** *Patterned paper:* The C-Thru Ruler Co. (floral), Pages in a Snap (David), Sandylion (Becky) and Karen Foster Design (Porter); *Computer font:* Century Gothic, Microsoft Word; *Tag, metal letters and metal word:* Making Memories; *Embroidery floss:* DMC.

Figure 5. Invite each of your baby's first visitors to have his or her picture taken. **Supplies** *Patterned paper:* SEI, Inc.; *Letter stickers:* Creative Imaginations; *Small circle punch:* McGill; *Computer font:* CK Fresh, "Fresh Fonts" CD, *Creating Keepsakes; Clear film:* F & M Enterprises; *Tiny eyelets:* American Pin & Fastener. *Ideas to note:* Becky cut circles from coordinating patterned paper to fill in some of the "white space" on this layout. She also punched smaller circles from the same colors. Becky printed her journaling on clear film.

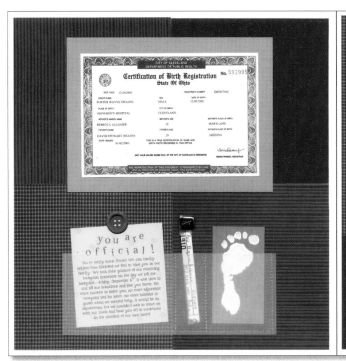
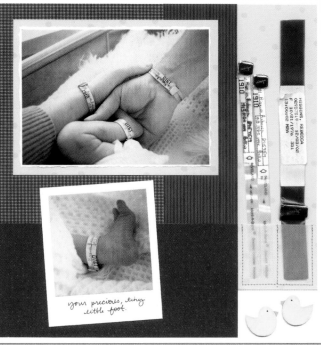

Figure 6. Showing a picture of your bracelets together in the hospital makes for a very special photograph. **Supplies** *Patterned papers:* All About Me Paper Co. (blue) and Lasting Impressions for Paper, Inc. (yellow); *Acrylic paint:* Delta; *Computer font:* CK Evolution, "Fresh Fonts" CD, *Creating Keepsakes; Letter stickers:* SEI, Inc.; *Button sticker:* Paper Patch; *Vellum:* Westrim Crafts; *Pop dots:* Mrs. Grossman's.

Share your thoughts about meeting each other for the first time.

- **Getting used to a new little person** in your life can be a dramatic change! Document your new schedule, adjusting to changes (and what those changes are), and be sure to include journaling about getting the baby on a schedule, feeding times, daily routines and favorite activities together.

- **Record your hopes and dreams** for your baby (see Figure 7). Don't forget to include letters from Mom and Dad, grandparents and other loved ones who cherish the baby.

- **Those little body parts** definitely need a place in your scrapbook (see Figure 7). When you're taking pictures, get close and use natural light, such as from a window. Every newborn deserves at least one roll of black-and-white pictures in the very beginning.

- **Another way to preserve little fingers and toes** is to make handprints and footprints (see Figure 6). To make it more interesting, include your own adult-sized impressions as well.

- **If you sent baby announcements** (of course you did—you're a scrapbooker!), don't forget to include an announcement in the baby's album.

- **Your baby's personality** is one in a million. As you begin to see individual traits, take pictures of the baby's expressions and journal about his or her unique qualities. Ask your parents and your husband's parents about what you two were like as babies and record this, too. Notice any similarities?

- **Create a "While you were sleeping" layout** that tells what you (Mom) do while your baby naps. It will be fun for your child to reflect on how you spend your time outside of feeding, burping, consoling and rocking. Do you take the opportunity to rest? Or do you catch up on chores, read a book or work on projects (like scrapbooking)?

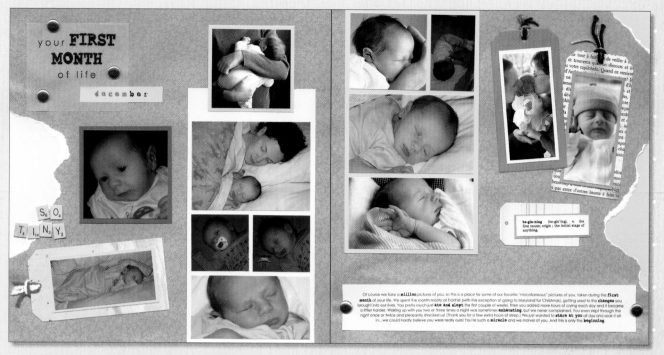

Figure 7. Include all those miscellaneous pictures in one place as you create a layout for each month of your baby's first year. **Supplies** *Patterned paper:* All My Memories; *Definition and tags:* FoofaLa; *Computer fonts:* Century Gothic, Microsoft Word; CK Typewriter, "Fresh Fonts" CD, *Creating Keepsakes*; *Vellum:* Paper Adventures; *Brads:* American Pin & Fastener; *Fiber:* Fiber Scraps.

plan ahead

If you want to keep up with your family albums while still maintaining the baby book, spend some time thinking about the big picture. If you only want your child to leave home with four or five books, you'll have to be super selective about what you include. Everything else will have to go in your family albums. In this example, you would have to squeeze about four years in one album. (It *can* be done!)

journaling perspectives

Because journaling is such a personal decision, I will share with you my philosophy for journaling in Porter's scrapbook. Please consider it a suggestion. As I make pages for Porter, the journaling will be in our perspective as his parents. For example, I'll include journaling such as "You were so adorable, your dad and I could hardly take our eyes off you!"

I don't want to put words in Porter's mouth such as, "I was so cute that day. Everyone kept staring at me." I believe maintaining a consistent voice on all the pages also helps the flow of your albums.

When it comes to creating an incredible scrapbook for your child, one consideration should guide you in your efforts. If you could have had the most wonderful presentation of your childhood, what is it you would have wanted your parents to include? Imagine all the details you'd want to know and the pictures you'd like to see. This is what you should do for your child.

If you feel overwhelmed at the thought of keeping up with your child's scrapbook, just remember that he or she won't care about elaborate accents or ingenious design. While these are nice enhancements, they shouldn't be the core of why you're creating pages for your child.

Continuously ask yourself why you're creating the pages. What is your motivation? This will be the foundation of every page you create for your little one, and it will certainly shine through in your work. ❤

10 terrific tips
for baby pictures

Set up a successful photo shoot

by Lisa Bearnson

My friend Jane recently had her sixth child, and I found myself offering to take pictures of her newborn son. Jane was thrilled, but I became uneasy as I realized how few pictures I'd taken of newborns. (I've had lots of practice with older toddlers and children.)

I thought about the incredible pictures Becky Higgins had taken of me and Baby Sage at the hospital, and how Becky had used natural lighting, different angles and various blankets for backgrounds during the shoot. But that was two years ago! I panicked and ran to the phone so I could call Becky for any last-minute advice. She wasn't available—she was at the hospital giving birth! So, I put on a smile and did my best to incorporate all the photo tips I've learned over the past few years. The results were just what I'd hoped they'd be.

Capture the delicate beauty of a newborn on film, and you'll capture something magnificent that's gone all too soon. The pictures are something that will be treasured, whether by you or someone else. Here are my top 10 tips for taking memorable photos of a newborn.

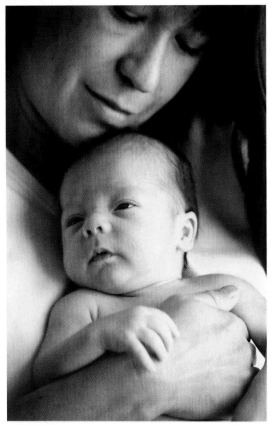

Figure 1. Capture your subjects in natural light, with light hitting them at a 45-degree angle. Take a closely cropped, vertical shot for visual interest.

10 TIPS TO GUIDE YOU

1. **Turn off your flash!** That's right—natural light on newborns' faces makes them look simply angelic (Figure 1). I opened the blinds on a large window and took the photos late in the morning while I stood directly beside the window. My subjects' shoulders were about three feet away from the window, and light was hitting them at a 45-degree angle.

   Note: Be sure to take the photos at the right time of day for the window you're using. Too much direct sunlight streaming through a window can create harsh shadows on your subject.

2. **Look through your viewfinder.** Is there enough light? Are there severe shadows, or does the subject's face look too dark? If so, try using another window or move your subject head-on toward the light.

3. **Go for black and white.** It's never been easier to take black-and-white photos thanks to Kodak's variety that can be processed the same way as color prints (C-41 process). Ilford and Moo Vue also make this type of film. Black-and-white film is more forgiving and smoothes out baby's blotchy skin. The film lends a timeless feel, and prints made on good paper generally last longer than color prints.

4. **Dare to get close.** That's right, extreme close-ups on baby's body parts and facial expressions are priceless (Figure 2). A telephoto lens on either your SLR or point-and-shoot camera is a must.

5. **Introduce variety.** In most of the shots shown here, I used different draped

Figure 2. Zoom in for an intimate look at baby's tiny feet cupped in an adult's hands. Note the interesting contrast in size and texture.

Figure 3. Introduce a variety of looks with blankets and a mix of textures in your picture's background.

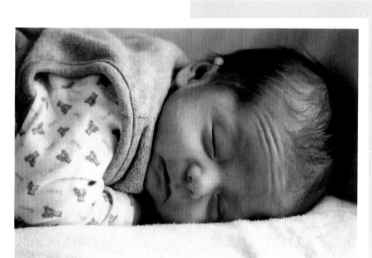

blankets for the background (Figure 3). However, on the shot with Jacob's feet cuddled in his mom's hands, I decided to use the existing background. It went a little blurry but created a nice effect. For most of these shots, Jane held Jacob while her arms and body were covered with fabric.

6. **Shoot lots of film.** Always have lots of film and extra batteries on hand. Not every picture will be perfect. Remember, the keepers will be worth the ones you toss.

7. **Get down on baby's level.** Although Jacob was lying on a chair so I could use the window's natural light (mom was close by), I still had to kneel and squat to get his precious expression in this photo (Figure 4).

8. **Don't be in a hurry.** I wanted photos of Jacob awake and asleep. While he was a little fussy, I'd scheduled plenty of time for the shoot and was able to get the shots I wanted.

9. **Take a few vertical shots.** (They're a nice change from the horizontal photos we all tend to take.) Also, an off-center shot like the horizontal one of Jacob wrapped in a blanket adds artistic interest (Figure 5).

10. **Study, study, study.** When you get your photos back from the lab, take time to examine each picture and learn from your mistakes. Does each photo capture an emotion? Does the lighting work? Is your background simple? Does it distract? Keep a portfolio of the photos that work and note special techniques used for those shots.

Figure 4. Get down on baby's level for some of your most darling, expressive shots.

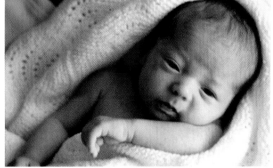

Figure 5. Remember the rule of thirds and take an off-center picture of the baby.

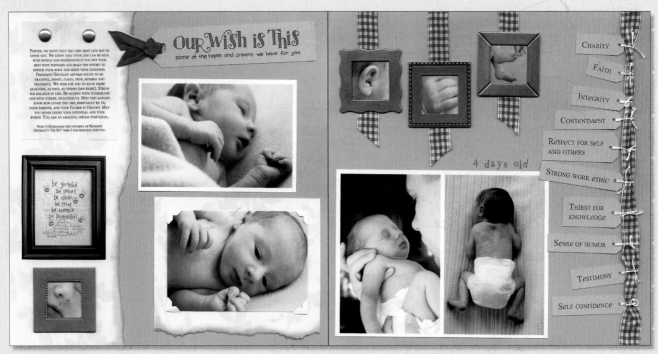

4 days old

CHARITY

FAITH

INTEGRITY

CONTENTMENT

RESPECT FOR SELF AND OTHERS

STRONG WORK ETHIC

THIRST FOR KNOWLEDGE

SENSE OF HUMOR

TESTIMONY

SELF CONFIDENCE

Figure 8. Share your thoughts about the desires you have for your child and his or her future. **Supplies** *Metal frames and nailheads:* Making Memories; *Patterned paper:* Liz King, EK Success; *Chalk:* Stampin' Up!; *Computer font:* CK Chemistry, "Fresh Fonts" CD, *Creating Keepsakes; Letter stamps:* PSX Design; *Stamping ink:* Stampin' Up!; *Photo corners:* Canson; *Colored pencils:* Prismacolor, Sanford; *White thread:* Kreinik; *Other:* Ribbon.

fun ideas for baby pages

Wondering where to begin? Consider creating some of the baby pages below.

First Year in Review
Create a layout that includes a block for each month with memories, milestones and accompanying photos. They will need to be small so you can fit the entire year on one layout. Work on the layout a month at a time, or wait and do it at the end of the year.

At a Glance
Show the growth of your child the first year on just one layout! Photograph the child with the same object at the same time every month. For example, since Porter's birthday is December 3, we photograph him with a favorite stuffed animal, in the same chair, on the third day of every month.

Made with Love
Did you make something special for your baby, such as a tied quilt, a crocheted hat or a cross-stitched sampler? Take pictures

of these special items and include them with pictures of handcrafted items from friends and family.

What's in a Name?
Choosing a name for a baby is a no-brainer for some and a long, complicated process for others. How was your baby's name determined? If the child is named after someone, try to include a picture of that significant person. Don't forget to mention the name's meaning, which can be found in baby name books or on the Internet.

Miscellaneous Pictures
If you take a lot of pictures but don't want to make a layout for each one, create a "Just Because" layout for every month or season. Include those shots that don't necessarily fit within a theme or event that you've already scrapbooked. I've started doing this (see Figure 7), and I

plan to have a layout for each month of Porter's first year. This is a great place to journal about your baby's memories from that month.

Baby's Firsts
First smile, first bath (see Figure 7), first time rolling over, first laugh. A person probably has more "firsts" in the first year of life than any other. What better way to preserve these milestones than to include them all together on a "First of Everything" layout?

MAY 0 3 2003

PRESTON

2003

PreCioUs

2
fub

angelic

cherished

heavenly

playful

sweet

THERE ARE TWO WAYS TO
LIVE YOUR LIFE.ONE IS AS
THOUGH NOTHING IS A MIRACLE.
THE OTHER IS AS IF EVERYTHING IS.
-ALBERT EINSTEIN

REPUB·FRANC·

2 ₵POSTES ₵ 2

"All Done!"

OCT 02

musing

pondering

thinking

"Those Beautiful Eyes"

by Mindy Bush
Idaho Falls, ID
Supplies *Computer font:* Hannibal Lecture, downloaded from the Internet; *Letter stickers:* Rebecca Sower, EK Success; *Flowers:* Nature's Pressed; *Page pebbles:* Making Memories.

Saige, you have the most gorgeous big blue eye's! I adore this photo of you because the window caught the light in your eye's and made them shine! What a perfect little sweetheart you are! How could I be more blessed?

"First Time"

by Helen Cruikshank Manly, NSW, Australia
Supplies *Patterned papers:* SEI (pink and purple stripe), Susan Branch (flower), Colorbök; *Computer fonts:* 2Peas Sugarplum, downloaded from *www.two-peasinabucket.com*; CK Cursive, "The Best of Creative Lettering" CD Vol. 2, *Creating Keepsakes; Other:* Buttons.

there's a first time for everything

Born @ 6:07pm
Weighed 3220g
Measured 50cm
Smiled @ 4 weeks
Clapped @ 7 1/2 months
Waved @ 7 months

Tooth @ 6 1/2 months
Rolled over @ 5 months
Crawled @ 7 months
Step @ 10 months
Word "ma ma"

first bed

first Mothers Day
first toast
first Birthday
first Christmas
first Bootscootin'

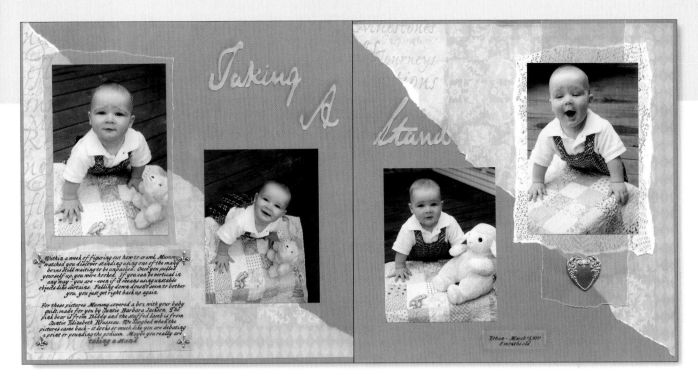

"Taking a Stand"

by Lynda Sturney
Brownsville, TX
Supplies *Patterned paper and vellum:* Hot Off The Press; *Computer font:* Texas Hero, downloaded from the Internet; *Metallic rub-ons:* Craf-T Products; *Nailheads:* Twopeasinabucket.com; *Chalk:* Artist's Choice; *Other:* Charm.

"Dreams"

by Cathy Blackstone
Westerville, OH
Supplies *Patterned papers:* 7 Gypsies (script), Autumn Leaves (under page pebbles); *Vellum tag, flower brads and "Dreams" metal word:* Making Memories; *Poemstones:* Sonnets, Creative Imaginations; *Letter and shadow stamps:* Hero Arts; *"Special" and "Precious" stamps:* Limited Edition Rubber Stamps; *Stamping ink:* ColorBox, Clearsnap; *Other:* Chalk.

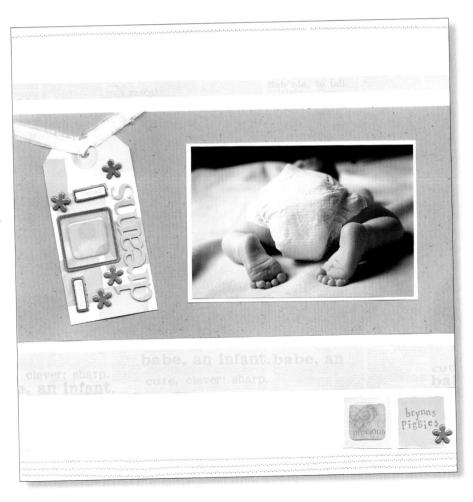

I tip-toe to your room,
checking on you
while you sleep.
You lay there like an angel
and the sound of your
sweet, fluffy breath
is the most beautiful music
I have ever heard.
Your feathery hair tickles
the nape of your neck and gives
you a downy crown.
An exquisite blush glows
from your porcelain cheeks.
How gentle you are in sleep.
How old will you be
before I stop checking on you
to make sure you are breathing?
Your very being amazes me.

I Thank God

FOR YOU.

I thank God that you exist,
that you are mine,
and just now,

after a long morning
of playing, learning
and challenging,

I am just simply thankful
that you are

FINALLY
ASLEEP

"Finally Asleep"
**by Jennifer Ditterich
Chokio, MN
Supplies** *Computer fonts:* Poor
Richard, LainieDay SH and Felix
Titling, downloaded from
www.dafont.com.

"All Done"
**by Ali Edwards
Eugene, OR
Supplies** *Vellum:* Paper Adventures;
Computer font: Fontdinerdotcom,
downloaded from
www.fontdiner.com; Pen:
Zig Millennium, EK Success.

"All Done!"

ANIMATIONS of a boy in his high-chair.

Some of your most hilarious expressions have come
upon us while you were seated in your old, wood, antique
high-chair... the same high-chair I used as a babe! This
set of photos was taken at Grandma and Grandpa's
house during our Christmas holiday in 2002... your Dad
can sure make you laugh... and oh the sounds that
come from that little body! You are just too silly!!!

The Case of the Bad Baby and Toddler Photographs

- **The Suspects:** Cluttered Clara, Red-Eyed Randi, Faraway Frank, Blurry Betsy
- **The Detective:** Licensed to Scrap, Marissa Perez
- **The Assignment:** We asked Marissa to scrapbook baby/toddler photographs with cluttered backgrounds and weak focal points.

Case Solved:

For her "Kailee" layout (Figure 1), Marissa cropped out the extra detail (the messy floor in the background) in three of the photos. Her placement of the three photos across the middle of the page creates a step-by-step scene for the eye to follow. The bow under the third picture of Kailee helps draw the eye to the best photograph. In addition, Marissa chose a complementary color scheme that makes the pictures of Kailee pop off the page.

For the birthday shots, Marissa used a similar technique, cropping and grouping the photos in a pleasing arrangement (Figure 2). She created a feminine, eye-pleasing design with the use of pink paper and beads.　→

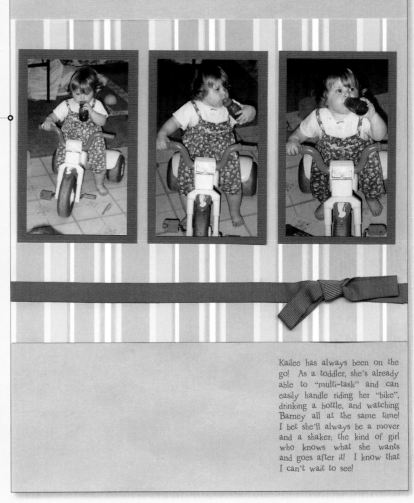

Kailee has always been on the go! As a toddler, she's already able to "multi-task" and can easily handle riding her "bike", drinking a bottle, and watching Barney all at the same time! I bet she'll always be a mover and a shaker; the kind of girl who knows what she wants and goes after it! I know that I can't wait to see!

Figure 1. A complementary color scheme can help your photographs pop off the page. *Page by Marissa Perez. Photos from Robbie McBride.* **Supplies** *Textured paper:* Bazzill Basics; *Patterned paper:* Treehouse Designs; *Computer font:* 2Peas Flea Market by Sharon Soneff, downloaded from *www.twopeasinabucket.com*; *Ribbon:* Michaels.

Happy
Birthday
Ashley!

Princess

Dear Ashley, You were so excited when you found out we were having a "Little Mermaid" birthday party for you! The shirts, the decorations, and even your birthday cake all carried the "Little Mermaid" theme. You loved pulling the seashells off the side of your cake and licking the frosting off of them. And of course, we all enjoyed it when you and your friend Brittany started dancing to the songs from the movie! I wonder if this is the start of the "princess" stage of your life? No matter, you'll always be special and unique to us! Happy Birthday, Love Mommy

Case Solved

Figure 2. Crop and group photos in an eye-pleasing arrangement. *Page by Marissa Perez. Photos from Joannie McBride.* **Supplies** *Patterned papers:* American Crafts; *Computer font:* Book Antiqua, package unknown; *Other:* Beads.

Top-Secret Tips:

For a stunning birthday photograph, Marissa suggests zooming in on the birthday child. In the photo in Figure 3, there's no doubt about the subject of the picture! In addition, zooming in will allow you to capture details such as frosting smeared across the child's face, hands and arms.

When photographing your child in motion, stay in motion yourself. Check the background of your picture and make sure it's free of clutter. Get down on the floor at your child's eye level, and take shots from different angles (Figure 4).

Figure 3. Zoom in close with your camera lens to capture your child's birthday joy. *Photo by Marissa Perez.*

Figure 4. Check all the angles to find the best shot of your child at play. *Photo by Marissa Perez.*

"Big Brown Eyes"

by **Erica Hernandez**
Fresno, CA
Supplies *Computer font:* Bookman Old Style, downloaded from the Internet.

Big Brown Eyes

Your eyes are so striking...everywhere we go people stop to comment on them. They're oh-so-big and this deep chocolaty brown color. You are so alert, always looking around, drinking in all that surrounds you, learning so much every second of the day. Definitely your dad's eyes. And boy-oh-boy, do you know how to work 'em. A ladies man at the ripe old age of 9 months, you have already mastered the art of the well timed glance. Windows to the soul...a beautiful soul at that.

6/11/03

"Gerber Baby"

by **Alice Merrill, Mishawaka, IN**
Supplies *Vellum:* The Paper Company; *Eyelets:* Simply Stamped; *Pop dots:* All Night Media.

When you were just over three months old Dr. Durham said we could try giving you baby cereal. The first time we tried it was a little bit that Aunt Stacie had given us from Ben's stash. We were so goofy. We thought we could just mix it into your bottle. Well, that didn't work so well, it wouldn't come out of the hole in the nipple. So, on January 9th we got out our little airplane spoon and placed you on your Boppy and successfully spoon-fed you for the very first time. You loved it! Mommy makes it with apple juice and water and warms it up nice and yummy for you. You and Daddy sure make a mess together!

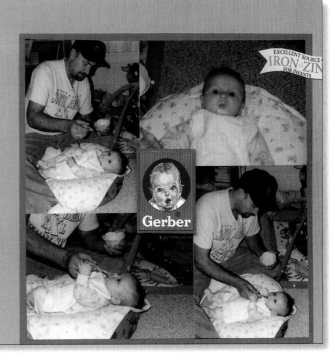

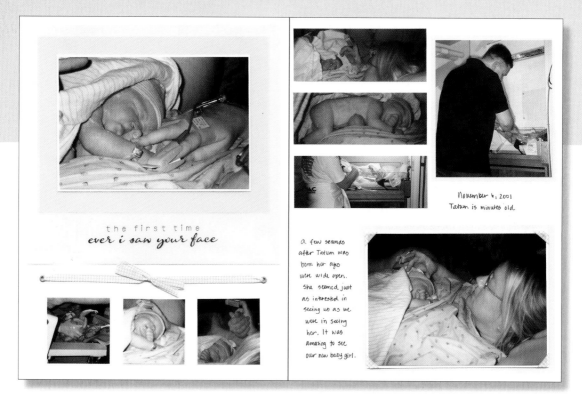

"The First Time Ever I Saw Your Face"

by Kim Heffington, Avondale, AZ

Supplies *Vellum:* Bazzill Basics; *Textured paper:* Source unknown; *Computer fonts:* Doodle Print, "PagePrintables" CD Vol. 1, Cock-A-Doodle Design, Inc.; Scrap Cursive, "Lettering Delights" CD Vol. 3, Inspire Graphics; *Ribbon:* Impress Rubber Stamps; *Square punch:* Marvy Uchida; *Eyelets:* Doodlebug Design; *Pen:* Zig Writer, EK Success. *Idea to note:* Kim used ribbon to make her own photo corners.

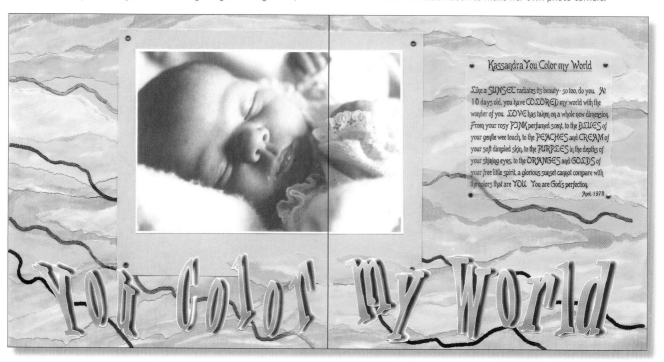

"You Color My World"

by Sharon Whitehead, Vernon, BC, Canada

Supplies *Vellum:* Paper Adventures; *Computer fonts:* Boomerang (journaling) and Jungle Juice (title), downloaded from the Internet; *Stamping ink:* Hero Arts; *Chalk:* Craf-T Products; *Fibers:* On the Surface; *Other:* Brads and eyelets. *Ideas to note:* Sharon created the sunset background with cardstock scraps in numerous colors, and added chalk, ink and fibers.

written in the stars...

Francesca Clare
May 5, 2000
1:15 a.m.

As a baby...
Loving caresses and a tender touch are what the Taurus baby lives for! This is a child who needs to be comfortable--a room and bed that are neither too hot nor too cold, food that is tasty (a budding gourmand has arrived!), soothing sounds, and whimsical toys will be necessities. When it comes to the learning curve, the Taurus baby is not in a hurry to grasp new concepts. She will learn things at her own pace and be unresponsive to pressure, yet persevering in the end. In light of this, a gentle manner to get her to react and respond is the sensible course of action. Also familial in nature, the Taurus baby will enjoy having the family in close proximity, especially siblings. You can consider this baby a people person. To sum up, the Taurus baby wants to be touched, will revel in delicious toys and, as an Earth Sign, will want to have both feet firmly planted on the ground!

The Bull
April 21 to May 21
Reliable, pleasure-loving, determined, conservative

As a child...
The Taurus child is steady and stable, taking his time with things and not rushing about. This is a child who will understand and appreciate process from the get-go! This youngster will also enjoy thinking about things and will generally appear consistent in her approach. A practical mind is a large part of the make-up here: When explaining things to a Taurus child, simply saying "This is how it is" won't do. This child needs to understand the "why" behind the rules, or she simply won't be able to live with them. The result is a well-adjusted kid. Another thing to keep in mind with this child is her need for affection. You can never hug the Taurus pup enough! This child is also quite domestic. You may well have a "Mother's Little Helper" in your midst, someone eager to mimic and learn from Mom. As the Taurus child is probably a future gourmet, expect this kid to spend a fair bit of time in the kitchen both cooking and eating! They're stubborn as well, making it pretty hard to sway the Taurus child once she gets an idea in her head. The flip side to this characteristic, however, is patience and persistence, something which renders the Taurus child a good student and an eager reader.

"Written in the Stars"

by Jennifer Bester, Somerville, MA
Supplies *Computer font:* Package unknown; *Charms:* All Night Media; *Constellation template:* From *Martha Stewart Baby* magazine; *Astrological information:* Downloaded from the Internet.

PAGE STARTERS

At 18 months old, my daughter routinely wowed us with her command of the English language. Strangers would comment on her verbal skills, and I'd bow my head modestly, acknowledging my firstborn's natural genius. At the same age, my second child was the proud owner of about three words. He was just too busy doing other things to work on language acquisition, but of course, he's a genius too!

I know it's considered taboo to compare siblings, but I decided it would be great fun to create a scrapbook page comparing my babies' development with that of a "typical" baby. By scrapbooking a development page or two, you can create an invaluable remembrance of what is actually just a snapshot moment in the timeline of your child's life. Here are some ideas to help you with your layout:

◆ Start with the chart. Babycenter.com features a free online chart for each month of baby's life.
◆ Include what it means to you when your baby makes those fledgling efforts to master new skills.
◆ Don't forget to focus on the milestones your baby is "behind" on, too. Be sure to record when your baby masters the skills and then some!

Record your baby's accomplishments on a layout based on child development charts. *Page by Allison Strine.* **Supplies** *Patterned paper:* Karen Foster Design (journaling and title boxes), Carolee's Creations; *Metallic paper:* Paper Adventures; *Stickers:* Magenta; *Ruler rubber stamp:* Planet Rubber; *Stamping ink:* ColorBox, Clearsnap, Inc.; *Embossing powder:* Judikins; *Computer font:* CAC Futura Casual, downloaded from the Internet; *Lettering template for title:* Wordsworth Chunkies, Wordsworth; *Other:* Tags, eyelets and beads.

◆ Include comparisons between your baby and you as a baby. How old were you when you first walked? Climbed up stairs?
◆ Keep a notebook in the kitchen where you can jot down baby's firsts. A chart layout is a great place to record those firsts that aren't big enough for an entire layout.
—*by Allison Strine*

"Wisdom Is to Wonder"
by Sherri Winstead, McChord AFB, WA
Supplies *Patterned paper:* Colors By Design; *Vellum:* Paper Adventures; *Mulberry paper:* PrintWorks; *Computer font:* Girls Are Weird, downloaded from the Internet; *Pen:* Zig Writer, EK Success.

"Muddy Puddle"
by Nicole Gartland, Portland, OR
Supplies *Patterned papers:* Hot Off The Press (burlap), Rocky Mountain Scrapbook Company (mud); *Computer fonts:* CK Print (journaling), "The Best of Creative Lettering" CD Vol. 1, *Creating Keepsakes*; Angelica (title), downloaded from the Internet; *Circle punch:* Marvy Uchida; *Craft wire:* Darice.

"Delaney"

by Danelle Johnson, Lindsborg, KS
Supplies *Patterned paper:* Colors By Design; *Vellum:* Paper Cuts; *Computer font:* Vivala, downloaded from the Internet; *Pop dots:* All Night Media; *Border photo:* Rocking Horse Shots, Danelle Johnson.

"Celebrating Amelia"

by Shannon Jones, Mesa, AZ
Supplies *Patterned paper:* Colors By Design; *Pen:* Zig Writer, EK Success; *Leaf and flower rubber stamps:* Close To My Heart; *Stamping ink:* Close To My Heart; *Square punch:* Family Treasures; *Embossing tool:* Lasting Impressions for Paper; *Mini album:* Kolo; *Chalk:* Craf-T Products. *Idea to note:* Shannon included more photos and journaling in the mini album she adhered to her layout.

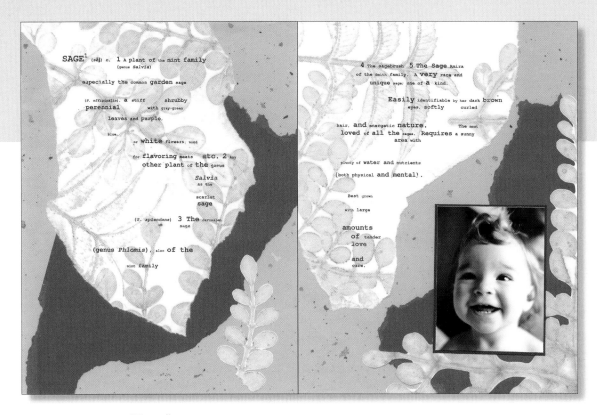

"Sage"

by Vivian Smith, Calgary, AB, Canada
Supplies *Handmade paper:* Source unknown; *Computer font:* Times Roman, Microsoft Word. *Idea to note:* Vivian looked up her daughter's name in the dictionary and included the definition in her journaling. She then expanded the definition with her own words in the same "dictionary" style.

"Max"

by Erica Pierovich, Longmont, CO
Supplies *Specialty paper:* Stamp Art, All Night Media (mulberry paper); Making Memories (striped vellum); *Lettering Template:* Fat Caps, Frances Meyer; *Computer font:* CK Script, "The Best of Creative Lettering" CD Vol. 1, *Creating Keepsakes; Other:* Erica used jute for the rope accents on her layout.

"Elizabeth"

by Jodi Olson
Redmond, WA
Supplies *Patterned paper:* Mara Mi; *Pens:* Zig Writer and Zig Scroll & Brush, EK Success; *Lettering idea:* "Concave," The Art of Creative Lettering, Creating Keepsakes Books; *Punches:* Forever Memories (square), Marvy Uchida (circle), All Night Media (spiral).

"Halle"

by Kristina Nicolai-White
www.TwoPeasinaBucket.com
Middleton, WI
Supplies *Patterned paper:* Colors By Design (vine), O'Scrap!, Imaginations! (striped); *Die cuts:* Accents, O'Scrap!, Imaginations!; *Lettering template:* Fancy Block, Provo Craft.

WHAT'S IN A NAME?

Create a keepsake for your child and design a page all about his or her name. Why did you choose the name? Does it have historic significance, or is it a name from your ancestry? What does the name mean? Was it a popular name when you chose it, or were you trying to choose something different? Writing the answers to questions like these will provide interesting, meaningful information for your child as he or she grows older.

"One Year Old's Pooh Party"

by Tawnya Rhode
West Linn, OR
Supplies *Scissors:* Seagull and Bubbles edges, Fiskars; *Letter stickers:* Creative Memories; *Punch:* Family Treasures; *Stickers:* Sandylion; Mrs. Grossman's; *Winnie the Pooh:* Traced from a "Pooh" book.

"Happy Birthday to Me"

by Tawnya Rhode
West Linn, OR
Supplies *Scissors:* Colonial edge,
Fiskars; *Stickers:* Disney;
Mrs. Grossman's.

"A Walk Through My 1st Year

by Deb Day, Coon Rapids, MN
Supplies *Letter stickers:* Creative Memories; *Die cuts:* Source unknown; *Paper:* The Paper Patch.

andrew and sydney

Check out how three scrapbookers juggle twins

WHEN MELISSA MORTENSEN of Louisville, Kentucky, takes her babies Andrew and Sydney out, she inevitably gets asked, "How far apart are they?" Not only do the two babies differ by several pounds and a few inches, they have different hair and eye colors and unique personalities. Melissa enjoys the reactions when she replies, "Thirty-eight minutes."

With twins to keep her constantly busy, Melissa asked *Creating Keepsakes* to find scrapbookers to create layouts for these adorable photos. Three talented scrapbookers—Kathy Petersen, Allison Strine and Melanie Pontius—accepted the challenge. Read on to see their approaches and why they chose them! ❤

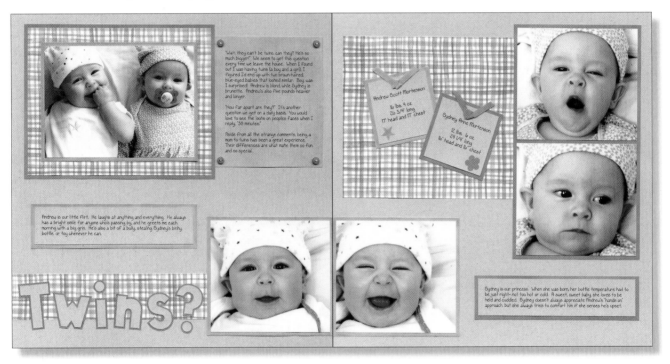

"Twins?"

by Kathy Petersen
Spanish Fork, UT

Supplies *Patterned papers:* Karen Foster Design (plaid) and Making Memories (green); *Punches:* Fiskars (star) and EK Success (flower and circle); *Lettering template:* ABC Tracers, EK Success; *Computer font:* DJ Jenn Pen, "Fontastics 2," D.J. Inkers; *Buttons:* Heartland Paper Co.; *Chalk:* Craf-T Products; *Other:* Thread.

KATHY'S APPROACH

With babies this cute, Kathy wanted to keep the layout simple. She chose papers and accents that coordinated with the green stars on Andrew's outfit and the purple flowers on Sydney's. "Because the children are twins, I wanted the focal point to be on both of them," Kathy says. She particularly liked how Melissa wrote about the babies together and separately.

With so much journaling, Kathy wanted to make sure the babies' differences in measurement weren't lost in the layout. She wrote the information on separate tags and matted each with paper that matched the outfit. She used star and flower punch accents on the tags to repeat the patterns in the babies' clothing.

"They can't be twins, can they? He's so much bigger!"

We seem to get this question every time we leave the house. When I found out I was having twins I figured I'd end up with two matching brown haired, blue-eyed babies. Boy was I surprised! Andrew is blond, while Sydney is a brunette. Andrew's also longer and five pounds heavier.

"How far apart are they?" is another question we get on a daily basis. I love to see the looks on people's faces when I reply, "Thirty-eight minutes".

Aside from all the strange comments, being a mom to twins has been a great experience. Their differences are what make them so special.

Sydney Anne Mortenson
Weight: 12 pounds, 6 ounces
Length: 24 1/4 inches
Head and chest are both 16 inches

Andrew Scott Mortenson
Weight: 16 pounds, 4 ounces
Length: 26 3/4 inches
Head and chest are both 17 inches

Sydney Anne

Sydney is our princess. When she was born, her bottle temperature had to be just right; not too hot or cold. A sweet, sweet baby, she loves to be held and cuddled. Sydney doesn't always appreciate Andrew's "hands on" approach, but she tries to comfort him if she senses he's upset.

Andrew Scott

Andrew is our little flirt. He laughs at anything and everything. He always has a bright smile for anyone who's passing by, and he greets me each morning with a big grin. He's also a bit of a bully, stealing Sydney's binky, bottle or toy whenever he can.

"Sydney Anne and Andrew Scott"

by Allison Strine
Atlanta, GA

Supplies *Patterned paper:* Karen Foster Design; *Vellum:* The Paper Company; *Silver paper:* Paper Adventures; *Flower die cuts:* Jolee's Boutique, Stickopotamus; *Punches:* All Night Media (hand and foot) and Marvy Uchida (circle); *Computer font:* CAC Leslie, downloaded from the Internet; *Glue dots:* Glue Dots International; *Pop dots:* All Night Media; *Fiber:* Fabulous Fibers; *Paper cord:* JudiKins; *Baby buggy:* Allison's own design; *Other:* Tulle.

ALLISON'S APPROACH

Allison found the twins' facial expressions so endearing that she wanted to make them the focal point of the layout. She worked with enlarged copies of three of the five photos to draw attention to the babies.

To represent the intimate bond between twins, Allison created half of a yin yang symbol with her textured background paper. She wanted a single, strong accent to finish the layout. The inspiration for the baby buggy came from a pre-made embellishment by Hirschberg Schutz & Co.

Snatch candid photos of your children's personalities.

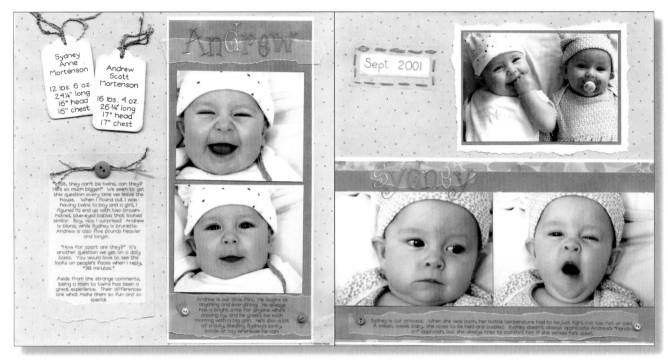

"Sept. 2001"

by Melanie Pontius
North Ogden, UT

Supplies *Patterned papers:* The Robin's Nest Press (purple) and Debbie Mumm, Creative Imaginations (dots); *Computer font:* CK Primary, "The Art of Creative Lettering" CD, *Creating Keepsakes; Buttons:* Making Memories (large) and Dress It Up (small), Jesse James Co.; *Heart punch:* EK Success; *Fiber:* On the Surface; *Vellum:* Paper Adventures; *Die-cut tags:* Stampin' Up!; *Letter stickers:* Provo Craft; *Embroidery floss:* DMC; *Chalk:* Stampendous!; *Foam tape:* Pop-It-Up; *Photo corners:* Pioneer Photo Albums; *Pen:* Zig Writer, EK Success.

MELANIE'S APPROACH

Melanie, who is expecting her first baby, was excited to scrapbook these photos. "It's the first baby scrapbooking I've done," she admits. With two adorable subjects to work with, she wanted to focus on the photos, individually and together.

"Since the babies are twins," she says, "I wanted to individualize each child, to show that even as tiny as they are, they are so different." Yet, because Andrew and Sydney are twins, Melanie knew she also had to show that they are alike. She positioned the individualized journaling under each child's pictures and set the other journaling off to the side.

The Simple Charms of Childhood

Illustration by Ann Boyajian

SCRAPBOOK THE FREEDOM AND FUN

In an ever-changing world, some things refuse to change—like the simple charms of just being a child. Aren't you glad?

EVERY NOW AND THEN, my children and I have a friendly argument over who can lay claim to the better childhood. For instance, how can you compare a grape Nehi in a glass bottle to a drink from a plastic pouch? Or riding in the front seat of the car, snuggled between Dad and Mom, to being strapped in your own bucket seat in the back of the minivan? Or shopping downtown with Grandma at the five-and-dime to fighting the crowds at the mall? >> by Rebecca Sower

Figure 1. Jot down random thoughts from your own childhood. If you don't, who will? *Page by Rebecca Sower.* **Supplies** *Handmade paper:* Books by Hand; *Stamping ink:* Creative Beginnings; *Alphabet rubber stamps:* Non Sequitur; *Mini hole punch:* McGill; *Pen:* Zig Writer, EK Success; *Colored inks:* Jacquard Products; *Brayer:* Speedball; *Hand-dyed ribbon:* ArtChix; *Other:* Eyelet and string. *Ideas to note:* The colored inks were applied to pieces of vellum with a brayer. Rebecca wrote the journaling after the inks dried.

The next time you notice a child simply being a child, take a minute to reflect, appreciate and refresh.

No Grown-ups Allowed

Thank goodness, some things never change. There's no substitute for making mud pies. Lying on your back in the grass, watching clouds roll by. Making daisy-chain necklaces. Creating a "no grown-ups allowed" clubhouse in the back of the barn. Lolling about on a do-nothing summer afternoon.

My only wish is that childhood would last much longer than it does. What if we could capture and hold on to fragments of our own childhoods as well as the flurry-by days of our offspring? That's what *scrapbooks* are for!

Let me offer some suggestions for pulling together your best possible memories of childhood pleasures.

Close Your Eyes

Most of us don't have thousands of pictures from our childhoods. Still, I've found that taking just one or two photographs of myself as a youngster, finding a quiet moment and reflecting, gives memories from long ago a passageway back.

Pick up a photo of yourself as a child and, without worrying about the particular event or place and time, close your eyes and

"become" that child again in your mind. I've surprised myself with the childhood memories that have sprung to life through this primitive exercise.

One at a time, as those random thoughts race across your memory, jot them down on a notepad. You don't need to worry if the memories are unrelated, the facts are sketchy, or they're from different points in time. Instead, just jot down what you recall. You can then create a "Random Memories from Childhood" layout (Figure 1) showcasing what you've remembered. Keep this in mind: If you

Figure 2. What is one of your favorite childhood memories? With or without photos, tell about it. *Page by Rebecca Sower.* **Supplies** *Alphabet rubber stamps:* PSX Design; *Stamping ink:* Close To My Heart; *Tree punch:* EK Success; *Pens:* Zig Writer (black) and Zig Scroll & Brush (brown), EK Success; *Postcard:* Iris Publishing; *Raffia:* Mudlark Papers; *Brown ink:* Sanford. *Idea to note:* To create the background effect, Rebecca placed a shipping tag randomly on her background paper and sponged around it with brown ink.

don't document these thoughts and memories, they may never resurface again. Only you can do this.

Who Needs Photos?

Allow me to jump onto my scrapbooking soapbox for a moment. *If the only memories we're capturing are those caught on film, we're leaving out significant portions of our legacy.* Okay, I'm back down now, so let's continue.

When you reflect back on your childhood, what are some of your fondest memories? Family vacations to the beach? A week each summer at your cousin's house in the country? Playing with neighborhood friends?

Some of my most enjoyable moments as a young girl were spent at summer camp with friends from church. To my knowledge, not one photo of this experience exists. Does that mean I shouldn't bother even touching on those moments in my scrapbooks? You know my answer to that. So, sans photographs, I created a layout (Figure 2) listing the highlights I recall from the rustic campground tucked up in the Smoky Mountains of Tennessee.

Childhood ✻ ✻ ✻ ✻ ✻ ✻ ✻ ✻ ✻ ✻ ✻ ✻ ✻ ✻ ✻ ✻

Figure 3. Don't you love the simplicity of childhood pleasures? Sometimes all that's required is a *tree*! *Pages by Rebecca Sower. Pages by Rebecca Sower.*
Supplies *Specialty paper:* Books by Hand; *Watercolors:* Winsor & Newton; *Alphabet rubber stamps:* Turtle Press; *Pen:* Zig Writer, EK Success; *Green stamping ink:* Ranger Industries; *Tree stamp:* PSX Design; *Library sleeve:* European Papers; *Coin envelope:* Silver Crow Creations; *Other:* Glassine envelope, mini kraft bag, twig, embroidery floss and oak leaf.

The Here and Now

Quite likely, you're already doing a super job capturing most of the simple pleasures of your child's life. You're snapping rolls of photographs at birthday parties, capturing memories from school programs, documenting family vacations, and even capturing those sweet, simple moments when your child is just being himself or herself around the house. That's terrific—keep up the good work! Still, don't overlook other opportunities to creatively capture the simple joys of carefree childhood.

Here are some ideas:

✻ Make a quick list of some simple childhood pleasures. Now, whether or not you have a picture for each activity, create a "Childhood Pleasures" layout showcasing miscellaneous photos of your little ones.

✻ Create a layout that focuses on the timelessness of an element, such as a tire swing or a sandbox. I chose to focus on a tree, any tree, for a layout about how childhood and trees seem to go hand-in-hand (see Figure 3).

I was lucky enough to find photos of my children in trees, but that wouldn't have been a requirement. Whether you're highlighting a sky full of fluffy clouds or a mud puddle, tie these unchanging foundations of childhood into a creative layout to express your appreciation for the simplicity of being a child.

✻ Consider creating a small album where the theme of each page is a simple childhood pleasure. Some suggestions? Flying a kite, wading in a creek, peanut butter and jelly sandwiches, lemonade stands, the ice cream truck, hide-and-seek, ghost stories, catching fireflies and more.

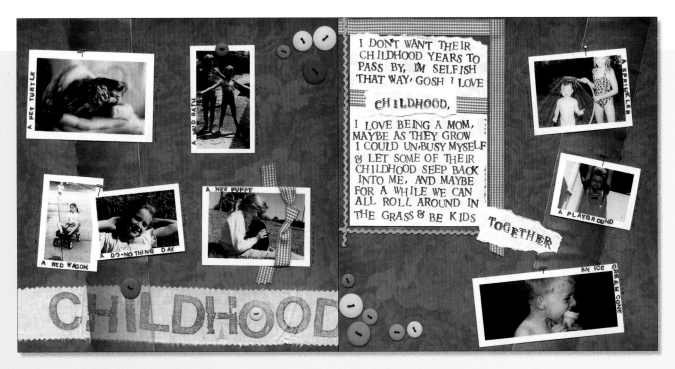

I DON'T WANT THEIR CHILDHOOD YEARS TO PASS BY, I'M SELFISH THAT WAY, GOSH I LOVE **CHILDHOOD**,

I LOVE BEING A MOM, MAYBE AS THEY GROW I COULD UN-BUSY MYSELF & LET SOME OF THEIR CHILDHOOD SEEP BACK INTO ME, AND MAYBE FOR A WHILE WE CAN ALL ROLL AROUND IN THE GRASS & BE KIDS TOGETHER

CHILDHOOD

Figure 4. What signifies childhood to you? Pen your musings about the fleeting years of youth. *Pages by Rebecca Sower.* **Supplies** *Patterned paper:* Design Originals (background), Anna Griffin (journaling block); *Alphabet rubber stamps:* Turtle Press; *Buttons:* Making Memories; *Stamping ink:* StazOn, Tsukineko; *Photo-editing software:* Adobe PhotoShop; *Other:* Ribbon, muslin and t-pins.

Childhood Connections

I'm a big believer in making connections through my scrapbooks. This means that anytime something happens today that brings to mind something from the past, I hone in on it. For instance, one day I stepped outside to find my children covered in mud. They'd discovered a squishy, messy kind of fun with a water hose and dirt.

After the shock wore off, I had a flashback to a time when my cousin and I found an almost empty pond. We were gradually up to our necks in cool, slimy *mud.* I took photos of my mud puppies, and when I create a layout for these photos, I will most definitely work into the journaling the story of my muddy adventure (yes, even without a photo of muddy me).

The Other Side

I don't have to watch a child playing for long before I wish I were a child again, too. From the desk where I work at my computer, I can watch through the window and see my children playing kickball, croquet or whatever the game of the day may be. It's difficult to resist the temptation to put down my work and run out there and join in.

Some days that's exactly what I do. And sometimes I just watch my kids and savor the moments of their childhood, their youth, because I know it's speeding past me. I chose to put down some of these thoughts on paper, then I created a layout (Figure 4) stating just what I was feeling about my own children's youth and my view from the other side of childhood.

Whether the child is your own or not, the next time you notice a child simply being a child, take a minute to reflect, appreciate and refresh. That's what childhood is all about—simplicity, freedom and pleasure. Come to think of it, that's what our scrapbooks should be about, too. ♥

Use WordArt in Microsoft Word to create a hand-drawn look. *Page and samples by Erin Lincoln.* **Supplies** *Patterned paper:* Chatterbox for EK Success (red) and Patchwork Paper Designs (yellow); *Computer fonts:* Nevermind and Think Small, downloaded from *www.two-peasinabucket.com*; *Pens:* Zig Writer and Zig Scroll & Brush, EK Success; *Punches:* EK Success; *Fiber:* Rubba Dub Dub, Art Sanctum; *Tags:* Making Memories; *Other:* Buttons and tag envelopes.

1 Choose and position your fonts.

2 Using the WordArt option, switch the word to outline form, leaving the middle blank. Increase the outline by 2 to 3 full points.

3 Go over the outline with black pen. Don't follow the lines too closely as you want it to look random.

4 Color between the lines. Don't be afraid to be sloppy!

Faux Hand Lettering

I've long admired hand lettering, but have a hard time getting it to look right. Not to be discouraged, especially after looking at my vastly underused collection of pens, I found an alternative to fool any observer into believing that I'm a whiz with a Zig marker. Here's a step-by-step list to help you master the art of faux (fake) hand lettering:

1 Using Microsoft Word, type the title you'd like to faux hand letter and select a font. (Thick fonts with soft curves work best.)

2 Select your word and open up your drawing toolbar. This can be found by right-clicking in your toolbar area and selecting "Drawing." Click on the "Insert WordArt" icon. A menu will appear and you can choose an outline format for your word.

3 Make the outline a little thicker by clicking the "Line Style" icon in the drawing toolbar. Your outline should be around 1.5 points.

4 Position the title on your page, choose an appropriate font size, then print it out.

5 Next, take a fine-tipped black marker and trace the outline. Don't follow the lines perfectly—you want what you're drawing to squiggle a little so it looks more hand-lettered.

6 Select a color pen and fill in your letters, the sloppier the better. This is your excuse to color outside the lines! I found a brush style marker works best because you can fill the letter with just one stroke, making it seem more natural. Shade and decorate the letters as desired.

—*Erin Lincoln, Frederick, MD*

5 Shade as desired.

field day

barbeque

reunion

recreation

relaxation

A boy and his trains

Elijah loves to play with his wooden "choo choo trains" set. He has always liked the set but recently it has started to border on obsession. Most days the first thing he wants to do when he wakes up is play with his trains. He has the tracks sprawled out across his room (and sometimes into the hallway), and throws a fit when we try to clean them up.

Since getting a Thomas trains set and videos from Nana for Christmas he has begun to play-act with the trains. He knows all their names and will have them converse with one another. It is the cutest thing to watch him hold a train in each hand and have one say to the other, "Hi, um watcha doin'? I goin' in da tunnel".

It is even more fun to play trains with him. I know the two of us could spend hours building and rebuilding tracks together, and some days we have come pretty close.

January 2003

chugga
chugga
choo!
choo!

"A Boy and His Trains"

by Shanté Welch
Mason, OH
Supplies *Letter stickers:* Sonnets, Creative Imaginations; *Letter stamps:* Hero Arts; *Stamping ink:* Source unknown; *Other:* Brads.

"Straight Talk"

by Ann-Marie Weiss
Oakland, CA
Supplies *Patterned paper:* 7 Gypsies; *Textured paper:* Bazzill Basics; *Letter stamps:* Wordsworth (large), Rubber Moon (small); *Stamping ink:* ColorBox, Clearsnap; *Ribbon:* C.M. Offray & Son; *Computer font:* Century Gothic, Microsoft Word; *Embroidery yarn:* Designs for the Needle; *Other:* Charm.

STRAIGHT talk

You just couldn't get your dad's hair. It had to be mine. Fine, straight, with bangs as sharp as razor blades. I never had blond hair, so the color must be from your dad. But where did his curls go? When you were babies, there was still hope. At bath time, I would play with the little ringlets, hoping they would stay after the hair dried. But no, the dry hair would just go limp and straight. Jessie, you always had the softest hair, even some locks, and I would beg the hairdressers to save "as much as possible." But each haircut left fever curls behind, as your hair went from baby wisps to toddler mane. This photo makes it all abundantly clear. Both of you have inherited my hair problems: hundreds of imprecise haircuts, shelves full of useless hair products, a couple of bad perms (if you feel brave), and many sad moments at the hairdresser await you. Sorry girls. Just wanted to give it to you straight.

"le Dita"

by Tracy Kyle
Coquitlam, BC, Canada
Supplies *Specialty paper:* Source unknown; *Computer fonts:* da Vinci and Soli, P22 Type Foundry; *Conchos:* Scrapworks.

It is just a silly little rhyme but it brings the biggest smile to Isabella's face. Nonna has been teaching her many Italian rhymes and stories, but this is her favourite. It gives me so much joy to watch them interact, and they are truly the best of friends.

Isabella does not understand that Nonna is getting old and her health is failing. In the past year Nonna has been hospitalized a few times and it just seems to make little things like this silly rhyme mean so much more. I am so thankful that Isabella has the love of a wonderful grandmother — I am thankful for this little rhyme — I am thankful for all that they share.

"Treasure Youth"

by Julie Scattaregia
Carmel, IN
Supplies *Patterned papers and wire expressions:* Sonnets, Creative Imaginations; *Vellum:* The Paper Company; *Computer fonts:* CK Script and CK Journaling, "The Best of Creative Lettering" CD Combo, *Creating Keepsakes;* Snaps, eyelet charms, eyelet letters, fibers and key tags: Making Memories; *Other:* Gems.

May you never lose your youthful desire to:

hang upside down
run through a sprinkler
go barefoot and blow bubbles
catch lightening bugs
whirl a lighted sparkler
enjoy a backyard picnic
lie on your back and look at the clouds

"Cousins"

by Mindy Bush
Idaho Falls, ID
Supplies *Patterned paper:*
7 Gypsies; *Computer font:* 2Peas
Flea Market by Sharon Soneff,
downloaded from *www.two-
peasinabucket.com*; *Microscope
slides:* FoofaLa; *Transparency:*
3M; *Other:* Machine stitching
and mini-brads.

Sarah, has

So much FUN with
her Cousins! These
photos were taken at
her very first slumber
party at grandma &
grandpa Linning's
house I'm so thrilled that they get along
So well because next fall we'll be living
across the street from them! They are
moving here from Arizona and just bought
the land across the street from where our
house is being built! I'm looking forward
to being near these little cuties as well!

IDEA TO NOTE: The
borders on the lay-
out were inspired by
the canvas tent in
the photos.

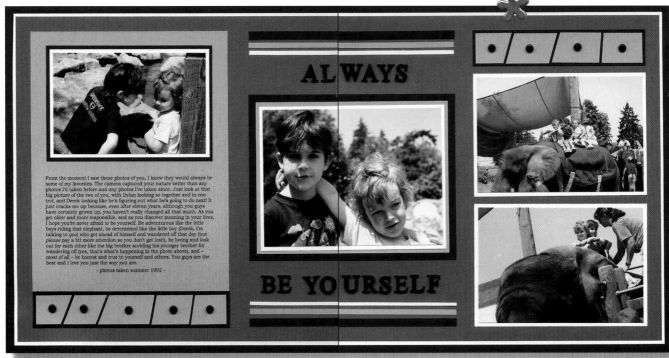

"Be Yourself"

by Maya Opavska, Redmond, WA
Supplies *Computer font:* Bookman Old Style, Microsoft Word;
Letter stickers: Colorbök; *Snaps:* Making Memories.

"Spark the Imagination"

by Kimberly Lund
Wichita, KS
Supplies *Patterned paper:* Sonnets, Creative Imaginations; *Computer fonts:* CK Primary ("the Imagination"), "The Art of Creative Lettering" CD, *Creating Keepsakes*; 2Peas Bad Hair Day ("Spark") and 2Peas Little Ladybug (journaling), downloaded from *www.two-peasinabucket.com; Fibers:* Fibers by the Yard; *Chalk:* Craf-T Products.

"Friendly Piggies"

by Nicole Gartland
Portland, OR
Supplies *Patterned paper:* Carolee's Creations; *Computer fonts:* CK Journaling (journaling), "The Best of Creative Lettering" CD Vol. 2, *Creating Keepsakes*; Freshscript (script subhead and main title), Spring ("Piggies") and Franks (small titles), downloaded from the Internet.

IDEAS TO NOTE: Karen created the frame for her focal-point photo by scoring and folding a Shotz photograph into a 3-D frame. To dress up the letter stickers, she placed a strip of tacky tape over the letters and added beads, shaved ice and foil.

"Impulse Buy"

by Karen Burniston
Littleton, CO

Supplies *Patterned paper:* Renaé Lindgren, Creative Imaginations; *Photograph, letter stickers and tag:* Shotz, Creative Imaginations; *Letter stamps:* Hero Arts (Tiny Cabaret), Rubber Stampede (Fun Type); *Computer font:* 2Peas Tuxedo, downloaded from *www.twopeasinabucket.com*; *Eyelets:* Scrappin' Fools; *Tacky tape, beads and shaved ice:* Magic Scraps; *Other:* Foil and fibers.

"Birthday Tea"

by Julie Scattaregia
Carmel, IN
Supplies *Patterned papers:* Bo-Bunny Press, me & my BIG ideas, Kangaroo & Joey; *Vellum:* The Paper Company; *Computer font:* CK Curly, "The Best of Creative Lettering" CD Combo, *Creating Keepsakes; Tags and brads:* Making Memories; *Stickers:* David Walker and Sonnets, Creative Imaginations; *Charms:* Card Connection; *Ribbon and ribbon accents:* C.M. Offray & Son; *Rubber stamps:* Stamp Craft; *Other:* Stamping ink.

"Family Movie Night"

by Mellette Berezoski
Crosby, TX

Supplies *Computer fonts:*
Mistral and Fusi, downloaded
from the Internet; *Fibers:*
Adornaments, EK Success;
Eyelets: Prym-Dritz.

"Grandma's Playdough"

by Amy Grendell
Silverdale, WA

Supplies *Patterned paper:* Keeping
Memories Alive; *Rubber stamps:*
PSX Design; *Pen:* Slick Writer,
American Crafts; *Computer font:*
2Peas Miss Happy, downloaded
from *www.twopeasinabucket.com*;
Buttons, stitches and bookplate:
Making Memories; *Mini paper
bag:* Impress Rubber Stamps.

Family Movie Night

Daddy
Favorite Family Movie: Ice Age
Favorite Snack: Ice Cream
Favorite Drink: Hot Chocolate with Marshmallows
Trademark: Gets up constantly for more snacks and can finish entire bucket of ice cream in one night

Mommy
Favorite Family Movie: The Prince of Egypt
Favorite Snack: Almond M&M's
Favorite Drink: French Vanilla Flavored Hot Chocolate
Trademark: Is most comfortable covered with at least four blankets

Maysie
Favorite Family Movie: Shrek
Favorite Snack: Pop Rocks
Favorite Drink: French Vanilla Flavored Hot Chocolate
Trademark: Sips hot chocolate with a spoon and watches with her blankie up to her nose

Dayton
Favorite Family Movie: Is there a Wheel of Fortune movie?
Favorite Snack: Popcorn
Favorite Drink: Ice Cold Whole Milk
Trademark: Talks through the first half hour and then falls asleep

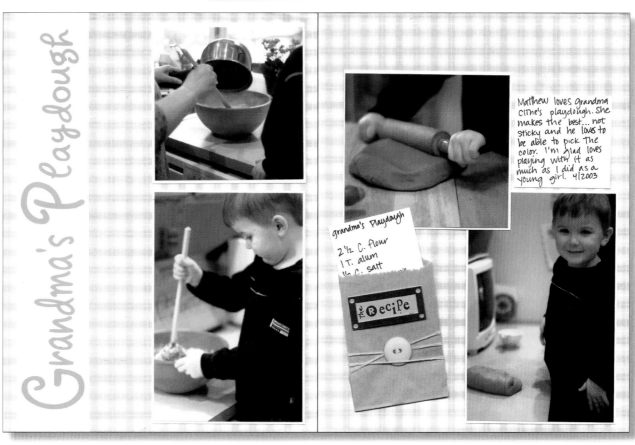

Grandma's Playdough

Matthew loves grandma Cline's playdough. She makes the best... not sticky and he loves to be able to pick the color. I'm glad loves playing with it as much as I did as a young girl. 4/2003

grandma's Playdough
2½ C. flour
1 T. alum
½ C. salt

The Recipe

Back to school

attire

Being the fashion forward 2nd grader that he is, Iain put a lot of thought into his "first day of school" outfit. The shirt was from Old Navy, the shorts were from Target (purchased by Dad) and the shoes were Vans. We bought the shoes earlier in the summer to attend a wedding (Brian and Charity's — our neighbors) and Iain grew out of them before the first day. We had to buy another pair after school. He picked out the Nikes.   August 2001

IDEA TO NOTE: Kim wrote the word "Attire" backward on black cardstock, then trimmed and adhered it to the layout.

"Back-to-School Attire"

by Kim Heffington
Avondale, AZ
Supplies *Vellum:* Bazzill Basics; *Computer font:* CK Handprint, "The Best of Creative Lettering" CD Combo, *Creating Keepsakes.*

"Our Wonderful Student"

by Christina Chrushch, Rocky Mount, NC
Supplies *Computer font:* Calvin and Hobbs, downloaded from the Internet; *Page accents:* Fresh Cuts, BumperCrops for EK Success; *Ruler button:* Source unknown; *Pop dots:* All Night Media; *Pen:* Zig Writer, EK Success. *Tip:* Christina scanned and reduced her son's progress report and report card, printed them on Kodak paper, and attached them to her layout.

"Car Wash"

by Suzanne Lopez
Denver, CO
Supplies *Computer font:*
Typical Writer, downloaded
from the Internet.

IDEA TO NOTE: Julie used
duplicate photos or parts of
"not so great" photos to
accentuate little body parts.

"Every Little Part"

by Julie Scattaregia, Carmel, IN
Supplies *Patterned paper:* Making Memories*; Vellum:* The Paper Company*; Computer font:* CK Script, "The Best of Creative
Lettering" CD Vol. 1, *Creating Keepsakes; Craft wire:* Artistic Wire Ltd.*; Square punch:* Marvy Uchida*; Gems:* Stampfetti*;
Alphabet rubber stamps:* Stamp Craft*; Stamping ink:* ColorBox, Clearsnap, Inc.*; Other:* Ribbon.

"Laugh"

by Jenny Benge
Battle Ground, WA
Supplies *Patterned paper:* Dana Simson,
Colorbök; *Computer font:* Unknown,
downloaded from *twopeasinabucket.com*;
Fiber: On the Surface; *Embroidery floss:*
DMC; *Jump ring:* Westrim Crafts; *Pens:* Zig
Writer, EK Success; *Chalk:* Craf-T Products;
Flowers: Jenny's own designs.

"Austin, Summer 2000"

by Yvonne Schultz
South Jordan, UT
Supplies *Mulberry paper:* Source unknown;
Computers fonts: Think Small, downloaded from
twopeasinabucket.com; Scriptina and Carpenter,
downloaded from the Internet; Times New Roman,
Microsoft Word; *Leaf rubber stamp:* Stampin' Up!;
Stamping ink: ColorBox, Clearsnap, Inc.; *Mesh:*
Magic Mesh, Avant Card.

"Moments"

by Irma Gabbard
San Diego, CA
Supplies *Textured paper:* DMD Industries; *Alphabet rubber stamps:* PSX Design; *Stamping ink:* Tsukineko; *Computer fonts:* Times New Roman, Microsoft Word; CAC Logo, downloaded from the Internet; *Fibers:* On the Surface; *Pebbles:* Halcraft; *Square punch:* Marvy Uchida.

JOURNALING TIPS

As I watched my daughter color the other day, I noticed something. The little rolls of chub that used to encircle her wrists were no longer there ... you know, the ones all pudgy babies seem to have? I tried to pinpoint when this transformation took place, when these new, slender wrists came to be. And I couldn't. It must have been a slow change that took place, unnoticed, as I was caught up in the day-to-day hubbub. I suddenly realized she had adopted several girl-like characteristics, seemingly overnight!

Most of our layouts document the events we see—firsts, birthdays, holidays. But what about the unseen transitions that mark the evolution from baby to child, child to young adult? These milestones are certainly as important, aren't they? Including them on layouts through journaling will allow your child's album to present the "complete picture."

Every now and then, write with the "when did you ..." or "what happened to ..." perspective to focus on the progress you *didn't* see. In the form of a letter, narrative or list, note your child's new looks, behaviors and accomplishments. Although we can't witness *every* change in our children, we can appreciate the differences—and I'm sure our kids will love to "hear" about them someday.

—by Denise Pauley

Journal about the sudden discoveries that convince you your child is growing up. *Page by Denise Pauley.* **Supplies** *Patterned paper:* Karen Foster Design; *White textured paper:* Scrap-Ease; *Computer font:* PC Script, Provo Craft; *Lettering template:* A Fancy Start, ScrapPagerz.com; *Pen:* Zig Millennium, EK Success.

"Playing with Fuzzy"

by Jodi Olson
Sammamish, WA
Supplies *Patterned paper:* Provo Craft; *Vellum:* PrintWorks; *Leaf punch:* Marvy Uchida; *Jar sticker:* Provo Craft; *Pen:* Pigma Micron, Sakura; *Other:* Yarn.

IDEA TO NOTE: Jodi put the leaf and caterpillar onto a piece of vellum, then placed the jar sticker on top and cut the sticker out.

"Jeepers, Creepers"

Sally Garrod, Haslett, MI
Supplies *Patterned paper:* Design Originals; *Lettering template:* Smarty, Déjà Views, The C-Thru Ruler Co.; *Computer font:* CK Handprint, "The Best of Creative Lettering" CD Combo, *Creating Keepsakes; Frog punch:* McGill; *Pop dots:* Cut-It-Up; *Other:* Raffia.

"Brenna Loves"

by Jennifer Wohlenberg
Stevenson's Ranch, CA
Supplies *Patterned paper:* Keeping Memories Alive; *Lettering template:* Kiki ("x"), ScrapPagerz.com; *Heart punch:* Emagination Crafts.

IDEA TO NOTE: Mary Anne created a photo collage on her computer using Adobe Photo Deluxe. She then printed the quote on transparency film to create an overlay for the collage.

"A Girl Is ..."

by Mary Anne Walters, Monk Sherborne, United Kingdom
Supplies *Computer font:* Girls Are Weird, downloaded from the Internet; *Other:* Quote by Alan Beck.

"Everyone Needs Their Own Spot"

by Tammy Krummel, Hancock, IA
Supplies *Patterned paper:* Bo-Bunny Press (green plaid); Mary Engelbreit, InterArt Dist./Sunrise (flowered); The Paper Patch (black checked); *Stickers:* Mary Engelbreit, InterArt Dist./Sunrise (puppies and flowers); Source unknown (black and white border); *Puppy die cuts:* Wallies, McCall; *Lettering idea:* "Classic," *The Art of Creative Lettering*, Creating Keepsakes Books; *Pen:* Zig Writer, EK Success.

"Hunter"

by Angie Pitre, Kentville, NS, Canada
Supplies *Lettering templates:* Scrapbook (title) and funky (journaling), Provo Craft; *Leaf template:* Leaves, Provo Craft; *Stamping ink:* Dauber Duos, Tsukineko; *Maple leaf punch:* Family Treasures; *Pen:* Zig Millennium, EK Success.

IDEA TO NOTE: Tammy used Pop Dots by All Night Media to add dimension to the title on the layout. She also included dried ferns as accents.

"Country Path"

by Tammy Krummel, Hancock, IA

Supplies *Patterned paper:* Provo Craft (green swirl), Keeping Memories Alive (green speckled); *Mulberry paper:* PrintWorks; *Lettering idea:* "Bouquet," *The Art of Creative Lettering*, Creating Keepsakes Books; *Pens:* Tombow.

IDEA TO NOTE: Sharon used Pop-It-Ups by Cut-It-Up to add dimension to the title and journaling block.

"Faith Is Like a Little Seed"

by Sharon Lewis, Mesa, AZ

Supplies *Patterned paper:* Source unknown; *Specialty paper:* Personal Stamp Exchange (mulberry paper), Making Memories (vellum); *Stickers:* Paper House Productions; *Memorabilia pocket:* 3L Corporation; *Pen:* Zig Scroll & Brush, EK Success.

"Sarah"
by Robin Johnson
Farmington, UT
Supplies *Patterned vellum:* Whispers, Starlit Studio; *Colored vellum:* Paper Adventures; *Pen:* Zig Millennium, EK Success; *Chalk:* Chalk Pencils, Stabilo.

IDEA TO NOTE: Robin placed a piece of colored vellum over half of the patterned vellum to create a "color block" effect.

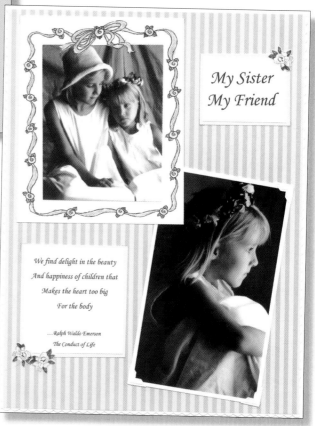

"My Sister, My Friend"
by Barbara Gardner
Scottsdale, AZ
Supplies *Patterned paper:* Paper Pizazz, Hot Off The Press; *Clip Art:* From My Hands to Your Heart, Provo Craft; *Computer font:* Source unknown; *Stickers:* Frances Meyer; *Scissors:* Scallop edge, Fiskars; *Photo corners:* Canson; *Ink pad:* Source unknown.

THREE WAYS TO CAPTURE YOUR CHILD'S PERSONALITY ON A PAGE

❶ Take a roll of black-and-white film of your child at least a few times a year. Turn off your flash and use soft, natural light to allow shadows to emphasize the contours of your child's face. You'll find that black-and-white pictures capture facial expressions and emotions you won't want to forget!

❷ Allow your child to become absorbed in an activity before taking pictures. Not every picture has to show your child's face looking at the camera. In fact, some of the most revealing pictures of children are taken without them even knowing it!

❸ Use journaling as a powerful tool to record things your child says or does that he or she may "grow out of." Tell stories, make lists, and have your child "narrate" a page or two.

sporting events & performances

turday morning trip to the football field so
major event.   Even though the football field
n field on campus.   The words: **Hut, Hike,**

time out

NOV   2002

Tee Ball

2
0
0

HOME

go

TOUCH DOWN

fight

02

play

LOCATION
GATE OR DOOR

UPPER

NORTHWEST
PRIDE
CRUSADERS

NORTHWEST
PRIDE
CRUSADERS

play har

applause

performers

competition

play-by-play

audience

"Soccer"

by Beth Rogers
Mesa, AZ
Supplies *Textured paper:* Bazzill Basics; *Computer fonts:* Times New Roman (title), Microsoft Publisher; Short Hand (journaling and title), package unknown; *Slide mounts:* Scrapworks; *Metallic rub-ons:* Craf-T Products.

"Tee Ball"

by Tonia Borrosch, Honeoye Falls, NY. Supplies *Patterned papers:* Karen Foster Design (red), 7 Gypsies (script), Creative Imaginations (blue); *Vellum:* The Write Stock; *Computer font:* 2Peas Hot Chocolate, downloaded from *www.twopeasinabucket.com*; *Tag:* Forget Me Not Designs; *Frame:* This & That, My Mind's Eye; *Slide holder and mini-brads:* Twopeasinabucket.com; *Letter stickers:* Nostalgiques, EK Success; *Rubber stamps:* All Night Media; *Letter stamps:* Stamper's Anonymous; *Stamping ink:* Memories (black); VersaMark, Tsukineko; *Embossing powder:* Ink Xpressions; *Tag:* Making Memories; *Paper clip:* Nunn Designs; *Baseball accent:* Shotz, Creative Imaginations.

"Cute"

by Donna Leslie
Tinley Park, IL
Supplies *Vellum:* The Paper Company; *Letter stickers and eyelets:* Making Memories; *Computer fonts:* PC Kick Plate, "Fontalicious" CD, Provo Craft; *Buttons:* Dress It Up; *Beads:* Westrim Crafts.

CUTE
don'tcha wish you
looked like me
I'm cute
Yeah, yeah, I'm cute
Whoo!!

You absolutely LOVE cheerleading! It all started with a summer pom-pom class. You had such a wonderful time. You memorized so many cheers and sang them all the time. Now you are a part of the Tiny Thunder Babes and look forward to cheerleading practice every week. Your favorite cheers are "I'm C-U-T-E" and "Firecracker". On this day you received your cheerleading award for the 2002-2003 season. Your squad performed for quite a crowd and the place went crazy! Everyone loved to watch the fabulous Tiny Thunder Babes! The best part was that Daddy and I got a chance to cheer for OUR favorite Thunder Babe!

"T-Ball"

by Cheryl Holzman
Tyngsboro, MA
Supplies *Patterned paper, stickers and eyelets:* Doodlebug Design; *Alphabet and metal tags:* Making Memories; *Computer font:* Garamouche, P22 Type Foundry; *Pen:* Zig Writer, EK Success; *Pop dots:* All Night Media; *Other:* Transparency.

Take me out to the ballgame...   May 03 '03
Katie, Mommy and Daddy were so surprised last fall when you mentioned that you wanted to play T-Ball in the spring. We signed you up and a few weeks before the start of the season, Daddy took you to Target to buy a glove. He also bought a bat and three balls, so excited to be buying sports equipment for his little ball-player. Paul Kyer, Dylan's Dad, called to let us know that you would be on his team, along with all of the other boys from the neighborhood. The name of your team is "The Marlins" and you chose number 11 for your shirt. The day of your first practice/game was a beautiful spring Saturday. Before the game, you and Daddy had a few practice throws in the front yard and then Daddy took you to the field and Mommy and Emily joined him later to watch you play. You did a great job paying attention to the coaches and showed great form on the ball field. Most of all, you had fun!

t BALL

"Ice Capades"

by Dino Watt, Newhall, CA
Supplies *Patterned paper:* K & Company; *Metal letters, snowflakes and tag:* Making Memories; *Letter stickers:* Shotz, Creative Imaginations; *Fishhook:* Dino's own design.

"Basketball Dreams"

by Angie Cramer, Medicine Hat, AB, Canada
Supplies *Computer font:* Arial, Microsoft Word; *Letter stamps:* PSX Design; *Circle punch:* Marvy Uchida; *Other:* Stamping ink.

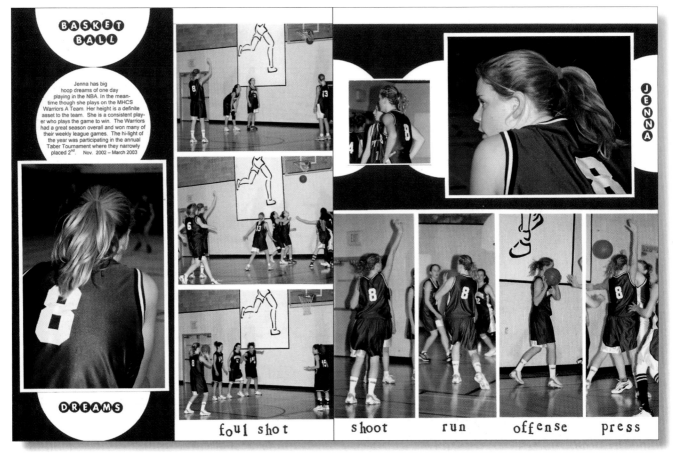

IDEA TO NOTE: Notice how Patricia extended the chalk lines from the baseball field outside of her photo to create a unique border on her page.

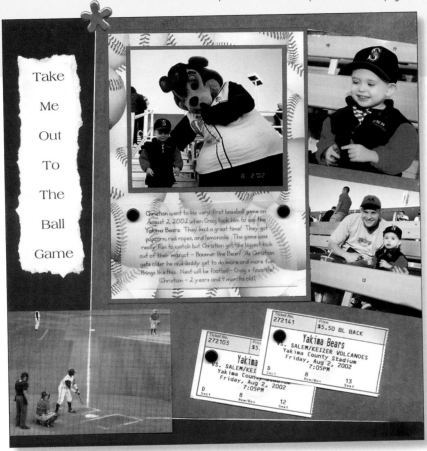

"Take Me Out to the Ballgame"

by Patricia Anderson
Selah, WA
Supplies *Patterned papers:* Sandylion (grass) and Frances Meyer (baseballs); *Vellum:* The Paper Company; *Computer fonts:* American Classic (title), Microsoft Word; CK Simple (journaling), "The Art of Creative Lettering" CD, *Creating Keepsakes;* *Brads:* Officemate; *Chalk:* Craf-T Products; *Other:* Tickets from the game.

"The Pool"

by Marnie Flores
Madison, WI
Supplies *Computer font:* Times New Roman, Microsoft Word; *Word rub-ons:* Simply Stated, Making Memories; *Other:* Pen.

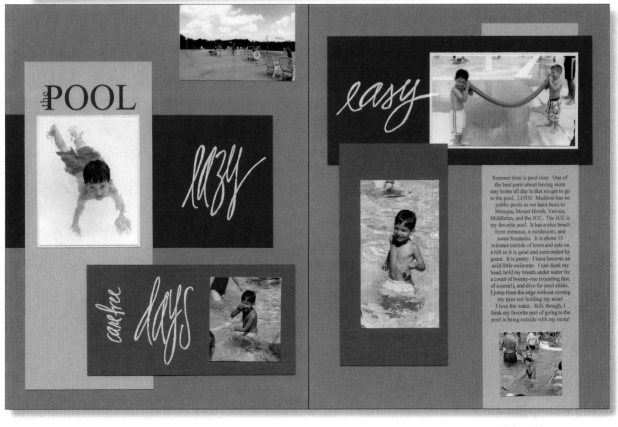

Marc 2002

IDEA TO NOTE:
Pam created her layout using Adobe Photoshop Elements 2.0.

"Life Is a Game"

by Pam Talluto
Rochester Hills, MI
Supplies *Computer font:* Bookman Old Style, package unknown.

"7 on 7"

by Darlena Campbell
Houston, TX
Supplies *Patterned papers:* Embossing Arts (lava rock) and Whole Paper (football); *Vellum:* The Paper Company (white) and A Labaster Vellum (translucent); *Computer font:* Unknown; *Mesh:* Magenta; *Pop dots:* All Night Media; *Square punch:* Source unknown; *Other:* Raffia.

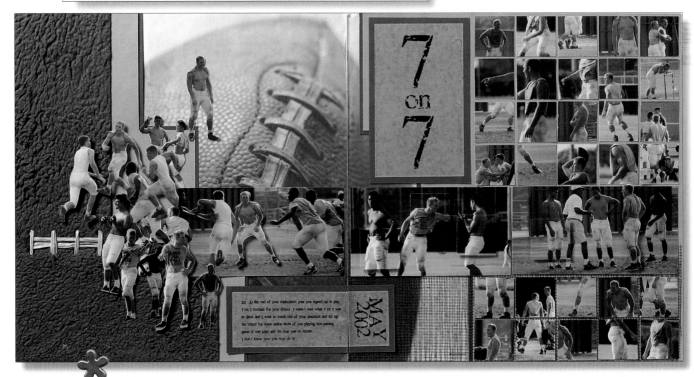

IDEAS TO NOTE: Darlena raised some of the photos on pop dots. To make the football, she punched holes on the backside of the lava rock paper and laced raffia through.

"The Agony of Defeat"

by Ali Moll
Bountiful, UT
Supplies *Vellum:* The Paper Company; *Computer font:* CK Newsprint, "Fresh Fonts" CD, *Creating Keepsakes; Title:* Simply Stated, Making Memories; *Brads:* Making Memories; *Ribbon:* Jo-Ann Stores.

M y favorite layouts are the ones that just seem to pop into my mind out of the blue, perfectly and completely designed. I don't know where those ideas come from, but I can't help but think my mind is constantly in "scrapbooking mode!" Realistically, those "out of the blue" ideas are few and far between.

So, what do I do the rest of the time? I start with my photographs. I'm a slow scrapbooker, and I won't work on a layout unless I'm completely inspired by the photographs. I really let my photos map out my layouts for me, from color choices to embellishments.

I usually work on a layout for a day or two. At night, when I'm in bed reading, I'll place my work-in-progress on my night table and glance over at it before I go to sleep. When I wake up in the morning, I often have a great idea for how to finish the layout. If the ideas still aren't there? Well, I have no problem setting a layout aside for several months, if need be! I've found that if I'm patient, the ideas will always come to me.

I don't rush myself. I hope that when I'm 80 I'll still have baby pictures of my children that I haven't scrapbooked yet. In fact, one of the things I love most about scrapbooking is telling a story from a perspective that may change from day to day, from year to year.

—*Karen Russell*

"I Hope You Dance"

by Karen Russell. **Supplies** *Patterned paper:* Daisy D's; *Computer fonts:* CK Gutenberg, "Fresh Fonts" CD and CK Bella "The Best of Creative Lettering" CD Vol. 3, *Creating Keepsakes;* Papyrus, downloaded from the Internet; *Conchos:* Scrapworks; *Clock:* 7 Gypsies; *Other:* Beads and hemp. *Idea to note:* Karen's photo lifts up to reveal journaling.

"Dance According to Emma"

by Shannon Taylor, Bristol, TN

Supplies *Patterned papers:* K & Company; *Velvet paper:* Sonburn; *Computer font:* Karaoke Superstar, downloaded from the Internet; *Letter stamps:* Source unknown; *Metal-rimmed tags:* Avery; *Charms:* Wisconsinplaza.com; *Embroidery floss:* DMC; *Thread:* Westrim Crafts; *Pen:* Zig Writer, EK Success; *Chalk:* Craf-T Products; *Other:* Beads and stamping ink.

"Passion for Dance"

by Tena Sprenger, Mesa, AZ

Supplies *Patterned papers:* Over The Moon Press (pink), EK Success; Paper Adventures (green); 7 Gypsies (script); *Embossed paper:* K & Company; *Vellum:* Paper Adventures; *Metal frames and heart eyelets:* Making Memories; *Letter stickers:* Flavia, Colorbök; *Quote sticker:* Wordsworth; *Dimensional adhesive:* Diamond Glaze, JudiKins; *Floral ribbon:* Wright's; *Mini-brads:* Boxer Scrapbook Productions; *Chalk:* Craf-T Products; *Computer font:* Dolphin, Microsoft Word.

The Case of the Bad Event Photographs

- **The Suspects:** Faraway Freda, Blurry Bonnie, Poorly Lit Paula
- **The Detective:** Licensed to Scrap, Kim Morgan and Licensed to Photograph, Stephanie Eldredge
- **The Assignment:** Take two sets of poor photographs (one from a baseball game, one from a dance recital) and scrapbook them on layouts that tell a story.

Case Solved:

Kim Morgan solved the case of the bad dance photographs by choosing her favorite shot of Danika, scanning it, cropping out the background and enlarging it. She trimmed the pictures of Danika on stage to place more emphasis on the girls and added them to the bottom of the page as a border (Figure 1).

The baseball solution? Kim didn't change the photographs; she just presented them in an appealing way. She chose a dark-red thread that matches Jordan's uniform. The color and the unique stitching draws the eye directly to Jordan and away from the imperfections in the photos (Figure 2).   →

Adorable!

Danika loved taking tap and ballet classes from Colette's Dancing School when she was three years old.

In these pictures, she performed on stage with her class to "Let's Dance" and "Kiss the Girl". All the girls were adorable, even as they invented their own dance routines to the program. Of course, as Danika's mom, I was sure that she was doing everything just right!

As you can see, Danika had stage presence even at the early age of three. Her love of dancing and performing lead to many more years of dance practices and performances.

June 6, 1995

Figure 1. Scan, crop and enlarge a photo of your subject to turn it into a focal point. *Page by Kim Morgan.* **Supplies** *Computer font:* Lucida Handwriting, Microsoft Word; *Chain:* Making Memories; *Paper charm:* Artsy Additions, Hot Off The Press; *Pop-up glue dots:* Glue Dots International; *Metallic rub-ons:* Craf-T Products; *Glue (for chain):* Scrappy Glue, Magic Scraps; *Other:* Ribbon.

The scrapbook page contains the following text elements:

Little League

It's not whether you win or lose... it's how you play the game.

Practice really works.

If at first you don't succeed... try, try again.

It takes a whole team to win a game.

Jordan learned so many valuable lessons from Little League this year. When I look back at his season, I can so clearly see how baseball was its own version of

Celebrate every success!

'Summer School'

Figure 3. Zoom your lens directly through the fence at the baseball field to get in close to the subject of your photograph. *Photo by Stephanie Eldredge.*

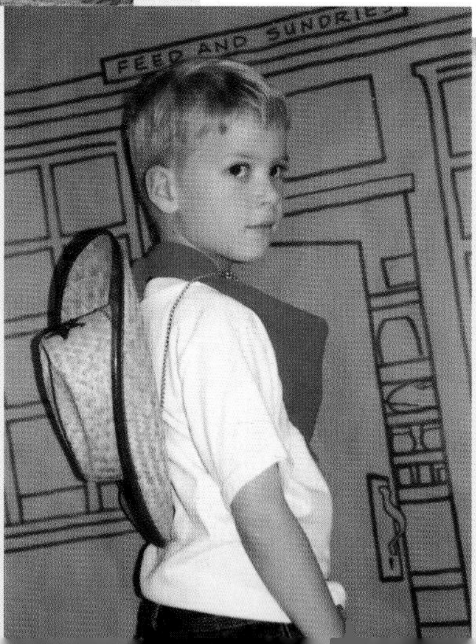

Figure 4. After the performance, snap a close-up of your child on stage. *Photo by Stephanie Eldredge.*

Case Solved

Figure 2. Use color to emphasize the subject of your photo. *Page by Kim Morgan.* **Supplies** *Computer font:* Poor Richard, Microsoft Word; *Brads:* Making Memories; *Embroidery floss:* DMC; *Square punch:* Marvy Uchida.

Top-Secret Tips:

Photographer Stephanie Eldredge captured Mitchell at bat by zooming the lens of her camera directly through the fence at the baseball field. Notice how Stephanie captured Mitchell's intense look of concentration and ready-to-swing stance as he prepares to swing the bat (Figure 3).

The photographers we talked with all admitted they have a hard time capturing excellent photos of dance recitals and school performances. As an audience member, you're often far away from the stage, and lighting conditions usually aren't optimal for good photography. Stephanie suggests taking several shots of your child on stage anyway (get to the performance early, get a seat in the front row, and use your zoom lens). After the performance, let the crowd clear out and then take a close-up shot of your child posed in front of stage props (Figure 4).

IDEA TO NOTE: Sharon cut the top-left photo and arranged the pieces to span the page.

"Painting Pictures"

by Sharon Whitehead, Vernon, BC, Canada
Supplies *Computer font:* Garamouche, P22 Type Foundry; *Flower die cuts:* Create-a-Cut; *Ribbon:* Welkmart; *Buttons:* Making Memories; *Chalk:* Craf-T Products; *Eyelets:* Impress Rubber Stamps; *Pop dots:* All Night Media.

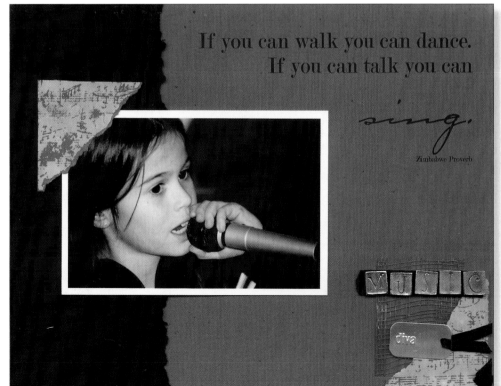

"Music"

by Dawn Brookey
La Crescenta, CA
Supplies *Computer fonts:* Modern No. 20, downloaded from the Internet; Carpenter, downloaded from *www.scrapvillage.com*; *Dog tag:* Clare Ultimo; *Pewter letter tiles:* Twopeasinabucket.com; *Rubber stamp:* Impression Obsession; *Other:* Handmade paper.

the big

Test

On November 17, Corey was tested for a higher rank in Taekwondo (the yellow belt). In order to move from a white belt to a yellow belt, Corey had to demonstrate Taekwondo "one-step" techniques. After three weeks of practice, he was ready.

"The Big Test"
by Shauna Devereux
Athens, GA
Supplies *Lettering template:* Blocky, Provo Craft; *Computer font:* Doodle Tipsy, "PagePrintables" CD Vol. 1, Cock-A-Doodle Design, Inc.; *Paper doll:* Paperkins, EK Success.

"What Gutter?"
by Kim Heffington
Avondale, AZ
Supplies *Wood paper:* Provo Craft; *Computer font:* Calendar, downloaded from the Internet; *Pen:* Zig Writer, EK Success.

FAMILY DATE NIGHT
DECEMBER 2000
Iain had been asking to go bowling for a while. We finally took him on our date night. His game has really improved. He picked up a few new moves & managed to keep the ball out of the gutter most of the night.

WHAT GUTTER?

IDEAS TO NOTE: The main photograph on the layout opens to reveal journaling and another photograph.

"Built for Champions"
by Jennifer Jensen
Hurricane, UT
Supplies *Vellum:* Paper Adventures; *Computer font:* CK Script, "The Best of Creative Lettering" CD Vol. 1, *Creating Keepsakes; Pen:* Zig Writer, EK Success; *Pop dots:* All Night Media.

PAGE STARTER: SCRAPBOOKING SPORTS

Whether you're scrapbooking your child's soccer season, your own softball victories or your favorite team's scores, chances are there's more to the story than you're telling on your pages! Sports and recreation are an important part of our lives, so try to capture what makes them so enjoyable. Here are a few ideas:

• Why did you choose the sports you play? Did you inherit your sporting abilities from your mother or father? Are you following a long-lived tradition of participating in a certain sport? Or did you branch out on your own and try something new?

• What aspects of your personality shine through while you're playing? Are there qualities you notice in your children as they participate in sports? What new things have you learned about yourself, your spouse or your children as you watch them play?

• How big a role do sporting activities play in your family members' daily lives? Do you incorporate recreation into every day, or does your family attend regular sporting events? Have certain sports become seasonal traditions for your family? Do you tend to participate in organized team sports or more leisurely individual activities? Does your choice in activities say something about the values you've tried to instill in your family?

try our spirit alphabet

Three cheers for your scrapbook pages

GIVE ME A "T"! Give me an "E"! Give me an "E"! Give me an "N"! What does it spell? Lots of friends, loads of fun and . . . serious scrapbooking potential!

Your teen years are packed with once-in-a-life-time experiences and a whole list of firsts—first driver's license, first car (or first accident!), first date, first dance, first kiss and first love, not to mention a few embarrassing moments along the way. I can't help but remember coming home from a school dance and learning later that my sisters had been watching the doorstep scene from a window overlooking the porch. Though I wasn't thrilled at the time, it's a funny memory that I now want to remember.

Teens today are definitely lucky when it comes to scrapbooking. With the industry overflowing with stylish products, there's no reason to save your pictures and memorabilia in a shoebox for years. You can turn them into "winning" layouts right now—and here's a creative lettering alphabet created just for you (Figure 1). Quick, grab a pen and we'll cheer you on to your next creative victory using the bold Spirit Alphabet.

Creating the Spirit Alphabet

❶ Using a pencil, write your word. Once the basic letters are drawn, add serifs at the ends of each line as shown.
❷ Create block letters by tracing around the letters

Figure 1. The academic Spirit Alphabet is perfect for all your school and extracurricular activity pages. **Supplies** *Patterned paper:* The Robin's Nest Press; *Pens:* Zig Millennium and Zig Writer, EK Success; *Colored pencils:* Prismacolor, Sanford.

ARTICLE BY HEATHER THATCHER

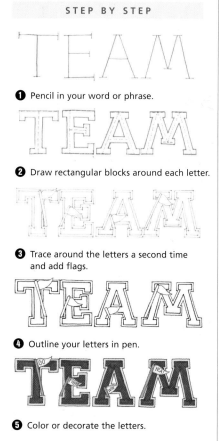

STEP BY STEP

❶ Pencil in your word or phrase.

❷ Draw rectangular blocks around each letter.

❸ Trace around the letters a second time and add flags.

❹ Outline your letters in pen.

❺ Color or decorate the letters.

Spirit Alphabet

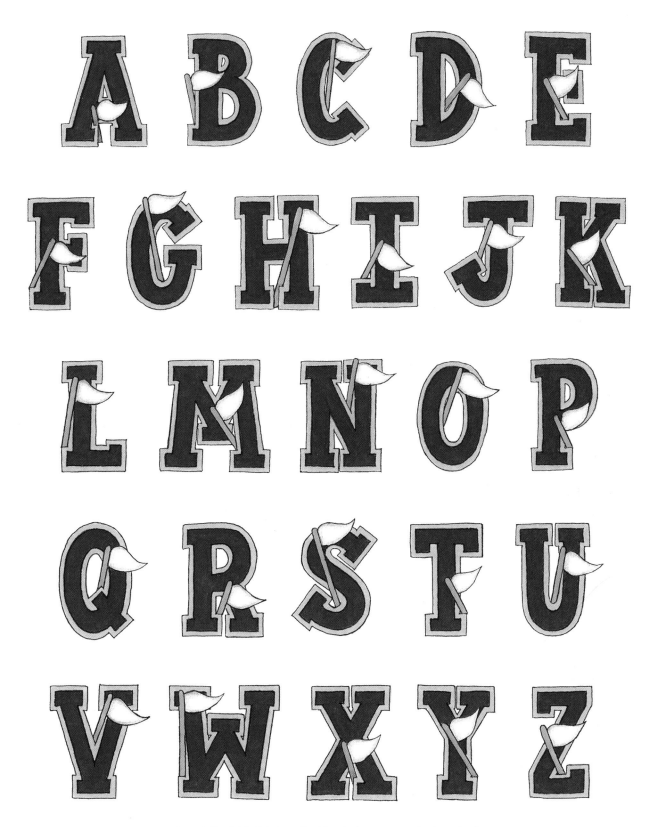

Figure 2. The Spirit Alphabet will add enthusiasm to your school scrapbook pages.
Supplies *Pen:* Zig Writer, EK Success; *Colored pencils:* Prismacolor, Sanford.

and serifs. Maintain even spacing as you draw around all sides of each letter.

③ Trace around the letters a second time just outside your first outline. Draw simple flags at random places and heights on the letters.

④ Once you've written the word the way you like it, outline the letters with a marker and erase the pencil lines.

⑤ Color and decorate the letters as desired (Figure 2).

It's really as simple as that! You can also change the look of your lettering by experimenting with various pen sizes, colors, outlines and flags (Figure 3). Play around and you'll find all sorts of variations you can use with the Spirit Alphabet (Figure 4).

If you start scrapbooking now, you'll not only have hours of creative fun today, you'll also have years of fun recalling all the ups and downs of your teen years. So . . . ready? OK. Get to work—you've got places to go, people to see and scrapbooks to create! ❤

Figure 3. Customize the Spirit Alphabet with your school colors. **Supplies** *Patterned paper:* Close To My Heart; *Pens:* Zig Millennium and Zig Writer, EK Success; *Colored pencils:* Primsmacolor, Sanford; *Raffia:* Paper Adventures.

Figure 4. Play with the Spirit Alphabet to find the right look for every page. **"BEST FRIENDS" Supplies** *Patterned paper:* Northern Spy (red), The Paper Patch (yellow); *Pens:* Zig Millennium and Zig Writer, EK Success; *Colored pencils:* Prismacolor, Sanford. **"REPORT CARD" Supplies** *Pen:* Zig Writer, EK Success; *Watercolor pencils:* Derwent. **"CLASS SCHEDULE" Supplies** *Pens:* Zig Writer, EK Success. **"LOGAN L" Supplies** *Pen:* Zig Writer, EK Success; *Watercolor pencils:* Derwent. **"POWDER PUFF" Supplies** *Patterned paper:* Keeping Memories Alive; *Pen:* Zig Millennium, EK Success; *Colored pencils:* Prismacolor, Sanford.

cape hatteras

POST CARD

DESTINATI

MAUI

of Interest

Pe'e Beach

ua Bay

rs Village Wha
of the Pacifi

a Bay

thames

EXPLORE

the untraveled paths

and secret garden

of this sweet life

journey

paradise

adventures

destination

excursion

COLONIAL
WILLIAMSBURG
2002

Some things Hannah learned:

Stop...Drop...Roll

Get out and call 911

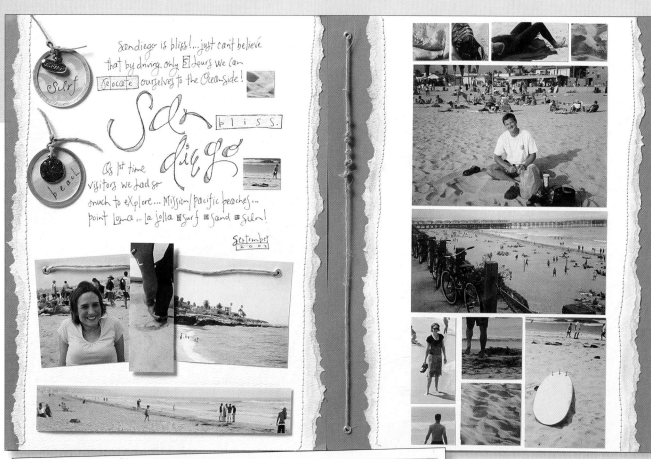

EcoTarium

When we visited the Ecotarium in Worcester, the big hit of the day was the polar bear. The boys watched, totally enthralled, as the bear made its circuit, swimming gracefully by the viewing window.

After he finished his ice cream, Nate entertained us with a little "mandolin music." Then we took a ride on the scale-model train, much to AJ's delight.

July 2002

"San Diego Bliss"
by Kelly Anderson
Tempe, AZ
Supplies *Metal-rimmed tags:* Making Memories; *Pen:* Zig Writer, EK Success; *Colored pencils:* EK Success; *Chalk:* Craf-T Products; *Hemp:* Westrim Crafts.

"Ecotarium"
by Judith Mara
Lancaster, MA
Supplies *Patterned paper and vellum:* Hot Off The Press; *Page template:* Deluxe Designs; *Computer font:* Times New Roman, Microsoft Word; *Chalk:* Stampendous!; *Pen:* Zig Millennium, EK Success; *Other:* Craft foam and jewelry.

"Ben"

by Kelly Anderson, Tempe, AZ
Supplies *Patterned paper, antique ruler, time stamp and circle frame:* Memory Lane; *Travel stickers:* Penny Black; *Clock hands and large paper clip:* Ink It!; *Gold embossing powder:* PSX Design; *Clock-face buttons:* Jo-Ann Stores; *Ceramic watch face:* Beads by Pamela; *Letter stamps:* Hero Arts; *Rubber stamps:* Ink It!; *Other:* Chipboard, hemp, old postcards, small clips and wire screen.

"Huckleberry Hill"

by Jocelyne Hayes
Trabuco Canyon, CA
Supplies *Vellum:* Accent Designs; *Computer fonts:* BudHand, downloaded from the Internet; 2Peas Gingersnap, downloaded from *www.twopeasinabucket.com*; *Other:* Brads.

I've
been
waiting
my
whole
life
to

MEET
YOU

One of the moments I looked forward to most when we planned our Disney trip was seeing Emily's face when she first met Mickey Mouse. We made reservations to have dinner at Chef Mickey's just after our arrival, so that Emily could meet Mickey right away. As we sat through dinner, Emily was greeted by all of the characters at the restaurant except Mickey. "Where's Mickey?" she kept asking. "He's the chef. He's making dinner in the kitchen," Daddy explained. Just as Mickey began making his way to the tables near us, Emily decided she needed to take a trip to the ladies' room. When we got back, Mickey had already passed our table and was getting ready to return to the kitchen. Daddy spoke to the manager and explained our situation. Moments later, Mickey came to our table and had a very special visit with Emily. He admired her Minnie ears, signed her autograph book and earned this adoring smile from Emily. Before he left, Emily thanked Mickey for cooking us dinner. It was an unforgettable encounter...and well worth the wait.

"I've Been Waiting My Whole Life ..."

by Jennifer Borowski
Princeton, NJ
Supplies *Patterned paper:* Sandylion; *Metal letters:* ScrapYard 329; *Computer fonts:* CK Stenography, "Fresh Fonts" CD, *Creating Keepsakes*; Times, package unknown; *Buttons:* Making Memories; *Snaps:* Doodlebug Design.

"Disney World Black & White"

by Amie Lloyd
Broken Arrow, OK
Supplies *Computer font:* Miss Brooks, downloaded from the Internet; *Date stamp:* Cosco; *Stamping ink:* Tsukineko; *Letter stickers:* Colorbök.

Disney World
BLACK **&** **WHITE**

IDEA TO NOTE: Glenda cut her photos into strips. She choose coordinating colors of cardstock and journaled the dates and names of the places she visited on her vacation.

kew gardens • JULY 17

london • JULY 22

dublin • JULY 27

ards peninsula • JULY 28

killyleagh • JULY 29

belcoo • JULY 31

carrickfergus • AUG 2

portrush • AUG 3

antrim coast • AUG 4

newtownards • AUG 6

"In Review"

by Glenda Van Engelen
Redmond, WA
Supplies *Vellum:* The Paper Company; *Computer font:* Festus, downloaded from the Internet.

"Spiderman"

by Heidi Steenblik, Salt Lake City, UT
Supplies *Patterned paper:* Club Scrap; *Vellum:* XPEDX; *Computer fonts:* Spiderman (title), downloaded from the Internet; 2Peas Nevermind (journaling), downloaded from *www.two-peasinabucket.com*; *Pen:* Zig Scroll and Brush, EK Success; *Flat-top eyelets:* Doodlebug Design; *Other:* Postcard from park.

Chapter 4
The Motor Scooter

One of the really nice things about Bermuda is that there is very little traffic. According to local law, there can only be one car per family! And many families use motor scooters to get about the island. Remember that Bermuda is only 21 miles long and one mile wide at its widest point. It's no surprise then, that tourists are not able to rent cars...its motor scooters, taxis or buses! George and I found a scooter shop not far from our inn.

We had to take a 'driving test' with the scooter before we were allowed to rent it. No surprise that George passed the driving test and I did not! Originally we had planned to rent two scooters, but tooling around on one together was actually more fun. And I'm proud to say that we did not get 'road rash'. That's the local term for getting scrapes and bruises from the pavement and rocks while riding the motor scooter.

Oxford House Clac
Box HM 374
Hamilton HM BX
809·295·0503
Summer '93

46

"Travelogue: Bermuda"

by Faye Morrow Bell
Charlotte, NC
Supplies *Patterned paper:* Source unknown; *Computer fonts:* Antique Type, Verdana and Book Antiqua, downloaded from the Internet; *Stamping ink:* Susan Branch, Colorbök; *Pens:* Zig Writer (brown), EK Success; Pigma Micron (black), Sakura; *Rubber stamps:* Inkadinkadoo and Stamper's Anonymous; *Other:* Paper clip and tea stain.

"Straw Market"

by Angie Cramer
Medicine Hat, AB, Canada
Supplies *Letter stamps:* Wordsworth ("Straw"), PSX Design ("Market"); *Flower stamp:* Stamp Craft; *Tag and buttons:* Making Memories; *Computer font:* 39 Smooth, downloaded from the Internet; *Embroidery floss:* DMC; *Other:* Ribbon and stamping ink.

Day 1 - Nassau - After breakfast we got off the ship and headed to the straw market. We stopped in a few stores along the way and bought some T-shirts and jewelry.

The Case of the Bad Vacation Photographs

- **The Suspects:** Color-Shift Carol, Disappearing David, Mysterious Martha, Landscape-Lovin' Lauren
- **The Detective:** Licensed to Scrap, Barbara Carroll
- **The Assignment:** We asked Barbara to solve the mystery of how to scrapbook blurry, far-away vacation photos and so-so scenic shots.

Case Solved:

Barbara transformed faded and far-away scenic photos into a gorgeous layout (Figure 1) by manipulating them in Microsoft Digital Image Pro 7.0. Note how she scanned, color-corrected and enlarged the family picture to put more emphasis on both the people in the picture and the beautiful foliage.

On her "Zoo" page (Figure 2), Barbara also manipulated the photos with Microsoft Digital Image Pro 7.0. Note how she cropped and enlarged the giraffe picture and turned it into a long rectangular photo along the right-hand side of the page. In addition, she used extra photos to create her title. →

Figure 1. Use photo-manipulation software to color-correct and enlarge imperfect vacation photos. *Page by Barbara Carroll. Photos from Leslie Miller.* **Supplies** *Computer font:* New Day Roman, downloaded from the Internet; *Tag:* 7 Gypsies; *Tiles:* Tile's Play; *Sticker:* Making Memories; *Other:* Fiber.

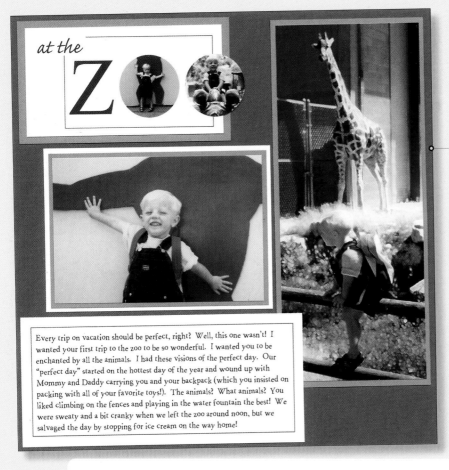

at the ZOO

Every trip on vacation should be perfect, right? Well, this one wasn't! I wanted your first trip to the zoo to be so wonderful. I wanted you to be enchanted by all the animals. I had these visions of the perfect day. Our "perfect day" started on the hottest day of the year and wound up with Mommy and Daddy carrying you and your backpack (which you insisted on packing with all of your favorite toys!). The animals? What animals? You liked climbing on the fences and playing in the water fountain the best! We were sweaty and a bit cranky when we left the zoo around noon, but we salvaged the day by stopping for ice cream on the way home!

Case Solved

Figure 2. Crop out extra detail in photos to turn them into stunning focal points. *Page by Barbara Carroll.* **Supplies** *Computer font:* Times New Roman and Garamouche, Microsoft Word; *Circle punch:* Whale of a Punch, EK Success.

Top-Secret Tips:

Looking for a great landscape photo? Barbara suggests that landscape photos are most attractive when the line of the horizon is not in the middle of the picture. She also says that the best time of day for taking landscape photos is in the morning or in the late afternoon (Figure 3).

Don't forget to include your family members in your vacation pictures! Zoom in close to capture their expressions on film, and have them turn slightly away from the sun to avoid squinting (Figure 4).

Figure 3. To capture a beautiful scenic shot, make sure the line of the horizon is not in the middle of your picture. *Photo by Barbara Carroll.*

Figure 4. Zoom in close to capture your subject's expressions. *Photo by Barbara Carroll.*

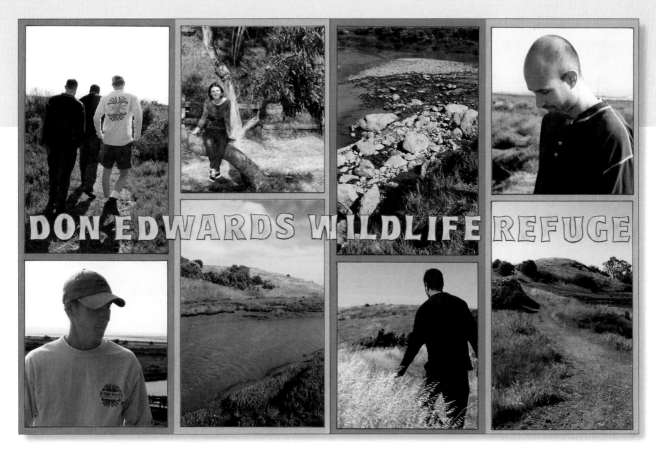

"Don Edward's Wildlife Refuge"
by Lisa Brown
Oakland, CA
Supplies *Pen:* Zig Writer, EK Success; *Lettering template:* The Crafter's Workshop.

PAGE STARTER: THE PLACES YOU GO

When, where and why you go on vacation can say a lot about you! Don't forget to include information on your vacation destinations as well as what you do there. Here are a few ideas:

• Why did you choose your particular vacation destination? Does it hold historical significance, personal meaning or have you always wondered what it would be like? How long have you been planning the trip? Was it a split-second getaway, or have you been working on the details for years?

• What vacation destinations do you visit year after year? Do you have a regular vacation spot, like a family cabin or a resort town you love? What activities do you do every time you're there? Who and what do you see during your visit?

• How do you travel to and from your destination? Was your family "born to travel," or is it torture to get everyone there in one piece? Do you have traditional stops along the way that add to the vacation experience?

"Kennedy Space Center"

by Kim Morgan
Pleasant Grove, UT
Supplies *Lettering template:* Rounded, ABC Tracers, Pebbles for EK Success; *Star punches:* Family Treasures; *Pens:* Milky Gel Roller, Pentel (white); Zig Writer, EK Success (black); *Vellum:* Frances Meyer.

The actual Saturn V Control Center (moved from Houston)

We spent an entire day here and enjoyed every minute of it (except perhaps the heat).
There is a fast food restaurant located underneath the Saturn V Rocket where we enjoyed a stellar lunch.

Ron standing beneath the Saturn V Rocket.

Parts of the International Space Center ~under construction.

"Our Future Astronauts"

by Vonda Kirkpatrick, Wenatchee, WA
Supplies *Lettering template:* Scrapbook, Provo Craft; *Alphabet stickers:* Fat Dot, Alphabitties, Provo Craft; *Chalk:* Craf-T Products *Corrugated paper:* DMD Industries; *Colored pencils:* Memory Pencils, EK Success; *Pens:* Zig Millennium, EK Success (black); Milky Gel Roller, Pentel (white); *Computer font:* CK Print, "The Best of Creative Lettering" CD Vol. 1, *Creating Keepsakes; Paper doll:* Paperkins, Pebbles for EK Success; *Hole punches:* Punchline, McGill; *Astronaut and space capsule:* Vonda's own designs.

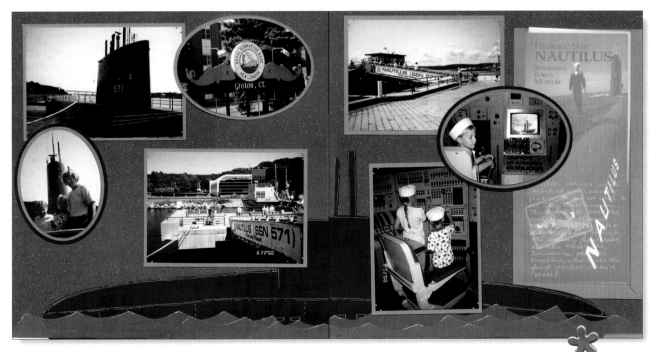

"Historic Ship Nautilus"

by Sandra Oehlert Yanisko, Barto, PA
Supplies *Patterned paper:* Keeping Memories Alive; *Vellum:* Paper Adventures; *Pens:* Milky Gel Roller, Pentel (white); Gelly Roll, Sakura (silver); *Colored pencils:* Prismacolor, Sanford; *Submarine and waves:* Sandra's own designs.

IDEAS TO NOTE: Sandra created a vellum pocket page on her layout to display a museum brochure. She also used the pocket as her journaling block.

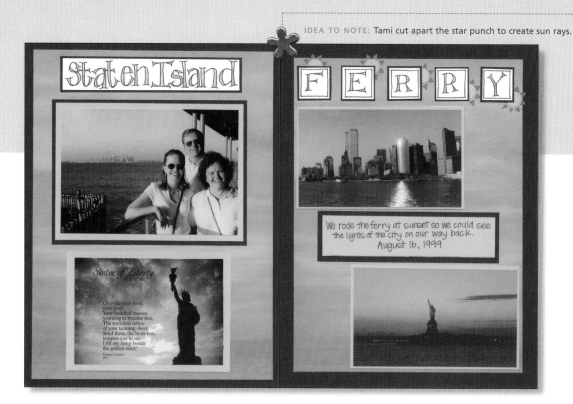

"Staten Island Ferry"

by Tami Beck, Salt Lake City, UT
Supplies *Sunset Stationary:* Geographics, Inc.; *Lettering Idea:* "Classic," *The Art of Creative Lettering*, Creating Keepsakes Books; *Star and circle punches:* Family Treasures; *Pen:* Zig Writer, EK Success; *Colored pencils:* Memory Pencils, EK Success. *Memorabilia idea:* Tami included the quote from the Statue of Liberty on the layout.

IDEA TO NOTE: Sandy used her baby's footprints as layout accents.

"Making Footprints in the Sand"

by Sandy Landon, Provo, UT
Supplies *Computer fonts:* CK Script (journaling) and CK Fill In ("Footprints"), "The Best of Creative Lettering" CD Vol. 1 and CK Cursive (title), "The Best of Creative Lettering" CD Vol. 2, *Creating Keepsakes; Vellum:* Paper Adventures; *Watercolor pencils:* Karat, Staedtler, Inc.; *Ink pad:* Stampin' Up!

A little messy, a little pricey, but more than a little tasty! Dad got a bushel of craps for us to share at Nissy's graduation.

WORKING 9 TO 5

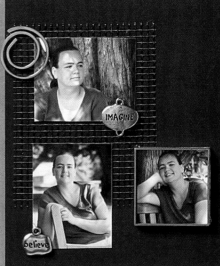

IMAGINE

believe

Two Classics

personality

friendships

dreams

education

aspirations

cyclist, ..."married" obsessed completed a grueling two-day charity ride Sunday (continued inside on 2A)

Latina

Nicole
Nicole you are such a special woman. I can't begin to describe all the qualities that make you the special woman you are. It all starts with your wonderful heart. continues with your compassion for others. This always makes me

"Heavy Pedal"
by Blair Blanks
Kingwood, TX
Supplies *Patterned paper:* Canson; *Computer font:* Walrod (title), downloaded from the Internet; Times New Roman (journaling), Microsoft Word; *Transparencies:* Pockets on a Roll; *Clip art:* Downloaded from the Internet; *Walnut ink:* Postmodern Design; *Other:* Paper clip and washers.

On April 15, 2003, Nikki got her braces off! While the rest of the country was upset because it was Tax Day, Nikki was anything but upset! After around two years of wearing her braces, she was so excited to get them off! Even though I think she looked very cute in her braces, she looks just beautiful without them! Dr. Belli was very proud of how well her teeth turned out, and our parents are thrilled that both of their daughters now have gorgeous smiles!

"Braces Off"
by Amanda Goodwin
Munroe Falls, OH
Supplies *Patterned papers:* KI Memories (yellow and aqua), Chatterbox (red); *Computer font:* 2Peas Flower Pot, downloaded from *www.twopeasinabucket.com*; *Circle die cut:* Sizzix, Provo Craft; *Circle stencil:* The C-Thru Ruler Co.; *Memorabilia pocket:* 3L Corp.; *Pen:* Zig Writer, EK Success; *Other:* Braces.

IDEA TO NOTE:
Jenni embossed the crabs several
times with various colors of
embossing powder to mimic the
look of the cooked crabs.

"Crabs!"

by Jenni Bowlin
Mount Juliet, TN
Supplies *Computer font:*
Teletype, Printmaster; *Sponge stamp:*
Fred Mullet; *Letter stamps:* PSX
Design; *Number stamps:* Turtle Press;
Charm: Giraffe Crafts; *Postage stamp:*
Art Accents; *Stamping ink:* ColorBox,
Clearsnap; *Laser cuts:* Li'l Davis Designs;
Embossing powders: UTEE, Suze
Weinberg; Ranger Industries (brown
and terra cotta); *Mini-brads:* American
Tag Co.; *Embossing ink:* VersaMark,
Tsukineko;
Other: Metal screen.

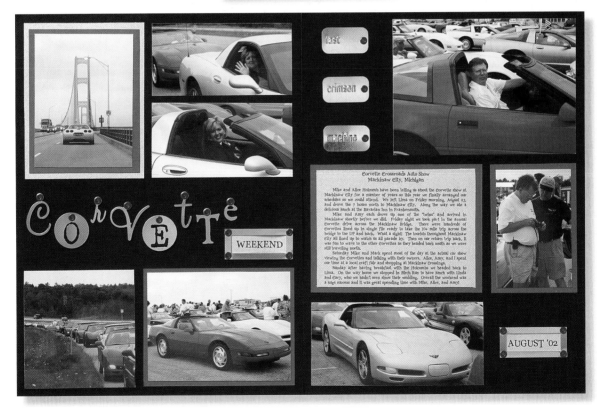

"Corvette Weekend"

by Candy Carpenter, Lima, OH
Supplies *Textured paper:* Bazzill Basics; *Metal letters and frame:* Making Memories; *Computer fonts:* CK Twilight
(journaling), "Fresh Fonts" CD, *Creating Keepsakes*; 2Peas Flea Market by Sharon Soneff (title and date), downloaded from *www.twopeasinabucket.com*; *Poetry dog tags:* Chronicle Books; *Color-blocking templates:* Deluxe
Designs; *Other:* Eyelets.

"Forever Friends"

by Barbara Carroll
Tucson, AZ
Supplies *Vellum:* The Paper Company; *Computer fonts:* Courier New, Microsoft Word; CK Cursive, "The Best of Creative Lettering" CD Vol. 2, *Creating Keepsakes;* *Tags:* Avery Dennison; *Alphabet rubber stamps:* PrintWorks; *Stamping ink:* Memories; *Punch:* Source unknown; *Other:* Button.

"An Old Friend"

by Loni Stevens, Gilbert, AZ
Supplies *Computer font:* CK Fun, "The Art of Creative Lettering" CD, *Creating Keepsakes; Pens:* Zig Writer, EK Success; The Ultimate Gel Pen, American Crafts; *Colored pencils:* Prismacolor, Sanford; *Embroidery floss:* DMC.

"Friendship"

by Cindy Schow
Cardston, AB, Canada
Supplies *Patterned paper:* SEI;
Stickers: Jolee's Boutique,
Stickopotamus; *Computer font:*
Twizot HMK, "Hallmark Card
Studio 2" CD, Hallmark.

This classy coin-holder border is perfect for prom pages and more. *Page by Lori Houk.* **Supplies** *Metallic paper:* Paper Adventures; *Handmade paper:* Paper Source; *Photo corners:* Kolo; *Sheer bag:* Paper Source; *Coin holders:* Craft Source; *Dried flowers:* Pressed Petals; *Silver leafing pen:* Krylon; *Silver glass beads:* Suze Weinberg; *Computer fonts:* Lemon Chicken (title), downloaded from the Internet; Crumbly Ginger (journaling), downloaded from *twopeasinabucket.com; 3-D foam dots:* Stampa Rosa; *Square punch:* Family Treasures; *Other:* Dog tag accent.

BORDER IDEAS

When our favorite baby-sitter got all dressed up for her senior prom, she looked incredibly beautiful! I found some pressed flowers that matched her dress exactly, so I knew I had to use them on a page. To dress up the pressed flowers even more, I found some silver coin holders—and a unique and classy border was born. Here's how you can create the same look:

❶ Cut a 2½"-wide strip of black cardstock. Cut a 1⅞"-wide strip of hand-made paper or lilac cardstock. Attach the smaller strip to the wider strip and set aside.

❷ Adhere the dried flower to the center of the coin holder. Adhere the coin holder shut with a strong adhesive (Glue Dots by Glue Dots International work well for this).

❸ "Paint" silver leafing onto the outside corners of the coin holders by "pumping" the tip of a silver leafing pen up and down to make the paint come out in spurts. This creates an authentic, mottled look. Repeat this step two or three times for a layered effect.

❹ Before the third layer is completely dry, daub the leafing pen in spots where you would like to apply beads. Sprinkle silver glass beads over the coin holders. Let dry overnight.

❺ Adhere the coin holders with 3-D foam dots to the strip of cardstock created in Step 1, then attach the border to your layout.

— *by Lori Houk*

"Class of 1993"

by Rachael Stone, Sandy, UT
Supplies *Computer font:* Old English, "500 Fonts" CD, Media Graphics International; *Letter stickers:* Geographics; *Chalks:* Craf-T Products; *Pen:* Zig Scroll & Brush, EK Success.

IDEAS TO NOTE: Rachael created a varsity letter on her layout using felt. She also included her diploma, tassel and a school pin on her layout.

"The Class of 1998"

by Cindy Schow, Cardston, AB, Canada
Supplies *Metallic paper:* Paper Garden; *Punches:* McGill (jumbo swirl), All Night Media (swirl border), Marvy Uchida (circle)

IDEA TO NOTE: Cindy ran the metallic paper through a Xyron 500 machine to apply adhesive to the back. Then she punched her small circles, making them easier to apply to her layout. She also used an actual graduation announcement to create the title and journaling on the layout.

"Graduation '95"

Karen Petersen, Salt Lake City, UT
Supplies *Metallic paper:* Accu-Cut Systems; *Graduation cap:* Karen adapted the idea from a thank-you note.; *Computer font:* CK Handmade, "The Best of Creative Lettering" CD Combo, *Creating Keepsakes*; *Number stickers:* Source unknown; *Memorabilia idea:* Karen included a miniature diploma, her tassel and her graduation announcement on the layout.

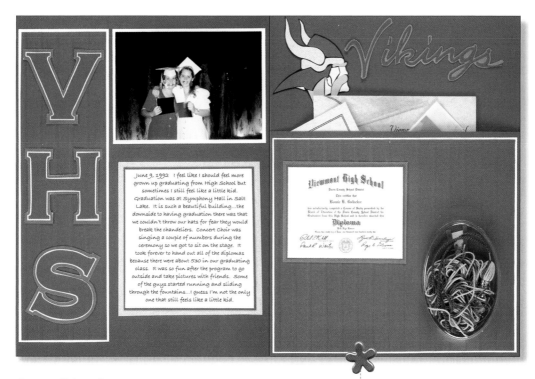

"VHS Vikings"

by Bonnie Lotz, West Jordan, UT
Supplies *Embossed paper:* Frances Meyer; *Computer fonts:* Unknown; *Metallic paper:* Paper Adventures; *Memorabilia idea:* Bonnie included a color copy of her diploma on the layout, and her graduation tassel in a 3D Keeper by Déjà Views.

IDEAS TO NOTE: Bonnie created a pocket page to hold her graduation program and other memorabilia. She also re-created the school mascot by paper piecing the design.

"Reach for the Stars"

by Ashley Schow
Cardston, AB, Canada
Supplies *Vellum:* The Paper Company; *Computer fonts:* Little Trouble Girl, downloaded from the Internet; Think Small, downloaded from *twopeasinabucket.com; Mini-star punch:* Darice; *Brads:* Westrim Crafts.

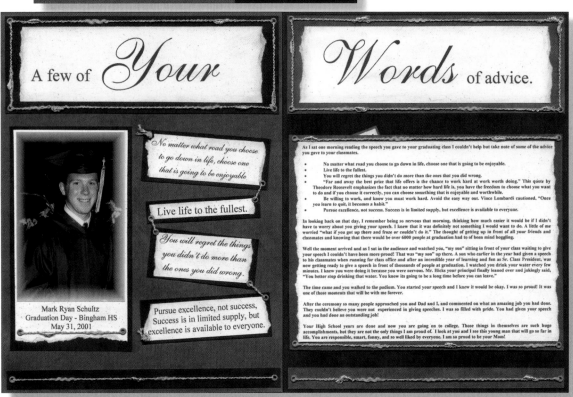

"A Few of Your Words of Advice"

by Yvonne Schultz, South Jordan, UT
Supplies *Computer fonts:* Shelley Allegro BT and Times New Roman, Microsoft Word; *Chalk:* Craf-T Products; *Fiber:* On the Surface; *Other:* Eyelets.

IDEA TO NOTE: Darcy color-copied her son's merit badge sash for the front panel of the fold-out page.

CAMBELL'S SCOUTING HIGHLIGHTS

*Oregon Troop 857 Scoutmaster, Mike Baird

*Intense "Capture the Flag" games on campouts

*Backpacking in the Cascade Mountains

* Summer scout camp

*Oregon Coast Bike Trip (rode the 500-mile Oregon Coast highway in two one-week segments-1998 and 1999)

*Snowcaving by Mt. Hood

*EAGLE SCOUT PROJECT: DESIGNING AND BUILDING BENCHES AND PLANTER BOXES FOR COMMUNITY GARDENS, FALL, 2000

*Philmont Ten-Day Trek, Troop 772, Summer, 2001

Eagle Scout Award Court of Honor, September, 2001

A SCOUT IS...

Trustworthy
LOYAL
Helpful
Friendly
Cheerful
Courteous
Kind

BRAVE
Clean
AND **REVERENT.**

-THE SCOUT LAW

MERIT BADGES EARNED

ASTRONOMY
BASKETRY
CAMPING
CANOEING
CITIZENSHIP IN THE COMMUNITY
CITIZENSHIP IN THE NATION
CITIZENSHIP IN THE WORLD
CLIMBING
COMMUNICATIONS
CYCLING
EMERGENCY PREPAREDNESS
ENVIORNMENTAL SCIENCE
FAMILY LIFE
FIRST AID
HORSEMANSHIP
LEATHERWORK
MAMMAL STUDY
PERSONAL FITNESS
PERSONAL MANAGEMENT
PIONEERING
ROWING
SAFETY
SKATING
SWIMMING
WOOD CARVING

RANK ADVANCEMENTS

SCOUT: 01/01/1996
TENDERFOOT: 09/15/1996
2ⁿᵈ CLASS: 07/15/1997
1ˢᵗ CLASS: 07/15/1997
STAR: 04/15/1998
LIFE: 11/15/1998
EAGLE: 07/11/2001

"Cambell's Eagle Scout"

by Darcy Christensen
Tucson, AZ
Supplies *Vellum:* The Paper Company; *Eagle Scout emblem sticker:* Boy Scouts of America; *Star accents:* Darice; *Computer fonts:* Unknown, Microsoft Word; *Eyelets:* Doodlebug Design; *Embroidery floss:* DMC; *Pop dots:* All Night Media.

JOURNALING TIPS

Teenagers. Who can figure them out? Well, we certainly try ... so often dubbing him "the shy one" or her "the artistic one." It's easy to put labels on kids that call out their predominant characteristics, but obviously quiet teens have moments when they're outgoing, and tough kids have their tender times, too.

To let your teen know that you notice his multi-faceted personality (and love him for it), do some journaling that goes against the grain. If you typically write about how funny he is, touch upon an instance when he was completely staid and serious. If he's known as a logical thinker, cite some examples of how artistic and creative he can be. Or even create an entire page devoted to qualities that are completely "unlike" how he is most often perceived.

Add richness to the journaling by quizzing your teen and including his answers in the text. Ask how he thinks others see him. If that's different from his self-image, discuss how he *wants* to be viewed and why. Find out his three favorite traits (they might surprise you) and others he wishes he did or didn't have.

By zeroing in on your teen's total personality instead of just the parts that we see most often, you'll create a treasure that he'll appreciate when he's older ... particularly when he has teens of his own!

— *by Denise Pauley*

Take your journaling beyond labels and record the multi-faceted personalities of the teenagers you know and love. *Page by Denise Pauley.* **Supplies** *Patterned papers:* Carolee's Creations (blue and yellow), Karen Foster Design (green); *Computer fonts:* Papyrus and Arial Block, Microsoft Word; *Square punch:* EK Success; *Pen:* Zig Millennium, EK Success; *Brad:* Impress Rubber Stamps.

"Self Portrait"
by Heather Murray
Ventura, CA
Supplies *Vellum:* Paper Adventures; *Computer font:* Think Small, downloaded from *twopeasinabucket.com.*

"Survey Says"
by Jennifer Wohlenberg
Stevenson Ranch, CA
Supplies *Patterned paper:* Magenta; *Computer fonts:* Enviro, downloaded from the Internet; CK Penman, "The Best of Creative Lettering" CD Vol. 4, *Creating Keepsakes; Fibers:* Rubba Dub Dub.

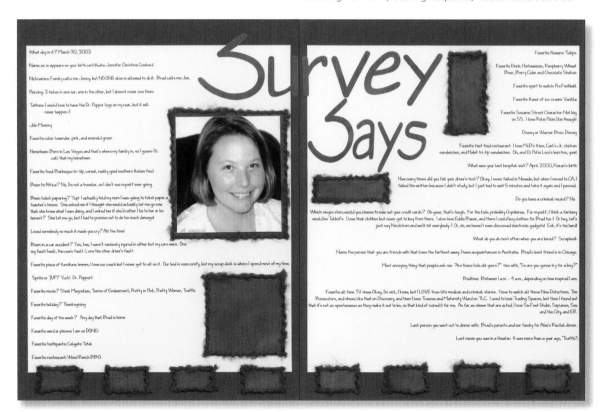

IDEA TO NOTE: Julie reduced and color-copied her bracelet to include on the layout.

Simply...

Charming

I had been wanting a charm bracelet for a while, but hadn't been able to find just the one I had in mind. During Amy's and My Christmas shopping trip, we found exactly what I had been looking for at the Ben. They had a good weight and look of the bracelet and a huge selection of charms. To make it even better, it was at 50% off, PLUS we had another 20% off coupon. For that day only at the Ben. I was pretty excited. Amy and the (nice!) saleslady patiently helped me choose my charms. They were all so adorable, it was hard to narrow down my choices. Each charm I choose has a special place in my heart (see below). When I got it home I showed Steve the gift he was giving me for Christmas – he thought it was great and put them all on for me (no easy task!) I just love my charms bracelet...it's one of my favorite things.

"Simply Charming"

by Julie Anderson
Renton, WA

Supplies *Patterned papers:* Bo-Bunny Press, Northern Spy, Karen Foster Design; *Lettering template:* Whimsey, ABC Tracers, Pebbles for EK Success; *Computer fonts:* Pookie (journaling), downloaded from *www.letteringdelights.com*; Lucida Handwriting, Microsoft Word; *Charms:* Impress Rubber Stamps.

Purse — Shopping trips with Amy
Bible — My relationship with God
Phone — Amy, and all the time we spend talking on the phone
Pig — The fun the girls and I had all the times we saw the Pigs. On Parade downtown and also my Grampa who collected "Pig Stuff"
Martini Glass — Fun nights out and lots of laughing
Visa — more shopping
Soccer Ball — Molly and Hannah playing soccer this past year (and Steve who loves soccer, too.)
Picnic Basket — Special family times. Being outdoors in the sun.
Teapot — My job at Pottery Barn Kids and Hannah + Madeline's room That is decked out in Teacups.
Ring — My marriage
Carriage — My three girls who are growing up so quickly
Ice Cream — The Anderson family staple and our kitten named Ice cream
Camera — My love of pictures and scrapbooking
Sandal — Lake Chelan and VACATION
Perfume — Smells that I love "girly" things and Steve's sense of humor
Carousel — Seaside, OR and how much the girls love to ride Merry-go-rounds

BORDER IDEAS

I love creating wedding albums for friends and discovered that the look of an embossed Cloisonné border lends just the perfect touch of elegance. I added tiny silver glass beads to the centers of the daisies in this border to keep it simple but beautiful. Here's how you can create this look:

❶ Tear a strip of black cardstock and adhere it to your background paper.

❷ Using an embossing pad or Boss Gloss, coat a 2" x 2" piece of chipboard.

❸ Apply a layer of Cloisonné powder over the wet surface. Heat with a heat-embossing tool until the powder melts and becomes glossy. Before the area cools, add more powder and heat again. Continue layering until you achieve the desired thickness (I used three layers).

❹ While the melted powder is still warm, press the rubber stamp into the surface to create the impression. Hold the stamp steady until the melted powder has cooled, then lift out the stamp.

❺ Apply clear-drying glue to the center of each daisy and pour glass beads over the glue. Shake the excess beads off and let dry.

❻ Adhere the squares to the torn strip of cardstock, spacing evenly.

—*by Lori Houk*

This modern, dressy Cloisonné border will add class to any wedding page. *Page by Lori Houk.* **Supplies** *Patterned paper:* Anna Griffin; *Embossing powder:* Cloisonné, Stampa Rosa; *Glass beads:* Global Gems; *Chipboard:* Magenta; *Paper clip:* Target; *Embossing pad:* Boss Gloss, Stamp-n Stuff; *Daisy stamp:* Impression Obsession; *Craft glue:* US ArtQuest; *3-D foam dots:* Stampa Rosa; *Other:* Beads and a charm (found at any craft store).

Now you will feel no rain,
For each of you will be shelter to the other
Now you will feel no cold,
For each of you will be warmth to the other.
Now you are two bodies,
But there is only one life before you.
Go now to your dwelling place
To enter into the days of your togetherness.
And may your days be good and long upon the earth.
-Apache Wedding Blessing-

"You Will Feel No Rain"
by Amy Jandrisevits
Woodridge, IL
Supplies *Computer font:* Girls
Are Weird, downloaded from the
Internet; *Charms:* Making Memories;
Fibers: On the Surface.

*True
Love*
Eric & Sharon

...and they lived
happily ever after.

"True Love"
by Cecilie Hudson
Chandler, AZ
Supplies *Patterned paper:* Anna Griffin;
Stickers: Mrs. Grossman's; *Ribbon:* C.M.
Offray & Son: *Tag:* Accu-Cut Systems;
Brads: Hyglo; *Eyelets:* Making Memories;
Pens: Zig Millennium, EK Success; Paint
Marker, Pilot; *Embroidery floss:* DMC;
Other: Button, twine, beads and chalk.

IDEAS TO NOTE: The book featured on Katherine's layout opens up and includes envelopes marked 1, 5 and 10 years. Katherine included journaling about "the ideal me" at each time in her life.

"Ideal Me"

by Katherine Brooks, Gilbert, AZ
Supplies *Patterned paper:* Anna Griffin; *Specialty paper:* Source unknown; *Computer fonts:* CK Constitution, "Fresh Fonts" CD and CK Journaling, "The Best of Creative Lettering" CD Vol. 2, *Creating Keepsakes*; Staccato, downloaded from the Internet; *Rubber stamps:* PSX Design; *Date stamp:* Staples; *Stamping ink:* Stampa Rosa (fresco); ColorBox (gold), Clearsnap; Ranger Industries; *Clasp:* 7 Gypsies; *Embossing powder:* UTEE, Suze Weinberg; *Modeling paste:* Liquitex; *Circle punch:* Family Treasures; *Craft wire:* Artistic Wire Ltd.; *Envelope tags:* Ink It!; *Tag:* Katherine's own design; *Other:* Jute, fibers, charms and ribbon.

"Work History"

by Kim Haynes, Harrah, OK
Supplies *Patterned paper:* Wordsworth; *Letter stickers:* Doodlebug Design (title) and Provo Craft ("Michaels '02"); *Computer fonts:* Batik Regular, downloaded from the Internet; 2Peas Bookplate, downloaded from *www.twopeasinabucket.com*; *Brads:* Karen Foster Design.

IDEA TO NOTE: Loni reduced and color-copied her dad's retirement certificates to include on her layout.

"Army National Guard"

by Loni Stevens
Pleasant Grove, UT
Supplies *Computer fonts:*
CK Toggle (title), CK Journaling
(journaling) and CK Monogram
(drop caps on title), "The Best of
Creative Lettering" CD Vol. 2;
CK Classic (fill font on title),
"The Art of Creative Lettering"
CD, *Creating Keepsakes; Star
template:* EK Success; *Colored
pencils:* Prismacolor, Sanford;
Pop dots: All Night Media; *Pen:*
The Ultimate Gel Pen,
American Crafts.

"A Dream Come True"

by Inge-Lise Bay MacFarlane
Southfield, MI
Supplies *Pens:* Pigma Brush, Sakura
(brown); Gel Xtreme (white) and
Metallic Marker, Yasutomo; Zig Writer,
EK Success (orange).

IDEA TO NOTE: To show the
passage of time, Inge-Lise
included childhood and current photos on the layout.

"Kiss"

by Melissa Okonski
The Colony, TX
Supplies *Vellum:* Paper Adventures; *Handmade paper:* NRN Designs; *Computer fonts:* Betty's Hand, Terry's Hand, Signature, Alex's Hand, Angela's Hand, Old Century and Bernhard Fashion, all downloaded from the Internet; *Embroidery floss:* DMC; *Pop dots:* Cut-It-Up; *Other:* Ribbon, charms and pearl strands.

"Melissa and Dave"

by Mechelle Felsted
Flagstaff, AZ
Supplies *Patterned paper:* Provo Craft; *Vellum:* Paper Cuts; *Computer font:* PC Script, "For Font Sakes" HugWare CD, Provo Craft ; *Punches:* Marvy Uchida (leaf, sun and corner rounder), Family Treasures (daisy).

"Celebrate"

by Nancy Maxwell-Crumb, Whitmore Lake, MI
Supplies *Patterned paper:* Karen Foster Design; *Gold paper:* Paper Adventures; *Lettering template:* Fat Caps, Frances Meyer; *Star template:* Frances Meyer; *Star and spiral punches:* Emagination Crafts; *Pen:* Gel Metallics, Marvy Uchida.

"Celebrating 50 Years"

by Lisa Brown, Oakland, CA
Supplies *Patterned paper:* Scrap-Ease; *Metallic paper:* Paper Adventures; *Gold handmade paper:* Source unknown; *Lettering template:* Calligraphy, ScrapPagerz.com; *Pen:* Zig Writer, EK Success; *Leaf punch:* Family Treasures; *Craft wire:* Amaco.

IDEAS TO NOTE: Lisa added "veins" to the leaf punches by scoring them. She also bent the craft wire to make part of the title

F R O M M Y

F A

C

Raymond Stanley Pasternak

Raymond Pasternak was born
Michigan on May 2, 1937. He
cond of two children. His
r Joe and Stella Pasternak,
er was named Dolores. For
two years he lived in Hamtramck,
mainly Polish town near Detroit.
as two years old his family
chester, Michigan and began
first home were they would
s. Dads parents both
automotive factories of
er Joe was a foreman at
n plant and his mother.
at GMC Truck and Coach
lating on the assembly
boys shown in these photos
are his cousin Joe Novak and
y. The white stuff on Dads
picture is calamine lotion,
poison ivy When this photo
family always ha

Sydney

1976

POST CARD

1942

CIRCA
1910

Faye & Joseph
Lyons

AUSTRALIA

heritage

traditions

history

yesteryear

reminiscence

"My Sister's My Teacher"

by Sharon Whitehead
Vernon, BC, Canada
Supplies *Computer font:* 2Peas Hot Chocolate, downloaded from *www.two-peasinabucket.com*; *Silhouette leaves:* Golden Oak Papers; *Letter stickers:* Pioneer; *Fibers:* Accents by Orchard; *Eyelets:* Impress Rubber Stamps.

"Scenes from My Father's Boyhood"

by Tena Sprenger, Mesa, AZ. **Supplies** *Patterned papers:* 7 Gypsies; *Rubber stamps:* Source unknown; *Embossing powder:* Stampin' Up!; *Key charm:* Embellish It!; *Mesh:* American Art Clay Co.; *Metal letters:* Making Memories; *Computer fonts:* Quixley LT (title) and Monotype Corsiva (title and journaling), Microsoft 2000; 39 Smooth (journaling), downloaded from *www.dafont.com*; *Bookplates:* Magic Scraps; *Tag:* American Tag Co.; *Metal rings:* Memory Lane; *Typewriter key inserts:* ARTchix Studio; *Photo corners:* Canson; *Hair spins:* Target; *Mini-brads:* Lost Art Treasures; *Other:* Stamping ink.

"Clyde"

by Carolyn Burt
Fisherville, VA
Supplies *Patterned paper:* Club
Scrap; *Computer fonts:* Cooper
MT Med, Andy, Campbell,
Typewriter, Technical, Brisk
Extended, Amazone BT,
Calligrapher, American Uncial,
Stewardson and Times New
Roman, downloaded from the
Internet; *Fibers:* Adornaments, EK
Success; *Stamping ink and eye-
lets:* Making Memories; *Pen:* Gelly
Roll, Sakura; *Charms:* Creative
Beginnings; *Other:* Letter beads
and gold chain.

"Anne, Lola, Deanna"

by Kimberly Kett
St. Catherine's, ON, Canada
Supplies *Patterned paper:* Hot
Off The Press; *Computer font:*
Scrap Cursive, "Lettering
Delights" CD Vol. 3,
Inspire Graphics.

IDEAS TO NOTE: Bethany embedded the leaves in several layers of UTEE and slightly cracked the embellishments for an aged look. To make the border around the vellum, she cut strips of corrugated paper and attached them to the page.

"Through Seasons and Stories"

by Bethany Fields
Amarillo, TX
Supplies *Patterned paper:* The Crafter's Workshop; *Vellum:* Sharon Ann Collection; *Corrugated paper:* DMD, Inc.; *Computer font:* Viner Hand ITC, Microsoft Word; *Stamping ink:* ColorBox, Clearsnap; *Leaves:* Nature's Pressed; *Embossing powder:* UTEE, Suze Weinberg; *Other:* Brads.

"Great-Grandfather"

by Leah Yourstone
Issaquah, WA
Supplies *Textured paper:* Club Scrap; *Lettering template:* Cursive, Wordsworth; *Letter stamps:* Hero Arts; *Letter cutouts:* Rubber Baby Buggy Bumpers; *Stamping ink:* StazOn; ColorBox, Clearsnap; *Clear envelope:* Card Connection; *Rub-on letters:* Bradwear, Creative Imaginations; *Mica tiles:* USArtQuest; *Brads:* Office Max; *Pen:* Zig Memory System, EK Success; *Other:* Mat board, twine and keys.

"The Fenton Family"

by Janelle Clark
Yorktown, VA
Supplies *Computer font:*
Harting, downloaded from
the Internet; *Border photo:*
Shotz, Creative Imaginations;
Other: Craft wire.

The Fenton family
on their Kansas farm
1925

All the world is God's own field, fruit unto His praise to yield;
Wheat and tares together sown unto joy or sorrow grown.
First the blade and then the ear, then the full corn shall appear;
Lord of harvest, grant that we wholesome grain and pure may be.

"Hazel"

by Colleen Macdonald
Calgary, AB, Canada
Supplies *Patterned papers:*
Anna Griffin (floral), Daisy D's
(green stripe); *Rubber stamp:*
Hero Arts ("Woman of
Spirit"), Art Accents (art col-
lage); *Stamping ink:*
Memories; *Frames:* Nunn
Designs; *Postcard sticker:* NRN
Designs; *Poem sticker:*
Wordsworth; *Oval nailheads
and conchos:* Scrapworks;
Number stickers: me & my BIG
ideas; *Ribbon:* Two Funky;
Tags: Source unknown; *Metal
sheeting:* Hot Off The Press;
Chalk: Craf-T Products; *Other:*
Pearl string and cameo.

HAZEL

Mother

a shoulder to cry on

a smile to count on

a love to live on

a woman of spirit and capacity

1976

On the day I was born, or shortly thereafter, who could have known that we would only have eight years together? Or that almost 40 years later, a relative would come across this photo of my mother and me? Yet both are true. On the 42nd anniversary of my birth, I am reminded of how much we are alike and how she shaped me during those short eight years into the wife and mother I am today. There was so little time, but I remember still...

Mother and Daughter
Ola and Diana
April 1960

"So Little Time"

by Diana Hudson
Bakersfield, CA
Supplies *Vellum:* Paper Adventures; *Letter stickers:* Flavia, Colorbök; *Computer font:* Gigi, downloaded from the Internet; *Eyelets:* Impress Rubber Stamps; *Clock sticker:* Jolee's Boutique, Stickopotamus; *Embroidery floss:* Westrim Crafts; *Other:* Foam board.

"Shirley Yvonne Garvey"

by Yvonne Schultz
South Jordan, UT
Supplies *Patterned paper:* Anna Griffin; *Computer fonts:* Allegro and Cottilion, downloaded from the Internet; *Stickers:* me & my BIG ideas; *Corner scissors:* Fiskars; *Corner punch:* Creative Memories; *Chalk:* Craf-T Products.

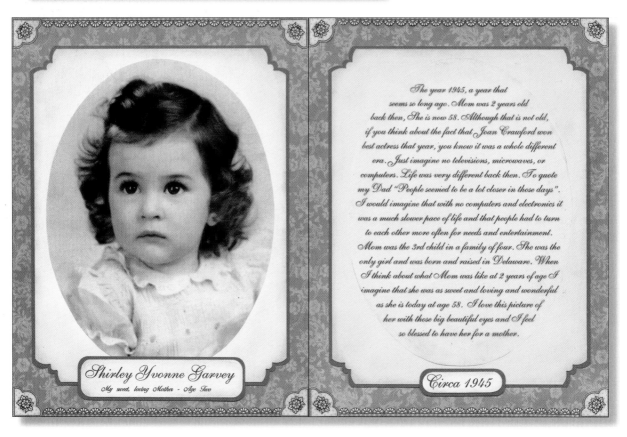

Shirley Yvonne Garvey
My sweet, loving Mother - Age Two

The year 1945, a year that seems so long ago. Mom was 2 years old back then. She is now 58. Although that is not old, if you think about the fact that Joan Crawford won best actress that year, you know it was a whole different era. Just imagine no televisions, microwaves, or computers. Life was very different back then. To quote my Dad "People seemed to be a lot closer in those days". I would imagine that with no computers and electronics it was a much slower pace of life and that people had to turn to each other more often for needs and entertainment. Mom was the 3rd child in a family of four. She was the only girl and was born and raised in Delaware. When I think about what Mom was like at 2 years of age I imagine that she was as sweet and loving and wonderful as she is today at age 58. I love this picture of her with those big beautiful eyes and I feel so blessed to have her for a mother.

Circa 1945

"Curtis Kids"

by Janice Curtis
Huntington Beach, CA
Supplies *Patterned paper:* Making Memories; *Computer font:* Humana Serif ITC-TT, International Typeface Corporation; *Lettering template:* Whimsy, Déjà Views, The C-Thru Ruler Co.; *Stickers:* The Okie Dokie Press; *Embroidery floss:* DMC; *Tags:* Janice's own designs.

IDEA TO NOTE: Janice cut 12" x 12" paper on one side to fit in the printer, then tore the paper after she printed on it.

PAGE STARTERS

Think you need to start with hundred-year-old photos to create a great heritage layout? Think again! Future generations deserve to know what was important to *you* as a child—what made you tick and what you understand about yourself now. When I think of my four grandparents and the wisdom I wish they could have passed on to me, I'm inspired to leave a legacy that my children will use as a springboard to understanding what kind of person I was. How about creating a page (or an album) describing lessons learned from some of your childhood experiences? Take some time to reflect on these ideas:

◆ As a child, what was one of your misconceptions about yourself?

◆ When were you the most proud of yourself as a child? When were your parents most proud of you?

◆ Describe your house. Where was it? What did it look like? Did you have a special corner or nook just for you?

◆ What things do you enjoy today that you loved doing as a child? Describe how the activities are different for you today.

◆ Devote an entire scrapbook page to describing your memories of some of the century's historic events. Where were you the moment you found out about the Challenger space shuttle explosion? Who told you about it and what were you doing? How has the event affected your life? Interview family members and include their memories on your page, too.

—*by Allison Strine*

You don't need to have photos from a century ago to create a heritage layout; create a layout about the heritage you'd like to pass on to future generations. *Page by Allison Strine.* **Supplies** *Patterned paper:* Colorbök; *Stamping ink:* ColorBox, Clearsnap, Inc.; *Computer font:* Festus, downloaded from the Internet; *Beads:* Art Accents; *Mesh and metal embellishments:* Scrapyard329.com; *Fibers:* Rubba Dub Dub; *Other:* Plastic.

A CUSTOM TOUCH

My family heritage album (with the paper of my choice) was custom-made by The Little Scrapbook Store (*www.thelittlescrapbookstore.com*; 864/228-6432). The company also has a large selection of papers available.

Faster Family History

4 IDEAS FOR COOL, QUICK-READ ALBUMS

About five years ago, I read something that had a profound effect on how I look at scrapbooking. In her book *Self Preservation*, author Anita Young Hallman said, "You are the link that ties the past and the future together. Think of how important your role is in giving continuity to your family's traditions and stories. Are you a strong link or a weak one?" I challenged myself with this question and invite you to do the same.

If the idea of preserving your family history feels daunting, relax. I've got four album ideas here that are doable and inspiring. They can help you, the family historian, be the important link your family needs and deserves.

BY BECKY HIGGINS

"Our Family Heritage"

BY BECKY HIGGINS

You may be lucky enough to have stacks of photos, documents and information about your ancestors, but it's unlikely your kids (especially when they're young) will want to sort through box after box to get the information.

My recommendation? Create an album that's all about your family's heritage at a glance. Your children will love this, as they gain a greater sense of their place in an extended family. They'll also love reading about their ancestors, especially as they learn what they may have in common with some of them.

ALBUM CONCEPT

Create a book that includes quick facts, stories and anecdotes about each individual in your family line. I covered three generations of my family and my husband's in one album. Each person has a page dedicated to him or her, complete with pictures and short snippets about his or her life.

I didn't have as much information for the third generation (our great-grandparents), so I dedicated those pages to married couples rather than individuals. The types of information I included on each person:

- Livelihood
- Personality traits
- Physical characteristics
- Modes of transportation
- Modes of communication
- Hobbies, skills and talents
- How they met and married their spouse
- Interesting stories about their life experiences

ALBUM DESIGN

I wanted the album to look consistent, so I changed any color photos to black and white with Adobe Photoshop software. I cropped and resized the photos as needed with the software, then used the same four decorative papers throughout the book and on the cover. Each page contains the same elements:
- A strip at the top, identifying the individual's relationship to our children (see facing pages)
- A row of four vertical pictures (each 2" x 3") ranging from childhood to adulthood, with one photo (that of the person at his or her most advanced age) highlighted on a decorative tag
- The individual's full name
- A pocket, sewn to the page for a secure hold. This is where facts, information and stories (printed on cardstock and cut into tag shapes) can be held for easy access. You can easily add items if desired.
- The individual's birth information, clipped to the front of the pocket

ALBUM OUTLINE

Include the following in your family heritage album:

- Title page
- Message from album creator (you)
- Table of contents
- Portrait pedigree charts
- A page per individual or couple
- Miscellaneous family pictures

Create a family heritage album to help you and others become familiar with past generations. *Pages by Becky Higgins.* **Supplies** *Custom-made album:* The Little Scrapbook Store; *Patterned paper:* Design Originals; *Computer fonts:* Maszyna Plus and Foxscript, downloaded from *www.free-typewriter-fonts.com*; Century Gothic, Microsoft Word; *Tags, clips and eyelets:* Making Memories; *Fibers:* FiberScraps (cover) and Timeless Touches (inside pages); *Tree accent:* Jolee's Boutique, Sticko by EK Success; *Hole punch on journaling tags:* McGill.

Note how each page contains a "relationship" strip at the top, four vertical pictures of the person at different ages, a pocket with tags of additional facts, and the individual's birth information.

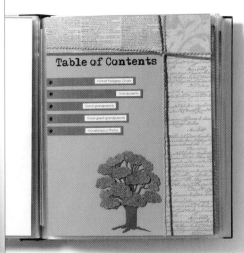

Create an "Our Family Heritage" title page (left), complete with family pictures and information on who compiled the book. A table of contents (right) can help guide viewers through the book.

Help others "see" family relationships with a pedigree chart that includes photos of individual family members.

"Research Diary"

BY RENEA BROOKS

Renea Brooks of Heatley, Australia, visited a town where she learned a lot about her ancestry. Notes Renea, "When I entered the little graveyard in Bauple, it epitomized the past where my paternal ancestry was all rooted to the one spot, etched in stone and there forever. I felt comforted in the presence of my past, by the sense of belonging. I am a part of it, a part of the place, and a part of the land, something my own children may never know except by word of mouth."

Renea chose to preserve her adventure, her findings and her feelings in this homemade book. She hopes it will help future generations appreciate their heritage.

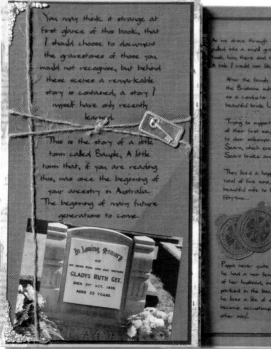

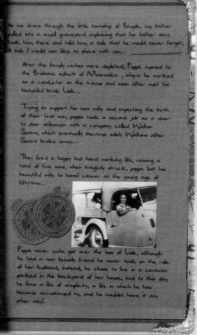

ALBUM CONCEPT

Whenever you find information about a particular ancestor or a "section" of your family history, put it in a theme album about your discoveries.

ALBUM DESIGN

Renea found a plain wooden book in her local thrift store. She covered the book's hardwood surface with decorative paper and embellishments.

ALBUM OUTLINE

When you open Renea's book you lift a flap on the right side; another flap opens downward (see next page). Instead of presenting her book in divided sections, Renea simply wrote the story of her experience, letting it flow throughout the book, section to section.

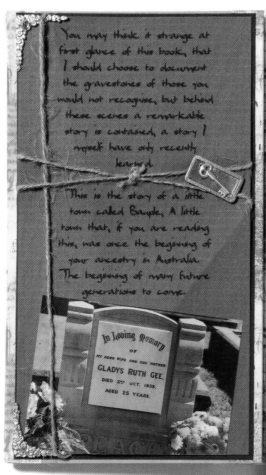

Family research can be inspiring and intriguing. Document the investigative process in a research diary. *Pages by Renea Brooks.* **Supplies** *Patterned paper for book cover:* 7 Gypsies; *Clear letter stickers:* Sonnets, Creative Imaginations; *Key charms and corner frames:* Crafty Things; *Wine hoops:* Arbee; *Turkish coins:* The Thread Studio (www.icenet.com.au); *Tags:* Making Memories; *Gold embossing powder:* Stamp-It Rubber Stamps (www.stampit.com.au); *Computer fonts:* Cursive Elegant, downloaded from the web site www.sparrowzcreationz.net/FontDownloads.htm; Scrap Cursive, "Lettering Delights" CD, Inspire Graphics; Dael Calligraphy, downloaded from *simplythebest.net/fonts/*; CK Gutenberg, "Fresh Fonts" CD, *Creating Keepsakes; Rubber stamp:* PSX Design; *Other:* Scrabble tiles, fiber, jute and Australian pennies. *Idea to note:* Renea altered the tags by embossing them with gold embossing powder.

"When We Were Your Age"

BY BECKY HIGGINS

As a long-term project, I'm working on childhood albums (three-ring, 12" x 12") for me and my husband, with pages being added all the time. For now, though, I've created a small "When We Were Your Age" album that can be enjoyed by my son and others. Sample pages follow.

Where to Find Interesting Facts

As you gather information about your childhood, consider including details from the following web sites:

- *http://dmarie.com/timecap/*
- *http://www.22cool.com/JoAnne/cpi.html* (Cost-of-living calculator)
- *www.historychannel.com* ("This Day in History" information)

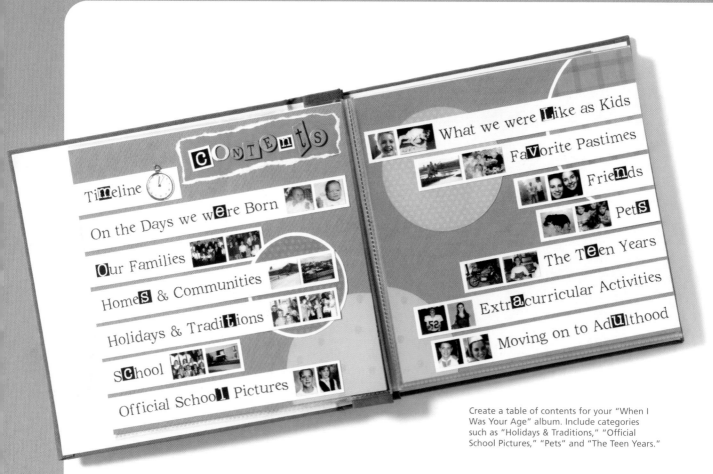

Create a table of contents for your "When I Was Your Age" album. Include categories such as "Holidays & Traditions," "Official School Pictures," "Pets" and "The Teen Years."

ALBUM CONCEPT

Create a summary of your childhood, complete with some of your favorite pictures, stories and memories. *Note:* This is not your all-inclusive childhood album. It should not include every picture ever taken of you or every report card received.

While you can focus on your childhood alone in a "When I Was Your Age" book, I chose to focus on the childhoods of my husband and myself. Either way, this album can help your kids understand that you were really once just like them. They may discover something you have in common, and that you had struggles and frustrations while growing up as well. Imagine looking through a book like this about your parents!

ALBUM DESIGN

First, remember who your audience is. If you want your kids to turn to this book time and time again, choose papers and embellishments you think your kids will like. I used an 8" x 8" canvas album (durable and great for small hands), plus the same lively colors and patterned papers throughout.

While I opted to leave each picture its original color, I did do some color restoration on color photos that needed help. For each layout, my husband, David, is featured on the left-hand side, and I'm featured on the right-hand side. Each page has a little "David" or "Becky" label in the top outer corner.

Note how the title is placed near the top and pictures are placed randomly, many of them treated as Polaroid snapshots. I used a circle theme throughout the book.

ALBUM OUTLINE

Include the following in your "When I Was Your Age" album:
- Title page
- Table of contents
- Timeline. On one layout, cover the span of your childhood. In our book, it begins in 1973 when my husband was born. The timeline continues until 1994, when I went to college.

Consider the following as well:
- On the Day I Was Born. This includes first photo, birth stats, world events at the time, and the story of when you were born.
- My Family. This includes various family photos, everyone's full names, and their birthdates.
- Homes and Communities. Share where you grew up, how many times you moved, and details (size, demographic, culture and traditions) about the town or city.

Share your favorite pastimes as a child. Family members will love learning about the games, toys and hobbies you enjoyed most.

- **Holidays and Traditions.** Reflect on favorite memories and most memorable holidays.
- **School.** Document what schools you attended, size, number of students, location, what classes and teachers were like, or what a typical day was like in class.
- **Official School Pictures.** Include one from every year available.
- **What I Was Like as a Kid.** Be honest. Tell your kids what you were really like, and include the perspectives of your parents and siblings as well. What did you want to be when you grew up?
- **Favorite Pastimes.** How did you spend your spare time? What were your skills and favorite hobbies? What were your favorite toys as a kid? What games did you play?
- **Friends.** Name your friends, tell why you shared a close relation-

ship, and detail what you did together.
- **Pets.** Document the pets you had, their names, how you acquired them and what you liked to do with them.
- **The Teen Years.** Cover dating, driving, pop culture, world stats at the time, your future plans, the music you listened to, the jobs you held, what you used for transportation, and more.
- **Extracurricular Activities.** What did you do outside of academics? Scrapbook what you were involved in, whether sports, musical instruments, debate club, foreign language, drama or art.
- **Moving on to Adulthood.** Include your first activities (college, moving away from home, joining the armed forces, traveling and more) as a young adult.

People love to compare "life then" with "life now." Create a "When I Was Your Age" album to help them see what's similar and what's different. *Pages by Becky Higgins.* **Supplies** *Album:* Scrap Artistry; *Patterned paper:* Lasting Impressions for Paper; *Metal frames, screw heads, and metal letters on cover page:* Making Memories; *Circle letter ("E") on title page:* Creative Imaginations; *Computer fonts:* GF Halda Smashed, downloaded from *www.free-typewriter-fonts.com*; Rubberstamp, downloaded from *www.scrapvillage.com*; CK Newsprint and CK Letter Home, "Fresh Fonts" and "Creative Clips & Fonts" CDs, *Creating Keepsakes; Clock accent:* Jolee's Boutique, Sticko by EK Success; *Circle cutter:* Fiskars.

"Interview Album"

BY ROBERT AND CLARINE DOWNS

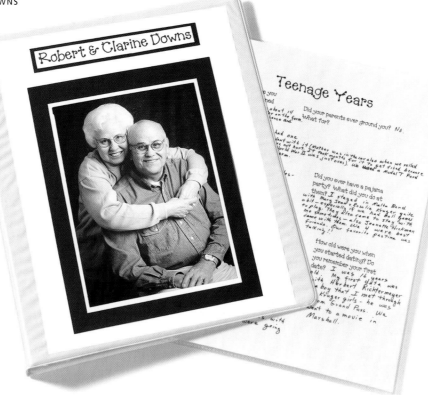

Three years ago, Lisa Bearnson's parents decided to break out of the "toy and clothing" category at Christmas and give each grandchild (26 total) a scrapbook that showcased the lives of Robert and Clarine. Even though they weren't sure if the kids would enjoy and appreciate this type of gift, the recipients couldn't wait to look at the interview books time and time again.

ALBUM CONCEPT

Create a book that's a series of questions and answers about you or a loved one. You can gather the information yourself, or enlist the help of the person being featured. Give him or her a list of questions and ask the person to write a response to each question. If you'd like to capture the person's handwriting, provide the actual album with space allotted for each answer.

A FUN TWIST

Create a *family* interview album. Prepare questionnaires, have family members fill them out at your next gathering (or via mail or e-mail), then compile everything in an album. Include a group photo if possible. ♥

ALBUM DESIGN

Robert and Clarine chose a simple, question-and-answer format, with pages that are three-hole punched and placed in a binder. They made one master book (complete with photos they wanted to include), then copied it 26 times. Choose the approach and presentation that will work best for you.

ALBUM OUTLINE

The Downs' interview album includes the following:

- Cover page, complete with photo
- Letter to posterity
- Favorite photos (categorized by childhood, marriage, career, children, etc.), complete with captions
- Questions and answers (the Downs' book contains the following categories: "Childhood," "My Home When I Was Small," "Growing Up," "School Years," "Teenage Years," "College Years," "Places I've Visited," "Celebrations," "Special Memories," "Dating Experiences," "As Time Goes By" and "Favorites")
- Closing page that tells more about the parent (the Downs' book includes answers to questions such as "What was my mom like as a baby?" and "What type of mischief did she get in?")

how will you be remembered?

Share what's important to you

Figure 1. Scrapbook the moments you want your children to remember. *Page by Tracie Smith.* **Supplies** *Patterned paper:* All About Me, Pebbles in my Pocket; *Watercolor paper:* Canson; *Watercolors:* Royal Talens; *Stickers:* Treehouse Designs; *Buttons and embroidery floss:* Making Memories; *Pen:* Zig Millennium, EK Success; *Craft wire:* Artistic Wire Ltd.; *Ribbons:* C.M. Offray & Son (orange gingham), Ink It! (yellow), raffitribbons (red plaid) and Stampin' Up! (green organdy); *Computer font:* CK Constitution, "Fresh Fonts" CD, *Creating Keepsakes.*

A FEW MONTHS AGO, my oldest son, Justin, went on his first field trip. As I packed lunch for the big day, I couldn't help but remember my fifth-grade field trip. I don't recall where we traveled or the name of the classmate who sat next to me on the school bus, but I remember the lunch my mom so lovingly packed for me.

At the time, we didn't have extra money so my mom rarely bought junk food. When she did, you can imagine how fast the treats disappeared with three kids in the house! You can imagine my delight when I opened my lunch pail and found a soda wrapped in foil.

Looking back now, my mom probably had to hide the soda so no one else would drink it first. Or, maybe she had to go to the store early that morning to buy the soda. Either way, I have a lasting memory of my mom and her thoughtfulness that I wouldn't trade now for the world.

My Legacy

After thinking about my mom, I couldn't help but wonder about my own children. What will

Figure 2. Tell someone how much you appreciate him or her by sharing the memories you treasure. *Book by Tracie Smith.* **Supplies** *Patterned paper:* K & Company; *Vellum and embossing powder:* Stampin' Up!; *Pen:* Zig Millennium, EK Success; *Embroidery floss:* DMC; *Charms and bookplate:* The Ink Pad; *Walnut ink:* Postmodern Design; *Ink technique for tags:* From *Designing with Textures* (Autumn Leaves); *Other:* Denim. *Idea to note:* To emboss her handwriting, Tracie traced over the title twice on vellum. Next, she poured clear embossing powder over it, then heated the powder with a heat tool.

Regardless of whether you choose to reflect or look ahead, be sure to record the way you'd like to be remembered.

Figure 3. Help your children remember special, shared moments by recording them on a layout. *Page by Alannah Jurgensmeyer.* **Supplies** *Handmade paper:* The Jennifer Collection; *Photo corners:* Canson; *Rubber stamp and stamping ink:* Stampa Rosa; *Computer font:* P22 Edward Hopper, downloaded from the Internet; *Gold frame:* Decorative Details, Nunn Designs; *Nailheads:* Jest Charming.

they remember about me? I know I'm not perfect, and unfortunately the bad moments seem easiest to remember. Will the sweet moments that mean so much to me follow my children into their adult lives?

I decided to try a little exercise. As part of it, I began writing down the little things I hope my children will remember. For example, a "tradition" of ours is to jump in the car on the first warm day of the year. We listen to the Beach Boys, volume cranked up, and every window in the car (moon roof included) has to be wide open. We drive and sing.

Figure 4. Create a page layout about your job and what you hope to accomplish there. *Pages by Tracie Smith.* **Supplies** *Watercolor paper:* Canson; *Watercolors:* Royal Talens; *Pen:* Zig Millennium, EK Success; *Rubber stamp and stamping ink:* Stampin' Up!; *Transparency film:* 3M; *Metallic rub-ons:* Craft-T Products; *Computer font:* CK Stenography, "Fresh Fonts" CD, *Creating Keepsakes; Label maker:* Label Buddy, Dymo; *Idea for name strips and dates:* From Heidi Swapp in Supply Savvy, March 2003 issue; *Other:* Denim. *Idea to note:* To create the name strips, remove the tape from a label maker and insert cardstock strips that are 3/8" wide. Press to emboss each letter of your name, date or journaling. Add metallic rub-ons to highlight.

The boys never believe me when I tell them that I used to be young. Or, sometimes I will be telling a story about when I was younger and Cole will ask, "Was that way back when you were skinny?" (KIDS...you gotta love 'em.) When I found this picture of myself with friends from high school, Barbara Dresser and Anne Johnson, I just had to show the boys that, yes, MOM was a young, thin, funny, & hip chick. I think it's good for them to see me in a different light than just ol' boring Mom. It's good for me to remember, too.

Is that REALLY you?

1984

MOM?

Figure 5. Reflect on your past by creating a scrapbook page for each era of your life. *Page by Lori Houk.* **Supplies** *Patterned paper:* Paper Source; *Textured paper:* Memory Lane; *Rubber stamps:* Antique and Link Letters, PSX Design; *Ribbon:* Tinsel Trading Co.; *Computer font:* 2Peas Evergreen, downloaded from *www.twopeasinabucket.com*; *Glue dots:* Glue Dots International; *Stamping ink:* Krystal Kraft; *Tag:* From an office supply store. *Idea to note:* Lori stained her tag and paper with coffee.

Once I started writing down little moments like these, I decided to create a scrapbook page (Figure 1) to preserve these memories in one place for my boys.

Your Legacy

Many of my friends have admitted, "I hope my kids forget their childhood. All I do lately is yell." If this is the way you're feeling, it's time to stop, reflect and regain perspective. Here's what I'd suggest:

❶ **Find a quiet spot where you can be by yourself.** (I do most of my thinking while jogging so no one is around to distract me.)

❷ **Think of the experiences that have touched you.** Often they're small and simple. For example, my mom used to check me out of school two or three days a year to go shopping. During our mother/daughter time, Mom and I shopped, ate Mexican food, and

had a blast together at a place we called the "shoe dump." I couldn't resist putting together a little book (Figure 2) to tell my parents what I remember and appreciate most about my childhood.

❸ **Think about the qualities you love in others.** This will help you discover what you hope others will remember about you. One quality I've tried to cultivate lately is a greater emphasis on enjoying time with my boys. Instead of insisting that we read something "appropriate," I've given in and read them *The Adventures of Captain Underpants* instead. My boys love it, we're reading, and we're happy. My friend Alannah feels the same way about sharing good times with her two boys. She created the layout in Figure 3 to help her family remember the special moments she cherishes. An example of her journaling? "If he's

feeling sad or sick, Carter loves to snuggle up in a little ball on my lap while I hold him tight."

❹ **Extend the concept to other relationships or your career** (Figure 4). Consider the legacy you'd like to leave through your job, church group, friends or community service. Journaling these thoughts and feelings is a great starting point for setting goals for your future.

❺ **Think about how much you change from one decade to the next.** I could do a completely different layout for each era of my life. So much changes, and it's often hilarious to look back in time.

I'm sure Lori Houk's children will laugh one day when they see her layout in Figure 5. Lori talks about being a young, hip and skinny chick back in high school. I remember high school and thinking my parents—in their late 30's—were so old they could never understand what I was going through. What a difference a decade or two makes!

Regardless of whether you choose to reflect or look ahead, be sure to record the way you'd like to be remembered. It's a wonderful way to convey what's most precious to you. ♥

playful designs for your pages

NOW THAT YOU'VE GOT some great ideas for your scrapbooks, we thought we'd give you an added boost—pre-designed titles and accents ready to be personalized and used on your layouts! On the next three pages, you'll find titles and graphics created by artist Karen Burniston. Check out her great examples of how to use the artwork in Figures 1 and 2, then gather your supplies and copy your favorite images with a copy machine or light box. Color and mat the designs, mount them on your page, and enjoy! ♥

Figure 1. Whimsical titles and accents are the perfect finishing touches for any layout. *Page by Karen Burniston.* **Supplies** *Handmade paper:* Source unknown; *Blue mesh paper:* Magenta; *Nailheads:* JewelCraft; *Colored pencils:* Prismacolor, Sanford; *Diamond punch:* Family Treasures; *Chalk:* Stampin' Up!; *Computer font:* Verdana, Microsoft Word.

Figure 2. Personalize titles and accents with watercolors, chalks or colored pencils. *Samples by Karen Burniston.*
"MEMORIES" Supplies *Chalk:* Stampin' Up!; *Fiber:* Rubba Dub Dub; *Photo corners:* Canson; *Black pen:* Pigma Micron, Sakura.
"KEY TO MY HEART" Supplies *Colored pencils:* Prismacolor, Sanford; *Chalk:* Stampin' Up!; *Heart buttons:* Source unknown.
"SPRING" Supplies *Colored pencils:* Prismacolor, Sanford; *Chalk:* Stampin' Up!; *Eyelets:* Creative Impressions.
"BIRTHDAY" Supplies *Colored pencils:* Prismacolor, Sanford; *Chalk:* Stampin' Up!.

FAMILY PORTRAIT

PLEASURES

Simple • Simple • Simple • Simple

Key to my heart

GAME
night

Memories